Studies in Immigration and Culture

Royden Loewen, series editor

7 *Ethnic Elites and Canadian Identity: Japanese, Ukrainians, and Scots, 1919–1971*
Aya Fujiwara

6 *Community and Frontier*
A Ukrainian Settlement in the Canadian Parkland
John C. Lehr

5 *Storied Landscapes*
Ethno-Religious Identity and the Canadian Prairies
Frances Swyripa

4 *Families, Lovers, and Their Letters*
Italian Postwar Migration to Canada
Sonia Cancian

3 *Sounds of Ethnicity*
Listening to German North America, 1850–1914
Barbara Lorenzkowski

2 *Mennonite Women in Canada*
A History
Marlene Epp

1 *Imagined Homes*
Soviet German Immigrants in Two Cities
Hans Werner

ethnic elites and Canadian identity

Japanese, Ukrainians, and Scots, 1919–1971

AYA FUJIWARA

UMP
University of Manitoba Press

University of Manitoba Press
Winnipeg, Manitoba
Canada R3T 2M5
uofmpress.ca

Printed in Canada
Text printed on chlorine-free, 100% post-consumer recycled paper

16 15 14 13 12 1 2 3 4 5

Cover design: Frank Reimer
Cover image: A Parade Float for the Japanese Community for a Royal Visit; Vancouver, BC, 1939. From the collection of the Japanese Canadian National Museum (2011.64.3.1)
Interior design: Karen Armstrong Graphic Design

Library and Archives Canada Cataloguing in Publication

Fujiwara, Aya, 1971–
Ethnic elites and Canadian identity : Japanese, Ukrainians, and Scots, 1919–1971 / Aya Fujiwara.

(Studies in immigration and culture, ISSN 1914-1459 ; 7)
Includes bibliographical references and index.
ISBN 978-0-88755-737-8 (pbk.)
ISBN 978-0-88755-427-8 (PDF e-book)
ISBN 978-0-88755-429-2 (epub e-book)

1. Multiculturalism—Canada—History—20th century. 2. Ethnicity—Political aspects—Canada--History—20th century. 3. Elite (Social sciences)—Canada—History--20th century. 4. Civic leaders—Political activity—Canada—History—20th century. 5. Japanese Canadians—Ethnic identity—History—20th century. 6. Ukrainian Canadians—Ethnic identity--History—20th century. 7. Scottish Canadians—Ethnic identity—History—20th century. 8. Canada—Ethnic relations—History—20th century. I. Title. II. Series: Studies in immigration and culture ; 7

FC104.F84 2012 305.8009710904 C2012-902596-8

The University of Manitoba Press gratefully acknowledges the financial support for its publication program provided by the Government of Canada through the Canada Book Fund, the Canada Council for the Arts, the Manitoba Department of Culture, Heritage, Tourism, the Manitoba Arts Council, and the Manitoba Book Publishing Tax Credit.

FSC
www.fsc.org
MIX
Paper from responsible sources
FSC® C016245

In memory of Professor Kazuo Kimura

CONTENTS

ACKNOWLEDGEMENTS

My first appreciation goes to Professor Frances Swyripa at the University of Alberta. As my PhD supervisor, she provided helpful suggestions and criticisms and shared her knowledge with me in numerous meetings, classrooms, and personal conversations. While I am solely responsible for any flaws in this study, this book would not have been completed had it not been for her guidance. Special thanks also go to Professor Royden Loewen at the University of Winnipeg. As an editor of the series, he gave me many invaluable suggestions and much support. Since the first time I met him, he has inspired me on a number of occasions, exchanging ideas and thoughts. I would also like to express my sincere gratitude to Professor Gerhard Ens, whose insights into the theories of ethnicity helped me improve the methodological aspects of this book, and to Professor Bob Irwin, who served on my PhD thesis committee. My thanks also go to Mykola Soroka, who assisted me in translating Ukrainian documents.

This book is a tribute to the late Professor Kazuo Kimura, who taught me Canadian history at the University of Tsukuba, Japan, and was an author of several books on Canadian history. As one of a few Japanese historians who specialized in Canada, he was not only instrumental to my knowledge, but also contributed greatly to the development of Canadian studies in Japan. It was not an easy task to keep faith and interest in this field, which was largely neglected outside Canada. But he never gave up and kept writing until 2007, when he passed away, believing that foreign scholars could add different perspectives to Canadian history. The legacy that he left to this field in Japan was profound, and certainly survives in my studies.

My special thanks also go to Douglas McCalla, Professor Emeritus at the University of Guelph, for his support; Professor Viv Nelles and the Wilson Institute for Canadian History at McMaster University for providing me with a place to complete this book; and to David Carr, Glenn Bergen, Cheryl Miki, and Dallas Harrison at the University of Manitoba Press for their great assistance in the publication process.

I would also like to thank the helpful staff at the following archives: the Library and Archives Canada, the Public Archives of Nova Scotia, the Beaton Institute at Cape Breton University, Acadia University Archives, the University of British Columbia Archives, the Presbyterian Church Archives, and the Japanese Canadian National Museum. Myron Momryk, who was a senior archivist at the Library and Archives Canada, provided me with an introduction to the available resources.

I am also grateful for several sources of funding that I have received as a doctoral student to complete this project. They include the scholarships and teaching assistantships at the Department of History and Classics, University of Alberta, the Darcovich Memorial Scholarship from the Canadian Institute of Ukrainian Studies, the Izaak Walton Killam Memorial Scholarship from University of Alberta and the Killam Trust.

Finally, I would like to express my appreciation to David R. Marples for his moral support at many difficult times, and scholarly insights for the entire course of completing this book. I also thank my parents, Kae and Katsuaki Fujiwara, for their encouragement.

A portion of Chapter 2 was first published as "The Myth of the Emperor and the Yamato race: The Role of the *Tairiku nippô* in the Promotion of Japanese-Canadian Transnational Ethnic Identity in the 1920s and the 1930s," *Journal of the Canadian Historical Association* 21, 1 (2010): 37–58.

LIST OF ACRONYMS

AUUC	Association of United Ukrainian Canadians
BCSC	British Columbia Security Commission
CBC	Canadian Broadcasting Corporation
CCF	Co-operative Commonwealth Federation
CCJC	Co-operative Committee on Japanese Canadians
CJA	Canadian Japanese Association
FLQ	Front de libération du Québec
JACL	Japanese American Citizens League
JCCA	Japanese Canadian Citizens Association
JCCC	Japanese Canadian Citizens Council
JCCD	Japanese Canadian Committee for Democracy
JCCL	Japanese Canadian Citizens League
JCRC	Japanese Canadian Research Collection
LAC	Library and Archives Canada
NATO	North Atlantic Treaty Organization
NJCCA	National Japanese Canadian Citizens Association
NMEG	Nisei Mass Evacuation Group
PANS	Public Archives of Nova Scotia
RCMP	Royal Canadian Mounted Police
UCB	Ukrainian Catholic Brotherhood
UCC	Ukrainian Canadian Committee
UCUSU	Ukrainian Canadian University Students' Union
UHO	United Hetman Organization
ULFTA	Ukrainian Labour-Farmer Temple Association
UNF	Ukrainian National Federation
USRL	Ukrainian Self-Reliance League
USSR	Union of Soviet Socialist Republics

argues, "immigrants come as individuals or families, rather than entire communities," but after immigration "such immigrants often coalesce into loose association," which he identifies as "ethnic groups."[2] Royden Loewen and Gerald Friesen referred to the space that was neither Canada nor any one ethnic group's homeland as "an imagined boundary zone."[3] It was under this condition that these elites found their new role through political activity, media, and personal networks. Often they were relative unknowns in their respective homelands yet gained power as self-appointed representatives of their ethnic communities in Canada. No matter which ideologies they supported, they possessed a dual identity that they tried to reconcile between two places. Whichever country they prioritized, either their homeland or Canada, their "transnational" identity shaped their roles, views, and missions. By nature, they were ambitious and diligent people who knew about the histories, politics, and languages of both Canada and their respective homelands, even to a greater extent than did their fellow countrymen. The majority were also better off than others and gained influential positions in Canada, such as ethnic press editors, presidents of ethnic associations, and small business owners. Yet being blessed with intellectual and material means did not necessarily guarantee them an elite status. They were also charismatic, exhibiting various skills of leadership in speaking, writing, and organizing.

Historians, political scientists, and sociologists have theorized the rise of this leadership class and its impact on ethnic peoples. Common to these theories is the portrayal of ethnic leaders as selfish and rational people who choose practical means to achieve their own economic, social, and political upward mobility. Scholars such as Orlando Patterson, Paul R. Brass, and Michael Hechter attribute the rise of such elites to intense political competition within and outside the ethnic group. For ambitious ethnic individuals, acquisition of political power in Canadian society was a major goal, but since influential positions in mainstream society were limited they had to use their ethnic backgrounds to bolster their positions. To do so, they first needed to become representatives of their ethnic communities by winning over or defeating rivals for the position. Then, by mobilizing and promoting their people's interests and ethnic consciousness, they could compete in mainstream society as legitimate voices of their ethnic communities.[4] A common basis of this theory is the conviction that ethnicity, to a greater or lesser degree, is constructed by choice and that, in Patterson's words, the ethnic "allegiance" of individuals is "in their own best social and economic interests."[5]

This theory, called "instrumentalism," has been used by Ukrainian-Canadian specialists such as sociologist Wsevolod W. Isajiw and political scientist Bohdan S. Kordan to explain the emergence and maintenance of

Ukrainian-Canadian ethnicity as a political phenomenon. Isajiw, for example, pointed out the particular tendency of the third or later generation of Ukrainians, who usually had little association with anything Ukrainian but relied on their ethnicity to gain access to and participate in higher strata of Canadian society.[6] Following the logic that ethnicity is an important element for politically weaker groups, instrumentalism is also useful in explaining why influential Scots did not overemphasize their ethnicity to attain individual and collective recognition and power in Canada. As part of "mainstream" leaders, they did not need to use ethnicity as a source of power.

Undoubtedly, ethnic leaders manipulated both Canadian and homeland politics to establish their power. Yet here I add a different angle, identifying them as individuals who devoted themselves to their communities, seeking the best ways by which their ethnic peoples could maintain their in-between identity and comfortably live in Canada. No matter how hard immigrants and their descendants tried to assimilate to Canadian culture and norms, learning English or French, anglicizing their names, or converting to Christianity, they faced the reality of being treated as second-class citizens. In the case of racial minorities in particular, skin colour always prevented them from participating in Canada fully. By creating a transnational space, ethnic elites provided a place in which ethnic peoples could belong. This does not mean that the grassroots always follow the leaders. As Franca Iacovetta points out, the political visions of ethnic elites did not always penetrate into their communities.[7] However, their role in the formation and maintenance of ethnic communities cannot be underestimated.

Three Groups and Their Historiographies

The three groups chosen for this study—Japanese, Ukrainians, and Scots—exemplify common and different patterns that emerge in terms of strategies of ethnic community building and maintenance and the construction of a multicultural Canada. Although my arguments here cannot necessarily be applied to all ethnic groups in Canada, I hope to provide useful clues to how other ethnic groups in Canada constructed and maintained ethnicity.

Obviously, the Scots belonged to mainstream Canada, not only sharing a sense of superiority with the "Anglo-Saxons" as the world's dominant race but also belonging to a primarily Protestant culture. Although Ukrainians were not part of Anglo-Protestant or Western civilization, the facts that they were Christian and white gave them an edge over Japanese in terms of accessing mainstream society. The Japanese, in contrast, believed mainly in Buddhism or Shintoism (except for a few converts to Christianity), were racially visible, and came from the "Orient." They were thus seen as unassimilable even if properly enlightened. The political implications of such differences were enormous, particularly with respect to equal participation in Canadian society.

The Scots helped to define what mainstream Canada should be, having a huge impact on its political, educational, and economic development and philosophical underpinnings as members of the dominant British group. Although they might not qualify as an ethnic group, they are significant from a comparative point of view since they still highlighted their ethnicity at times. For both reasons, I treat the Scots differently from the other two groups, which are central to my analysis. Ukrainians, whose Old World political ideologies and involvement were never accepted by mainstream Canadians before World War II, were more or less acknowledged for their economic contribution as prairie farmers and allowed naturalization and the franchise. Their European origin and white skin also made them culturally and racially assimilable. The dividing line from mainstream Canada was the most persistent in the case of Japanese because of their race and non-Christian culture and traditions. Japanese, except for a small number who settled outside British Columbia, came under the close influence of the consulates of Japan until World War II and were denied the franchise until 1948.

Regional differences also affected how these three groups perceived themselves and their significance in Canadian nation building. The fact that until 1942 the great majority of Canada's Japanese population was concentrated in "marginal" British Columbia reinforced their sense of otherness. Ukrainians, conversely, cultivated and exploited the notion that they were a founding people of the economically significant prairie provinces. For Scots, who settled across Canada, regional boundaries often did not matter, weakening ethnic cohesiveness. Yet, as with the other two groups, Scottish identity was fortified where populations were concentrated and somewhat marginalized, as in Nova Scotia. Patterns of geographical concentration among the three groups became less distinctive after World War II, yet myths and memories of the ethnic regions survived and even flourished.

At the official level, both Ukrainian and Japanese elites pressured the federal and various provincial governments to be recognized as full-fledged citizens without any official or unofficial discrimination. Broadly speaking, internal competition—between nationalists and communists among Ukrainians and between *issei* ("the first generation") and *nisei* ("the second generation") among Japanese—created four camps in the interwar period, each of which sought to build a better relationship with mainstream leaders, proving that they were "real" and "fit" representatives of their ethnic communities who shared democratic and liberal ideals with other Canadians.

At the same time, all four camps tried to insert their own political ideals and agendas into Canadian politics. Specifically, nationalist Ukrainians campaigned for the independence of Ukraine in Europe, while communist Ukrainians tried to build socialist democratic principles in Canada. *Issei* Japanese campaigned for a better relationship between Japan and Canada, an end to occupational restrictions, and the franchise, especially for World War I veterans who fought for Canada, while *nisei* Japanese lobbied for their enfranchisement as their birthright. Ultimately, Ukrainian nationalists and *nisei* Japanese, advocating democracy and freedom, which were closest to mainstream Canadians' definitions of the two concepts, won the competition with their respective rivals and became important factors in shaping Canada's multiculturalism.

At the unofficial level, the integration of ethnicity into Canadian identity, or the fusion between mainstream and ethnic identities, began during the interwar period and accelerated after World War II. As part of this process, Ukrainian and Japanese elites both injected Canadian elements into their traditional homeland myths, symbols, and collective memories and constructed new, distinctively "Canadian" ones that reflected life in the adopted homeland. Scots focussed on making Canada Scottish, which was always part of mainstream Canadian identity. Myths, symbols, and collective memories represented areas where mainstream and ethnic boundaries became indiscernible more quickly than in official Canadian identity.

Theoretically, instrumentalism, which focuses only on the ambitions of ethnic elites, has been reinforced by classic modernist theories of ethnicity. They tie the ethnic elite to its grassroots. Benedict Anderson's "imagined communities" provide a great example. Although a primary goal of this concept is to answer a much larger question—whether or not the nation is a phenomenon constructed as a result of modern technological and economic developments—its understanding of ethnic community has repercussions for Canada. Anderson's theory asserts that "all communities," including ethnic ones, "are imagined" by their members mainly through the rise of "print capitalism" and the decline of kingdoms.[8] Implicitly, it stresses the impact that ethnic individuals who filled up the early vacuum of power where no obvious leaders existed, and produced ideas on paper, had on the formation of ethnic groups. Thus, the theory provides great insights into how both Ukrainian- and Japanese-Canadian elites promoted ethnic consciousness, largely constructed after immigration, through their own presses, which eliminated the need for face-to-face encounters in a vast land. For the individuals who initiated and controlled these presses, the role that "imagination" played was of great significance.

In this context, Anthony D. Smith's ethnosymbolism discounts the role of ethnic elites in the formation of ethnic communities by focussing on grassroots transfer of myths, symbols, and shared memories. Smith sets out to refute the overwhelming importance placed on modern changes in technology and capitalism. Although he admits that nation and ethnicity are modern phenomena, he stresses an essential historical continuity between premodern *ethnie* and modern ethnicity and the modern nation. For him, the profound attachment that ethnic groups have to their traditions and culture derives from the myths, symbols, and memories that group members have nurtured for a long time.[9] Yet, applied to the modern era, his theory implicitly anticipated the emergence of individuals who adopted and selected those myths, symbols, and memories. "Myths of common descent," in particular, constitute a crucial part of ethnic consciousness since they provide a sense of security and meaning for a group and its members. Specifically, such myths include temporal origin, location and migration, ancestry, the heroic age, and regeneration.[10]

This ethnosymbolist theory explains well why both Ukrainian and Japanese elites constantly produced or reproduced their own homeland and Canadian myths and collective memories, which provided them with what Smith calls a sense of distinctiveness as "chosen peoples."[11] This theory also explains why the Scottish elite, who defined much of the Canadian mainstream, sometimes needed to emphasize their Scottishness: for them, ethnicity was strongly tied to a sense of mission and pride as a superior people who designed much of the modern world and built the foundation of Canada as a colony. In this sense, Herbert Gans's "symbolic ethnicity"—whereby the ethnic group focuses on ethnic traditions, food, music, and arts as its members become integrated into mainstream society[12]—always contains a political message.

In Canada, ethnic histories, especially in the 1990s, highlighted the role that ethnic leaders played in the creation and maintenance of ethnic communities. Ethnic scholars began situating elites in the larger Canadian context, applying the traditional single-group approach to studies that noted marked distinctions among groups. Of the three groups concerned here, Ukrainian-Canadian historiography is the most advanced, not only in the incorporation of the larger Canadian context into ethnic history, but also in the attention to the impacts of both community elite and mainstream-Ukrainian negotiations. *Canada's Ukrainians: Negotiating an Identity* (1991), a collection of essays edited by Lubomyr Luciuk and Stella Hryniuk, Luciuk's *Searching for Place: Ukrainian Displaced Persons, Canada, and the Migration of Memory* (2000), and Bohdan S. Kordan's *Canada and the*

Ukrainian Question, 1939–1945 (2001) provide insights into how Ukrainian elites responded to and shaped the federal government's external and internal policies.[13]

Studies that pay more attention to the constructed nature of ethnicity, and examine the role of elites in promoting ethnic identity, are Orest Martynowych's *Ukrainians in Canada: The Formative Years, 1891–1924* (1991) and Frances Swyripa's *Wedded to the Cause: Ukrainian-Canadian Women and Ethnic Identity, 1891–1991* (1993). Martynowych's monograph, which demonstrates how Ukrainian individuals, motivated by ambition, clashing ideologies, and competition for power, rose as self-appointed intermediaries between their immigrant people and the mainstream society, illustrates their centrality to creating and defining a Ukrainian community.[14] Swyripa's study, which explains how an ideologically divided Ukrainian elite manipulated ethnic myths, symbols, and collective memories to mobilize women on behalf of the community agenda, incorporates gender, class, ethnicity, and region into its analysis. While Martynowych emphasizes the process by which socialist and nationalist Ukrainian leaders gained power as community representatives, Swyripa adds an ethnosymbolist analysis to the entire history. She regards the myths and symbols—such as the glorious past of the Cossacks and a traditional icon such as baba—as particularly significant elements of shaping Ukrainian-Canadian identity. Both nationalist and socialist elites competitively constructed, maintained, and reinvented these myths and symbols.[15]

Approaches that tackle the complexity of viewpoints of ethnic elites and conceptualize ethnicity theoretically are rare in both Scottish- and Japanese-Canadian historiographies. The writing of Scottish-Canadian history has, from the beginning, tended to problematize Scottishness as a grappling with identity in which Scots sought to distinguish themselves from other British settler peoples through their symbols and cultural traditions. Multiculturalism in the late twentieth century only encouraged this tendency to further cement the link between writing Scottish-Canadian history and creating Scottish identity. For Japanese Canadians, the situation was the opposite; long marginalized, they established a historical tradition around the collective memory of "injustice" associated particularly with prewar racism and internment during World War II. The impact of this event was so strong that other facets of their past often received little attention until recently. For example, few studies examine how Japanese-Canadian elites emerged in the late nineteenth and early twentieth centuries and how they conceptualized their place in Canada.

Scottish-Canadian history has been regarded as an integral part of mainstream Canadian history, and thus any attempt to write a separate history for Scots inevitably highlights distinctively Scottish elements and impoverishes the common narrative. D. Campbell and R.A. Maclean in *Beyond the Atlantic Roar: A Study of the Nova Scotian Scots* (1974) adopt conventional themes such as settlement, literature, education, and politics. *Beyond the Atlantic Roar* illustrates the dilemma in treating Nova Scotian Scots as an ethnically identifiable group, arguing that Scottishness remained "in the realm of attitudes," while Scots themselves were politically and culturally assimilated by 1940.[16] The Scottish elite thus were often ethnically invisible since they were mainstream. Publications on Scots in Canada outside mainstream Canadian historiography often celebrate things Scottish—historical personalities, cultural traditions, education, and folk arts, for example—without any attempt at analysis.[17] A number of books appearing after the introduction of official multiculturalism in the 1970s reinforced this emphasis on the maintenance of "symbolic ethnicity" among Scots while commemorating their strong political, social, and cultural impacts in Canada. *The Scottish Canadians* (1981) by Allen Andrews is an illuminating example in which political success is highlighted. He writes that "our nation's first Prime Minister, John A. Macdonald, was of Scottish descent, as were a third of the Fathers of the Confederation. This Scottish tradition in politics has continued till the present."[18] This tendency to valorize and even romanticize the Scottishness of Canada continues in the twenty-first century. Jenni Calder in *Scots in Canada* (2003) writes that, "wherever there were Scots, it seems, there was music.... It is often said that Scottish Canadians cherish the culture of the Gael more enthusiastically than do the Scots in Scotland."[19] Similar approaches can be seen in Matthew Shaw's *Great Scots! How the Scots Created Canada* (2003) and Paul Cowan's *How the Scots Created Canada* (2006), intended for a popular readership.[20] Ken McGoogan's *How the Scots Invented Canada* (2010) represents the field better in that it celebrates Scottish contributions to Canada. The book, which he calls "deliberately less academic," traces the Scottish origins of Canada's first settlers, inventors, and political figures.[21]

Yet some scholars have addressed the frequently blurred boundary between mainstream and Scottish identities and examined how Scottishness became an integral part of Canadian identity. Ian McKay, for example, has insightfully demonstrated the artificial and constructed nature of Scottish ethnicity in Nova Scotia, noting the promotion of Scottishness, imbued with antiquity and exoticism, between 1933 and 1954, in particular by the "antimodernist" premier Angus L. Macdonald.[22] According to McKay, Scottishness was designed by Macdonald to ethnicize the province, in which

Scots were not numerically dominant, for both economic and promotional reasons, incorporating Scottish symbols such as the tartan, Gaelic songs, Highland games, and bagpipes into the province's identity. Focussing on the academic efforts to maintain Gaelic, Gilbert Foster's *Language and Poverty: The Persistence of Scottish Gaelic in Eastern Canada* (1988) makes a similar point, arguing that "the cultural tradition manifested by Angus W. R. McKenzie and the Gaelic College at St. Ann's Nova Scotia, with respect to the common Gaelic heritage, emerges as one of romanticization."[23] Two collections of essays, *Transatlantic Scots* (2005) and *A Kingdom of the Mind: How the Scots Helped Make Canada* (2006) inquire into the complexity of Scottish ethnicity as a symbolic phenomenon that often exists in the mind. Celeste Ray's article in the first collection, for example, theorizes "Scottish Americans" or "hyphenated Scots" as "imagined" and historically rooted.[24] Significantly, both books recognize the strong influence of Scots in every sphere of life in Canada, thereby underscoring the fact that their strong power as nation builders rarely hurt their desire to remain Scottish.[25]

Japanese-Canadian historiography, as opposed to its Scottish counterpart, which was shaped by positive myths, evolved around recollections of the negative past mainly by those who witnessed or experienced the wartime evacuation from British Columbia. The earlier books thus concentrated on grassroots experience. Often written as first-hand accounts, these books on internment in the 1940s are valuable personal records, but their focus on the narrative of the event avoids an in-depth analysis of the role of the elite. Illuminating examples include Barry Broadfoot's *Years of Sorrow, Years of Shame: The Stories of Japanese Candians in World War II* (1977), Keibo Oiwa's *Stone Voices: Wartime Writings of Japanese Canadian Isseis* (1991), and Takeo Nakano's *Within the Barbed Wire Fence: A Japanese Man's Account of His Internment in Canada* (1980).[26] The triumph in 1988 of the redress movement seeking compensation for wartime losses also produced a series of books that extended the collective memories of the evacuation beyond World War II. Maryka Omatsu's *Bittersweet Passage: Redress and the Japanese Canadian Experience* (1992), for example, provides a first-hand account of experiences in the evacuation and the redress movement, tying the two events into a long history of "struggle."[27]

Among the earlier books on Japanese Canadians, Ken Adachi's *The Enemy that Never Was: An Account of the Deplorable Treatment Inflicted on Japanese Canadians during World War Two* (1976) and Ann Sunahara's *The Politics of Racism: The Uprooting of the Japanese Canadians during the Second World War* (1981) were exceptions in terms of their inclusion of analysis into the story and the pre-World War II period that they cover. While Adachi provides regarded an ethnic boundary as a political construct, had a great impact on the study of ethnic groups. Barth argued that ethnic boundaries existed independently and were never defined by such biological and cultural elements but drawn by social interactions that distinguished the members of one ethnic community from those of another. Once ethnic boundaries were built, they could survive despite the decline in cultural distinctiveness, and people could move across the boundaries.[35] In Canada, the ethnic boundaries once created by the elite were no doubt persistent, as Barth suggests, but their survival was due in part to ethnic elites' consistent efforts to maintain them.

The development of ethnic histories is an example of how ethnic boundaries have been maintained by ethnic leaders. Especially after the implementation of official multiculturalism in 1971, ethnic historians produced ethnic histories artificially, focussing on a single group and often deliberately disassociating ethnicity from mainstream Canadian identity. Historians such as Howard Palmer, Roberto Perin, and Franca Iacovetta pointed out the static nature of early Canadian ethnic histories, which adopted ethnicity as their predetermined conceptual framework. Perin's 1990 article, which criticized the "static" and "dry" nature of the monographs in the state-funded Generations Series, attributed the problem to the official mentality to recognize and commission ethnic history.[36] Most of these books, which appeared in the 1970s and 1980s, used a similar framework, organizing their chapters around themes of immigration, settlement, politics, religion, secular community life, and socioeconomic issues, and they defined ethnic boundaries artificially. But by implication these studies conceived of ethnicity as common descent rather than a political construct emerging out of ethnic elites' interactions with mainstream society.[37]

Undoubtedly, certain traditional tendencies in the study of Canadian identity have hindered the investigation of the mainstream/ethnic boundary as flexible and dynamic. Yet, more significantly, ethnic historians are often part of the ethnic elite. Their early efforts to write ethnic histories were intended to create, maintain, and emphasize ethnic boundaries, just as all historians make claims to national, regional, and local histories. Although ethnic historians can be distinguished from ethnic activists, who are much more politically focussed and methodologically untrained, both bodies are influential agents in ethnic boundary creation and maintenance.

Ethnic historians alone, however, have not created the mainstream/ethnic boundary. Although a number of studies have made significant contributions to the understanding of how Canada adopted ethnic pluralism as the official mainstream identity, the study of Canadian identity has traditionally belonged to intellectual history, where the evolution of British Protestant ideas has been a major focus. These studies have underestimated the impact of "ethnic" perspectives on Canadian identity. While this tendency has been challenged traditionally by historians such as Palmer, who incorporated ethnic elites into the picture after the official introduction of multiculturalism, such elites are not yet regarded as full participants in the evolution of Canadian identity. José E. Igartua's *The Other Quiet Revolution: National Identities in English Canada, 1945–71* (2006) reveals that, since the end of World War II, mainstream politicians, presses, and commentators broadened Canadian identity, moving from an emphasis on British "common ancestry" to "universalistic moral values of equality."[38] It is perhaps understandable that, in an analysis of mainstream Canadian views, how ethnic leaders saw Canada is overlooked.

Yet the rise of "equality" in Canada's political discourse would never have been possible without the long-term interaction between mainstream and ethnic perspectives. Igartua regards "the emergence of civic representations of Canadian identity as the foundation of Canadian political discourse" as "sudden."[39] His argument is convincing if political discourse does not include the ones produced by ethnic elites. Such elites in Canada had been promoting the idea of a "liberal-democratic" and "all-inclusive" Canada, which he examines already between the wars, and thus were agents in shaping its modern identity. Similarly, C.P. Champion's *The Strange Demise of British Canada: The Liberals and Canadian Nationalism, 1964–1968* (2010) provides an insightful account of the process by which mainstream "Anglo-Celtic" Canadians dismissed their ethnicity as "something that was not truly Canadian" in the late 1960s.[40] Like Loewen and Friesen, Champion emphasizes the idea of "Canadian hybridity," which includes Britishness as a core element that shaped Canadian identity in the post-1960s era.[41] As he rightly asserts, "Britishness" was "a constitutive and animating element deeply embedded in the Canadianism of hybridized individuals and groups of a variety of ethnic backgrounds, not only those of British ethnicity."[42] Yet, while Champion incorporates ethnic elites into the story briefly, his focus remains the views of Anglo-Celtic Canadians.[43] My study builds on these two scholars and pushes their points further, arguing that non-British ethnic leaders indeed contributed to the consolidation of both Britishness and hybridity of Canada since the interwar period. The Britishness at the core of Canadianism was also a "core element" of ethnic identity.

Some recent studies successfully demonstrated the impact that ethnicity had on the evolution of human rights and multiethnic identity in Canada. Due to both the decline of ethnic historiography and the popularity of research topics concerning the notions of citizenship, human rights, and democracy, these studies promoted the fusion between mainstream and ethnic histories. Examples include Ross Lambertson's *Repression and Resistance: Canadian Human Rights Activists, 1930–1960* (2005) and Franca Iacovetta's *Gatekeepers: Reshaping Immigrant Lives in Cold War Canada* (2006). Lambertson shows how Japanese and Jewish elites independently nurtured a clear notion of human rights. Their activism, he argues, became the driving force behind passage of the Canadian Bill of Rights in 1960.[44] Focussing on the impacts that new immigrants of the post-World War II period had on the increasing awareness of Canadian citizenship and democracy in the Cold War context, Iacovetta reveals that ethnic elites' ideas helped to define what Canada should be. Her study, by implication, suggests that no clear-cut boundary existed between ethnicity and the mainstream. This is well illustrated by her analysis of citizenship official Vladimir Kaye, who worked for the integration of new immigrants into Canada, emphasizing "unity in diversity" and the "anti-Communist position."[45] Iacovetta rightfully treats him as a mainstream officer rather than an ethnic elite. Yet Kaye, Ukrainian in origin and an active nationalist, also successfully incorporated his nationalist Ukrainian agenda into the very idea of Canadian citizenship.

Within the above theoretical and historiographical framework, my study tries to provide a way to conceptualize ethnic histories in larger Canadian and transnational contexts. Quite naturally, it builds on the aforementioned studies as well as Ukrainian and Japanese sources. It shows that the strategies and discourses on which Ukrainian and Japanese ethnic leaders, as members of minority groups, relied were similar. For them, ethnic pluralism was always the only way to achieve and legitimize the desired dual identity that drew on both the homeland and Canada. Both groups needed to maintain ethnic boundaries and attach various meanings to them to participate in Canada politically. Yet race as a category constructed on people's physical appearance and discrimination urged Japanese Canadians to identify ethnicity as race to create a single ethnoracial boundary so that ethnic pluralism would not exclude non-white groups.

Organization and Themes

Chapter 1 outlines the formation of Japanese, Ukrainian, and Scottish ethnic communities in Canada and describes their changing profiles. Significantly, though both Ukrainian and Japanese communities displayed inconsistency in membership in organized activities, widespread integration at elite and grassroots levels, and geographical migration of members, the transformation rarely pointed to the decline of ethnicity.

Chapter 2 examines the consolidation and factionalism of the three ethnic communities between the wars, when elite mobilization of the masses produced a number of self-serving ethnic myths and first introduced the concept of ethnic pluralism, their notions of democracy, and homeland imperialisms into Canadian discourses.

Chapter 3 focuses on World War II, when the mainstream/ethnic boundary was most visible and rigid because of suspicion and discrimination against suspect ethnic groups. Scots fully supported Canada's war effort, pushing its universally Western causes for democracy. While both Ukrainians and Japanese faced a test of loyalty, marginalization of Japanese took official form after Japan attacked Pearl Harbor and became belligerent. Although Ukrainians were expected to participate in Canada's war effort, they too were affected by international developments, especially events in Ukraine.

Chapter 4 argues that the mainstream/ethnic boundary became more flexible after 1945 for two main reasons. First, wartime atrocities dramatically changed attitudes toward ethnic minorities across the globe—reflected, for example, in the Citizenship Act of Canada in 1947 and the Universal Declaration of Human Rights in 1948. Scots were part of this mainstream development. Second, both Ukrainian and Japanese elites accelerated their campaign for full recognition as well as the specific goals of the admission of Ukrainian refugees and limited compensation for Japanese losses during the war. Increasing appreciation of democracy provided both groups with the best opportunity in Canadian history to lobby the federal government on behalf of their particular goals.

Chapter 5 posits a merger between ethnic and mainstream identities. As participants in this process, all Japanese, Ukrainian, and Scottish elites attached new "democratic" meanings to their homeland symbols and myths, thereby Canadianizing them. At the same time, they produced their Canadian symbols and myths, ethnicizing specific places, events, and historic figures.

Chapter 6 focuses on the period when lobbying for multiculturalism gained momentum, triggered by the rise of French-Canadian nationalism and the appointment of the Royal Commission on Bilingualism and Biculturalism by the federal government in 1963. Yet it was also during this period that a divergence between Ukrainians and Japanese became obvious in terms of ethnic activism. While Ukrainians were in the vanguard of the multiculturalism movement, Japanese lost much of their organized power. As part of English-speaking Canada, Scots were least active during this period.

Scope and Limitations

As an examination of the evolution of Canadian identity over five decades, my study has its limitations. First, its focus is on how ethnic elites perceived and defined the role that "their" people should play rather than on how the masses responded to these leaders or thought independently. Given that my primary interest is more a comparison among ethnic groups in their negotiations with Canada than an in-depth examination of a single ethnic group, this approach seeks to be more fruitful in a particular way. Most significantly, a mosaic identity or ethnic consciousness was, if not invented, at least crystallized and articulated by community elites, who generally had a better knowledge of and familiarity with Canadian mainstream and homeland politics through education and interest. Most scholars of nationalism, including Anthony D. Smith and Eric J. Hobsbawm, agree that the initiative of elites is necessary in the formation of ethnicity or the nation.[46] Often members of a rising and ambitious middle class, living in urban centres and acquiring influential positions as newspaper editors, businessmen, and teachers, these leaders were anxious to improve political, cultural, and economic conditions both for themselves and for the group. As such, they played an important role as self-appointed mediators between mainstream society and the ethnic community, seeking upward mobility and defining ethnic boundaries by mobilizing "their" people behind their group's goals.

Second, some chapters focus on Ukrainians and Japanese and make only occasional references to Scots since the nature of Scottish ethnicity differed. While Scottish ethnicity, to some extent, was politically motivated and influential, Scots did not need to take advantage of or exploit their ethnicity to participate in mainstream society. Certainly, they did not face the political inequality and/or marginalization that Ukrainians and Japanese confronted for most of the period concerned. Yet Scots' ethnicity provides a valuable conceptual perspective when used to highlight the differences from Ukrainians and Japanese since Scots continued ethnicizing themselves and Canada. In a sense, they demonstrated an extreme case in which ethnicity defined Canadian identity without any difficulty—a state that Ukrainians and Japanese reached only in 1971 when Canada introduced multiculturalism.

Despite these parameters, my study posits an alternative ethnic view of Canada in an effort to stress the significance of ethnic elite activism for democratic and liberal principles and to pinpoint when and how ethnicity began defining Canadian identity. Rejecting the single interpretation of the evolution of Canadian identity from Anglo-conformity to liberal-democratic ethnic pluralism defined by mainstream Canadians, the study recognizes multiculturalism as a principle that ethnic elites possessed before World War II and with which they began to challenge mainstream Canadians after the war. In the process, the latter recognized ethnicity as a significant component of Canadian identity, while ethnic leaders accepted, broadened, and redefined narrowly defined Canadian identity and democracy.

CHAPTER 1

Changing Ethnic Profiles: Scots, Ukrainians, and Japanese

Ethnic boundaries have always been dynamic and fluid and cannot be defined by pre-existing national, religious, and racial backgrounds. These factors, however, determined primarily how wider Canadian society perceived the nature of each ethnic group. They also affected its position in the country's ethnoracial hierarchy, which favoured those of British origin. Ethnic leaders constantly sought to redefine the nature of their ethnic communities, both responding to political and economic conditions of the new land and negotiating old stereotypes imposed on them.

This chapter outlines the backgrounds of three ethnic elites, which shaped the wider society's first impressions of them. It also focuses on change and continuity within Ukrainian, Japanese, and Scottish ethnic communities over approximately a century, investigating two simultaneous but contradictory forces: segregation and integration. In the first decades of the twentieth century, discrimination dominated public attitudes toward ethnic communities, which tended to distance themselves from the wider society. In the post-World War II period, prewar ethnic community boundaries collapsed or shifted considerably, leading ethnic elites to become integrated into mainstream politics. Undoubtedly, Scots created close-knit circles among themselves, yet their nation-wide "imagined" Scottish community was not as consistent and cohesive as those of Ukrainians and Japanese and often overlapped with that of Canada. Although in different ways and at different paces, both Ukrainian and Japanese imagined communities dramatically transformed their outlooks over the years, becoming increasingly open and minimizing the distance from mainstream society.

The Era of Segregation and Alienation

The great surge of immigration to Canada in the late nineteenth and early twentieth centuries was crucial to ethnic community building. While pre-existing national, racial, and religious biases determined the hierarchy of ethnic groups, other factors, such as the scale of immigration and the place and size of settlement, reinforced it. These biases and factors not only influenced the agenda of ethnic elites in Canada but also had a persistent impact on negotiations between ethnic groups and mainstream society.

The first and most significant factor, placing Scots in a different cultural location than Ukrainians and Japanese, was racism. The old but powerful concept that categorized humans by skin colour and physical features into "Caucasian, Mongoloid, and Negroid" believed in the superiority of the Anglo-Saxon, Celtic, and other northern European races.[1] Racism emerged as a scientific doctrine mainly from the increasing contact between Europeans and others as a result of colonialism in the eighteenth and nineteenth centuries, and it dominated public discourses in North America into the early twentieth century.[2] Mainstream Canadian politicians, philosophers, and commentators believed that people's racial or physical characteristics determined their group nature in other respects. They thought that Canada should remain an Anglo-Celtic or at least a "white" nation because the race represented both physical and moral strengths. James S. Woodsworth's 1909 immigration study, for example, classified immigrants into ethnoracial categories and perceived both Ukrainians and Japanese as inferior to Brits. Still, there was a clear difference in his attitudes toward the two groups. For example, he portrayed Galicians (Ukrainians) as "quarrelsome and dangerous" but also "patient," "industrious," and "eager to become Canadianized."[3] Japanese and other Asians, in contrast, tended to maintain "their own virtues and vices" and "constitute an entirely distinct class or caste," and they could not "be assimilated."[4]

A second crucial factor was the particular roles that the homelands of the three groups played on the world stage, for they predetermined how their people would be perceived in Canada. Politically united with England since 1707, Scotland wielded considerable influence in the world. Not only did Scots expand geographically around the globe as part of the British Empire, but they also contributed fundamentally to modern science and technology and to the British-based legal, political, and educational systems like those in Canada. As Arthur Herman has shown, Scotland thus became a symbol of modernity and hegemony for Scottish immigrants overseas.[5] Neither Ukraine nor Japan could make such a claim on behalf of Western civilization.

The contemporary territory of Ukraine, which had known periods of statehood in medieval Kievan Rus' and under the Cossacks, was divided among neighbouring powers and subject to foreign rule.[6] The provinces of Galicia and Bukovina in Western Ukraine, where most Ukrainians in Canada originated, were part of the Austro-Hungarian Empire, then interwar Poland and Romania, and then the Soviet Union, except for the short period between 1917 and 1920. Statelessness and national oppression disadvantaged both Ukrainian immigrants and their descendants as a sign of cultural and political weakness and galvanized them to help the homeland. Statelessness also led to confusion, so that when Ukrainians first came to Canada they were identified by various names as Austrians, Ruthenians, Galicians, and Bukovinians. In contrast, Japan had existed as an isolated realm since ancient times and developed as a strong modern nation-state after the Meiji Restoration in 1868. But in light of its seclusion from the world for a long time and localism in the Far East, Japan was regarded in Europe and North America as backward economically, politically, and culturally. Its attempt at colonial expansion was viewed as neither equally influential nor benevolent as the British Empire. Ukrainians and Japanese, then, were placed below Scots in the world's hierarchy of power, even before they immigrated to Canada.

A third important factor was the sheer scale and timing of Scottish immigration—both much larger and earlier than Ukrainian and Japanese immigrations. Scots not only constituted a dominant group numerically in Canada but also were initial builders of the new colony following the British conquest of New France. For them, British North America was a logical place for emigration and an extension of their homeland. During the eighteenth century, Scots in Canada included often transient fur traders, soldiers, merchants, labourers, and adventurers as well as more permanent settlers of Loyalist stock. Large-scale immigration and settlement occurred after 1815, nearly a century before Ukrainians and Japanese began arriving in Canada en masse, thereby consolidating the Scottish imprint on British North America. Between 1815 and 1870, approximately 170,000 Scots immigrated to Canada; another 326,000 arrived between 1870 and 1918.[7] Although the reasons for this movement were often associated with economic conditions in Scotland, such as overpopulation and lack of land, they also represented imperial expansionism politically, culturally, and economically.

British Canada's deeply rooted ethnoracial biases allowed more Ukrainians than Japanese to immigrate, thereby securing for the former greater numbers and political influence. Even though Ukrainians would later promote themselves as co-builders of western Canada, British immigrants

Table 3. Ukrainian population in Canada, 1931–71.

	1931	1951	1971
British Columbia	2,583	22,613	60,150
Alberta	55,872	86,957	135,510
Saskatchewan	63,400	78,399	85,920
Manitoba	73,606	98,753	114,410
Ontario	24,426	93,595	159,880
Quebec	4340	12,921	203,25
Atlantic	883	1,431	3,215

Source: William Darcovich and Paul Yuzyk, eds., *A Statistical Compendium on the Ukrainians in Canada, 1891–1976* (Ottawa: University of Ottawa Press, 1980).

Table 4. Japanese population in Canada, 1931–71.

	1931	1951	1971
British Columbia	22,205	7,169	13,585
Alberta	652	3,336	4,460
Saskatchewan	114	225	315
Manitoba	51	1,161	1,335
Ontario	220	8,581	15,600
Quebec	43	1,137	1,745
Atlantic	4	19	140

Source: Dominion Bureau of Statistics, Census of Canada.

Both discrimination and internal group dynamics (often Old World in origin or character) determined the cohesiveness and nature of ethnic communities and their associations in Canada, with Ukrainians and Japanese establishing much more close-knit institutions than did Scots. As new immigrants, elites of the three groups had helped them to create local and regional organizations for the purpose of mutual support, which marked a significant first step in the formation of identifiable ethnic communities outside the common society. The first Scottish association, the North British Society of Halifax, was established in 1768, and several St. Andrew's societies appeared in the late eighteenth and early nineteenth centuries in cities such as Saint John, Montreal, and Ottawa.[15] Undoubtedly, these voluntary associations helped newcomers to get used to Canada. But politically speaking, because Scots experienced little discrimination given their background, their associations tended to focus on recreational activities, often combined with charity and/or promotion of ethnic identity, such as celebrating St. Andrew's Day or Robert Burns Day and hosting Highland games. Some attempts were made to recreate the Scottish clan system, which represented kinship and geographical links in the old country, yet it was often done for symbolic purposes, including the celebration of more localized roots. Among Ukrainians and Japanese, pioneer secular institutions were more than opportunities for socializing. Facing prejudice because of their ethnic or racial origin and difficulties in communicating in English, both Ukrainians and Japanese regarded their countrymen, friends, and neighbours as crucial sources of assistance. By the end of the 1920s, a number of Japanese and Ukrainian secular institutions, which followed homeland models, emerged at the local level. Ukrainians formed *chytalni* ("reading clubs") and *narodni domy* ("community halls") for mutual support, enlightenment, and preservation of Ukrainian culture, while Japanese established *kenjinkai* ("countrymen's clubs"), similar to the Scottish clan system yet more practical in promoting cooperation among fellow immigrants from the same prefectures. The first Ukrainian reading club was organized in Winnipeg in 1899, and dozens of others or related institutions had appeared in both prairie cities and the rural Ukrainian blocs by the 1930s.[16] Japanese *kenjinkai* existed mainly in Vancouver and southern Alberta; the first to be formed was the Hiroshima *kenjinkai* in 1902, followed by the Shiga *kenjinkai* in 1905, both in British Columbia.[17]

Religion also functioned as a natural focal point of ethnic identity as well as spiritual faith and practical collaboration. Yet religion was also subjected to Canada's pre-existing ethnoreligious hierarchy, which placed Christianity, and Protestantism in particular, at the top, thus reinforcing the marginalization of Greek Catholics and Orthodox Ukrainians but especially Buddhist/Shinto Japanese. As J.M. Bumsted has shown, the Protestant Scots, who were mostly Presbyterian, played a significant role in the consolidation of Protestant traditions and values in Canada. Presbyterianism had its roots in the Scottish Reformation led by John Knox in the sixteenth century and was strongly tied to Scottish identity. The Presbyterian Church was established in Canada in 1875 and merged with the Congregational and Methodist Churches to form the United Church of Canada in 1925. Catholic Scots, who came mostly from the Highlands, maintained their ethnoreligious identity, particularly in Cape Breton, eastern Nova Scotia, and Prince Edward Island.[18]

A Scottish minister of the Presbyterian Church, Alexander MacMillan, for example, recalled in his memoir written between 1940 and 1945 that Presbyterian influence had already had a great impact on Canada in the late nineteenth century. As a divinity student, he had travelled throughout Canada and wrote that "I reported faithfully to the Theological Society of the College concerning the great and growing work of the Presbyterian Church in Canada throughout the Dominion. From what I had learned I determined to apply to the Colonial Committee of the United Presbyterian Church of Scotland for a colonial commission."[19]

Establishing and securing their religious institutions in Canada were more complicated for Ukrainians and Japanese, whose respective faiths were regarded as foreign and inferior. Protestant missionaries, inspired in part by a sense of British superiority, worked among both peoples, hoping to proselytize them, while the Roman Catholic Church, tied to French linguistic and cultural survival, tried to win Ukrainian converts in particular to consolidate its influence in the west.[20] For example, the French Latin-rite Catholic archbishop of St. Boniface, Adélard Langevin, opposed the establishment of an independent Greek Catholic Church under a Byzantine-rite bishop for Ukrainians until 1912, trying to keep Roman Catholic order in Canada. Similarly, the construction of Japanese Buddhist or Shinto institutions in British Columbia was not welcomed by white Canadians. In fact, Protestant missionaries worked intensively among Japanese immigrants, trying to enlighten them by instilling Christian morality and values. The most successful denomination was the Methodists, who had built eight Japanese churches in British Columbia by 1921.[21]

Ukrainians and Japanese, however, never abandoned the desire to worship in their own faiths and eventually succeeded in building their own religious institutions. Moreover, their leaders saw religion, with its familiar ritual and language, as a tool to reach out to the masses. The Ukrainian pioneer nationalist intelligentsia, for example, opposed the appointment of foreign priests and the Latin-rite influences because of the important connection that they made between ethnicity and religion.[22] They established the independent Ukrainian Greek Orthodox Church in 1918, overtly tying religion to their secular nationalist agenda, especially the retention of Ukrainian identity. During the 1920s and 1930s, both the Greek Catholic and the Ukrainian Greek Orthodox Churches successfully promoted Ukrainian ethnoreligious consciousness and enjoyed the support of most Ukrainian Canadians. In 1931, 58 percent of all Ukrainians were Greek Catholic, while approximately 24 percent were Ukrainian Greek Orthodox.[23] For the

Japanese elite, who came from the non-Christian world, religion created a much clearer split within their community. While the majority of Japanese retained Shintoism and Pure Land Buddhism (*jôdo shinshû*), some converted to Christianity, which became a symbol of Canadianization. Shintoism, originating as a folk faith that possessed neither a founder nor scriptures, was closely intertwined with people's internal being and lives, while Buddhism was more organized institutionally. The Buddhist elite built their first temple in Vancouver in 1905 under Sasaki Senju, a temporary priest from Japan, hoping to block further expansion of Christianity among their people. The first temple was established in 1910, also in Vancouver. Buddhism was further promoted by associations that targeted specific age and gender groups, such as the Buddhist Women's Organization (1913) and the Buddhist Youth Association (1915). By the 1930s, Buddhism had five missions and six branches served by Japanese priests and twenty-eight associations organized by secular priests.[24] Japanese Christians focussed on the Methodists did exert some pressure on Buddhist temples, however. For them, Christianity was a way to interact with mainstream society, whose acceptance provided them with a special status in the Japanese community.

These ethnic and/or religious societies at the local level were established mainly by the initiative of individuals who, in many cases, were more highly educated or economically better off than other immigrants and demonstrated leadership qualities. They provided assistance and guidance to members of local communities in the early stages of settlement, and they were admired as leaders if not recognized officially. Although these men played significant roles in the formation of identifiable ethnic communities, the concepts of creating nation-wide networks and "imagined" communities emerged from a rising middle class.

While Scots, whose leaders became Canada's leading politicians and even prime ministers, did not create a distinctive pan-Scottish community in Canada, a pan-Ukrainian consciousness and a pan-Japanese consciousness gradually crystallized. The new elites, upwardly mobile and often politically ambitious, were educated either in the homeland or in Canada and moved into influential occupations such as newspaper editors, businessmen, and teachers. They also founded their own bases for activity in Winnipeg (Ukrainians) and Vancouver (Japanese). Because they were familiar with conditions in both Canada and the homeland, they tried to educate and guide their peoples as their self-appointed representatives. The emergence of such a leadership core of Ukrainians and Japanese sooner or later led to sharp competition as they sought power and respect within both mainstream and ethnic communities.

How and when these conflicts emerged were affected by the political situation surrounding and energizing the larger group. Polarization occurred much more quickly among Ukrainians, organizing around competing solutions to the unresolved Ukrainian question in Europe, and thus accelerated the mobilization of Ukrainian masses behind community building. Before World War I, a rivalry had gradually emerged between nationalists and socialists, the former defending Ukrainian independence and cultural and linguistic survival, the latter seeking workers' rights and the construction of an international proletarian world.[25] They laid the foundations of two large, conflicting, nation-wide camps in the interwar period, pulling Ukrainians together beyond the local community, for example, around nationalist bilingual teachers and the Federation of Ukrainian Social Democrats and establishing their own presses.[26] Japanese also experienced minor internal rivalries before the war, but they did not import such clear ideological conflict from Japan. Their competitions were between regional and clan groups, Christians and Buddhists, and Vancouver-based elites and local community leaders. Yet the prewar urban and rural associations and their presses, which appeared in both British Columbia and Alberta and initiated antiracist activities, helped Japanese elites to broaden their influence among their people in the interwar period. For example, the Canadian Japanese Association (CJA) was established in Vancouver in 1897, followed by the Calgary Japanese Association in 1909 and the Raymond Japanese Association in 1914 in Alberta. Rural Japanese, mainly farmers and fishermen, established cooperatives all over British Columbia, such as the Fraser River Japanese Fishermen's Cooperative, established in 1900.

The first common challenge for ethnic elites in terms of situating their own positions in Canadian society was World War I, in which British Canadian leaders, including Scots, participated as one of the British dominions. It was the first and only period in the twentieth century during which Japanese and Ukrainians reversed their positions in the ethnic hierarchy. Japanese, whose homeland fought on the Canadian side, saw the war as an opportunity to improve their status in Canada. As a group who did not have the vote, however, their enlistment in Canadian military forces often caused dilemma and contradiction in terms of sense of duty.[27] One hundred and ninety-six Japanese volunteers[28] no doubt had a great impact on ethnic leadership, receiving respect from their community and the franchise in 1931. Ukrainians, most of whom came from Austria-Hungary, now a German ally, faced a different challenge. The War Measures Act categorized approximately 80,000 people who retained their citizenship with enemy countries as "enemy aliens" and interned approximately 6,000 Ukrainians.[29] Such action by Canada no doubt restricted organized Ukrainian activities, particularly those by pro-German or pro-Austrian leaders. Yet scholars regard their internment as a result of crossing borders in search of jobs rather than of leading ideologically suspicious activities. Many of them were ordinary labourers and farmers.[30]

From the 1920s through the mid-1940s, internal conflicts and power struggles among Ukrainians and Japanese went through a number of stages. After the Bolshevik revolution in 1917 and the failure of Ukraine to become independent, the earlier Ukrainian rivalry between nationalists and socialists intensified, pitting those who sought statehood for a non-communist Ukraine against communist sympathizers who worshipped the Soviet Union, which included the bulk of Ukrainian territory. Among Japanese, tensions emerged mainly due to differences of opinion over assimilation. The *issei* or immigrant generation was divided between Buddhist traditionalists who insisted on the preservation of Japanese cultural and linguistic traditions in Canada and assimilationists who converted to Christianity and stressed the significance of Canadianization. The former, which constituted the majority, increasingly found their views at odds with those of the *nisei* or Canadian-born generation.

In general, nationalist Ukrainians and *nisei* Japanese, both strong advocates of democracy at any time, found it easier to adapt their principles to Canada's values and goals. Although Ukrainian nationalists were split into pan-Canadian homeland-oriented and Canadian-oriented factions—the monarchist United Hetman Organization (UHO, established in 1924), the Canadian-oriented Ukrainian Self-Reliance League (USRL, established in 1927), and the right-wing émigré Ukrainian National Federation (UNF, established in 1932)—they all saw their search for freedom and democracy as overlapping with British and thus Canadian political ideals. *Nisei* Japanese also stressed their loyalty to Canada and claimed their natural rights as Canadian citizens, establishing the Japanese Canadian Citizens League (JCCL) in 1936 to further their goals. In comparison, communist Ukrainians and *issei* Japanese experienced more difficulty in fitting into Canadian society, even if they had great impacts on their respective communities. Their ideologies—Ukrainian communism and Japanese nationalism tied to colonialism—were often regarded as being incompatible with Canadian values or even dangerous. While the nation-wide communist Ukrainian Labour-Farmer Temple Association (ULFTA, established in 1918 as the Ukrainian Labour Temple Association) was active in the rural Ukrainian blocs, the cities, and the resource towns in support of the Soviet Union and promotion of workers' rights, its activities were viewed as suspicious and often inspected by the Canadian police. *Issei* Japanese carried the memory of official and unofficial discrimination, including the Vancouver riot of 1907, in which Canadian anti-Asian organizations attacked the Chinese and Japanese quarters in Vancouver. Thus, during the interwar period, *issei* Japanese continued fighting overt discrimination against Japanese at the same time as trying to promote Japanese consciousness among *nisei*.

A final factor affecting the behaviour and agenda of Ukrainian and Japanese elites as community leaders was their relationship with the Canadian mainstream. As Orest Martynowych suggests, Ukrainians, as voting citizens, had a better chance of negotiating with Canadian political leaders, developing, for example, a system of "party agents" already in the period of initial immigration. These agents, affiliated with the mainstream Conservatives or Liberals, campaigned in the Ukrainian blocs in the prairie provinces on behalf of their parties, playing an intermediary role that promoted their status both in their own communities and in mainstream political circles.[31] Without the ballot, Japanese elites had limited methods by which to form bridges between their community and mainstream society.[32] One of them was through formal representatives from their homeland; Japan opened its first consulate in Vancouver in 1889, followed by one in Montreal in 1902. Another possible way for Japanese leaders to build a better relationship with the Canadian government was to exploit a formal relationship between Japan and Britain. The Anglo-Japanese Alliance of 1902, a military agreement between Japan and Britain against Russian expansion, for example, provided them with a strong backbone.

During World War II, nationalist Ukrainians and *nisei* Japanese focussed on building stronger negotiating bodies with mainstream society for different reasons. The former were united for the first time under the government-sponsored Ukrainian Canadian Committee (UCC, established in 1940) to facilitate their cooperation with the mainstream Canadian war effort. The latter, facing internment, sought a better deal with the Canadian government, forming new organizations such as the *nisei* Japanese Canadian Citizens Council (JCCC, established in 1942), the Nisei Mass Evacuation Group (NMEG, established in 1942), based in Vancouver, and the Toronto-based Japanese Canadian Committee for Democracy (JCCD, established in 1943).

The Era of Assimilation and Integration

Although the origins of the Scottish, Ukrainian, and Japanese ethnic communities determined their fundamental roles and positions in Canadian society, their appearances changed over the years. Naturally, as members became more integrated into Canadian political and economic structures, the size and number of ethnic associations tended to shrink, and geographical concentration became less obvious. In addition, old ideological tensions did not always function in the same way as they had in the past. Recognizing such changes is significant when ethnicity as a political phenomenon is under investigation. First, integration of ethnic elites into the higher levels of Canadian society increasingly changed the notion of "mainstream" Canada. Second, decline in the membership of ethnic associations did not necessarily correspond to a decline in ethnicity or ethnic consciousness, which continued to shape Canadian identity after World War II. Third, diffusion of ethnic populations did not necessarily affect the impact of ethnicity on Canadian identity either. After World War II, people increasingly moved out of traditional ethnic clusters, a voluntary process separate from the coercive policy of diffusion imposed on Japanese in the internment camps. This section touches on these issues, focussing on differences and similarities between the Ukrainian and Japanese communities after World War II and drawing in Scots where relevant.

The integration of ethnic leaders into influential positions in Canadian society did not always lead to the demise of ethnic activism in politics. Traditionally, historians, social theorists, and others argued that such upward mobility resulted in the loss of political motivation and an emphasis on the symbolic aspects of ethnicity, such as cultural traditions, ethnic foods, and folk arts. Although this argument can be applied to Scots, it does not explain Ukrainian or Japanese ethnicity. Even though prominent Ukrainian individuals emerged as members of Parliament, cabinet ministers, and senators, they never lost their commitment to ethnic causes. As Isajiw points out, they were still a minority among policy makers, and they needed to use their ethnicity to gain more power.[33] For example, Anthony Hlynka, elected to the House of Commons for Social Credit in the Vegreville constituency in 1940, keenly worked for the acceptance of Ukrainian displaced persons after the war,[34] while Paul Yuzyk, appointed to the Senate in 1963, frequently spoke up for Ukraine in Europe and Ukrainian rights in Canada. Not surprisingly, Japanese participation in Canadian politics was very slow, yet after the mid-1960s individuals emerged locally as mayors, magistrates, or judges who also chose to work for the betterment of their people in Canada. Lucien Kurata, appointed a deputy magistrate in 1966, for example, identified the promotion of "human rights" as his top priority.[35] For Ukrainian and Japanese elites, whose chances to climb to the top were not as great as those of Scots, ethnic agendas and their peoples' support served as significant means to gain and retain power. Their integration, in turn, thus played a significant role in defining the Canadian mainstream as multicultural.

Decline in ethnic organizational membership after World War II was particularly true for *issei* Japanese and communist Ukrainians, whose falling fortunes changed the tone of ethnic activism within their respective communities as the competition among ethnic leaders for group loyalties became less intense. In the Japanese community, the shift in leadership and power from *issei* to *nisei* was inevitable since between 1957 and 1961 the proportion of *issei* in the Japanese-Canadian population dropped from 29 percent to approximately 21 percent.[36] After the end of World War II, *issei* did not establish any new large-scale independent associations and were, in fact, incorporated into the *nisei*-oriented, nation-wide body, the National Japanese Canadian Citizens Association (NJCCA, established in 1947). By the 1960s, the old *issei-nisei* rivalry had virtually died out, and *nisei* did not compete with their subsequent generations in the same way that they had with their parents' generation. After 1962, when most racially discriminatory policies were removed from Canada's immigration policy, Japanese immigrants to Canada gradually increased, yet they were neither ideologically oriented nor closely united. The NJCCA's struggle for survival, which became the largest community issue during the 1960s, largely reflected the lack of appealing agendas, competition among leaders, and enthusiastic mobilization of the masses. After 1945, the communist Association of United Ukrainian Canadians (AUUC, established in 1945) peaked quickly and then lost both members and branches, affected by the growing antagonism toward communism during the Cold War. Between 1954 and 1970, approximately ninety-one AUUC branches closed.[37] Yet, while the communists posed no serious threat to the far more popular nationalists, the fact that the USSR continued to control Ukraine kept animosities high. Reinforcing these tensions, as well as national consciousness among Ukrainians already in Canada, was the immigration of postwar displaced persons, anticommunist refugees from former Nazi camps.

Finally, physical concentration was not a prerequisite for the existence of ethnic communities, especially when means of communication through the ethnic press and other media were available. Despite the flourishing of Ukrainian myths that focussed on rural communities in the Prairies in the postwar period, the reality was that many Ukrainians lived neither in the Prairies nor in rural areas. In 1941, approximately 80 percent of all Ukrainians lived in Alberta, Saskatchewan, and Manitoba, but this figure dropped to 58 percent by 1971. By 1951, approximately half of the Ukrainian population was urban.[38] For Japanese, the evacuation from the West Coast in 1942, and the postwar policy to resettle them east of the Rockies, destroyed their political base in British Columbia completely. In 1941, 95 percent of all Japanese lived in British Columbia, while in 1951 only 15 percent could be found in that province. The Japanese population in British Columbia recovered to some degree and reached 35 percent in 1961, but the Japanese dispersal across the country was obvious: another 40 percent lived in Ontario and about 13 percent in Alberta in that year.[39]

The positions of Scots, Ukrainians, and Japanese in Canada were determined by their race, religion, ranking in the country's ethnoracial hierarchy, place of settlement, and size and timing of immigration. Together these factors made Ukrainians and Japanese second-class citizens and favoured Scots, who were entrenched in the mainstream. Both Ukrainian and Japanese elites focussed on improving their status inside and outside their groups and on gaining negotiating power with the mainstream society, expanding their ethnic communities nation-wide throughout the interwar period. Major changes after World War II in geographical distribution, ideological rivalries, and elitist political integration of Ukrainians and Japanese could have meant the demise of ethnicity. Yet the reality was that Ukrainian and Japanese elites, to a greater or lesser degree, maintained ethnic identity as a means to obtain greater power, lobbying the federal and provincial governments for their specific agendas and producing various collective memories and myths. Integration, in fact, increased such opportunities for both elites and had more ethnic impact on mainstream politics and culture. The following chapters thus demonstrate that ethnicity, despite the changes that occurred throughout the fifty years, continued to shape Canadian identity.

CHAPTER 2

The Consolidation of Ethnic Boundaries and the Rise of the Mosaic

The 1920s and 1930s witnessed a consolidation of ethnic boundaries because of the intensive activities of ethnic elites and the rise of the "mosaic" as the basis of Canadian identity. During this time, ethnic elites expanded their influences over the majority of late-nineteenth- and early-twentieth-century immigrants, who were usually apolitical and lived in close-knit circles of fellow countrymen. This crystallization of ethnic communities is particularly significant because, as powerful categories of identity, they determined how political leaders and scholars conceptualized Canadian identity in the past and present. In other words, the roots of ethnic pluralism, which preserves ethnic boundaries, lay in this period. This chapter examines the nature of consolidating ethnic boundaries in light of the roles that factors such as homeland and host society politics, ideological competition within an ethnic group, region, and ethnic myths and symbols played in ethnic community building, and it questions how the mosaic became the dominant view of Canada among ethnic elites. In fact, it was the dramatic interplay among these factors that defined ethnic boundaries.

Through a comparison of Ukrainians, Scots, and Japanese, I can make some observations. First, while their elites, to a greater or lesser degree, all found instrumental advantages in ethnicity, Ukrainian leaders had the prerequisites to organize a more politically distinctive community than the other two. One reason was their political oppression in Ukraine, and the other was their "middle" status in the ethnic hierarchy between "mainstream" Scots and "marginalized" Japanese. Their middle status, in particular, allowed Ukrainian elite to consider active political negotiation with mainstream society. Second, the prototype of ethnic pluralism as understood in Canada can be found in the ideals of Ukrainians and, to a lesser degree, Japanese during the interwar period. In this sense, the notion of multiculturalism or ethnic pluralism, which not only preserves the cultural heritages of ethnic groups but also respects ethnic individuals' right to keep loyalty to homelands, is by no means a postwar concept. Ukrainian nationalists and *issei* Japanese, in particular, regarded Canada as neither a British country nor a Canadian melting pot at any time. Third, ethnic and mainstream visions of Canada never met during the 1920s and 1930s, and the mainstream/ethnic boundary remained in force. Although a few British-Canadian scholars and writers—including Kate A. Foster and John Murray Gibbon[1]—did suggest that a cultural mosaic could distinguish Canada's identity, they tended to confine their discussions to cultural and philosophical matters and never incorporated homeland politics, racial and/or ethnic equality, and the political recognition of ethnic groups into their ideas of the mosaic.[2]

Ethnic Elites and the Crystallization of Ethnic Communities

The roles of ethnic leaders in Canadian society and in individual ethnic communities were key factors in determining the nature of ethnic boundaries. In interwar Canada, Scots, Ukrainians, and Japanese were all represented by self-appointed ethnic leaders. Yet various factors left nationalist Ukrainians in a better position to gain influence among their people as representatives than either their rival communists or the other two groups. Of fundamental importance was the distance of Ukrainians and Japanese from the British-Canadian mainstream and Scots' closeness to it, which made a difference in the effectiveness of elites in mobilizing their people.

Unlike Ukrainian and Japanese elites, regarded as second-class citizens, Scots occupied politically, economically, and culturally influential positions in Canada, and their elite included in many cases national leaders. Thus, they lacked strong motivation and incentive to become "ethnic" representatives. In this context, the few individuals who stressed their Scottish roots were rarely seen as organized voices for Scottish people in Canada. They included, for example, Gaelic scholars such as J.G. MacKinnon, A.M. Sinclair, and James MacNeil and politicians such as Angus L. Macdonald, premier of Nova Scotia, who began a Gaelic and/or Scottish revival movement particularly in Nova Scotia during the 1920s and 1930s.[3] Gaelic or Scottish scholars were academics more than political activists, and their focus on the promotion of Scottish culture and folklore was motivated by their scholarly interests in culture and language. A politician such as Macdonald was more politically motivated and active than academics, but he represented all people in Nova

Scotia, not just Scots. Similarly, Lord Tweedsmuir, a Scot and an influential advocate of Scottish history and heritage, appointed as governor general of Canada in 1935, was a symbol of English Canada and Britain.

Prominent Ukrainian and Japanese individuals, in contrast, regarded ethnicity as a significant means to gain full participation in Canadian political and economic structures. Ukrainians, however, possessed the franchise, constituted a majority in some prairie ridings, and did not have to deal with any official non-Soviet representatives from their homeland[4] who could overshadow or contradict them. These factors made it easier for their leaders than for Japanese leaders to climb the ladder as influential spokespersons. The turning point for Ukrainian leaders came when they recognized the need for their own elected representatives instead of imposed ones. They increasingly began "to take their destiny into their own hands" to further their ethnoreligious goals, rejecting the Anglo-Protestant agenda of assimilation,[5] and advanced their own candidates in federal and provincial elections, particularly in the prairie provinces with their sizable Ukrainian populations. The emergence of a "formal" political elite had two consequences. It not only helped to mobilize the grassroots but also facilitated the Ukrainian elite in bringing their ethnic agenda to the attention of mainstream provincial and national governments. The Edmonton-based newspaper *Zakhidni visty*, for example, repeatedly stressed that the economic and political interests of Ukrainians, "equal rights" in particular, would be fought for only by Ukrainian candidates, and it argued that "solidarity and unity among the Ukrainians" were crucial for the success of a Ukrainian candidate.[6] It was imperative, therefore, to remind Ukrainian people of their right to vote at every election and to urge immigrants to take out naturalization papers and be eligible.[7] Obviously, such priorities subordinated general political ideals and party affiliations to ethnicity and the ethnic agenda.

Japanese leaders, on the other hand, were disenfranchised in every federal, provincial, and municipal election in British Columbia throughout the interwar period.[8] Unlike Ukrainians, they could neither mobilize their people as voters nor have themselves elected to any body. Unlike Scots, who had both official representatives of their homeland and influential Canadian-made elite, they had no choice but to rely on Japanese delegates in the Consulate of Japan and, after 1929, the Legation as their only "official" representatives who possessed some influence with Canadian governments. Yet, due to differences between official homeland delegates and Japanese-Canadian immigrants in priorities and opinions, internal conflicts were common during the interwar period.[9] One consul, Tatsuo Kawai, for example, was a controversial figure. His understanding that "all Japanese in

Canada were under his control," and the Canadian Japanese Association's (CJA) compliant attitude toward him, divided the Japanese community in 1926 when sixteen executive members left the association in anger.[10] Kawai's attempts to directly govern the CJA and a Japanese-language school (Japanese public school),[11] plus other issues, caused dissent between CJA members who believed in their "autonomy" and those who supported the consul.[12] The frustrated sixteen members contended that "the CJA only existed for the consul's satisfaction and personal interest in power" and that the consul's overt belief that the CJA and all Japanese in Canada belonged to Imperial Japan fuelled pre-existing anti-Japanese sentiment among white British Columbians.[13] Their memoranda, which outlined Kawai's lack of effort to bridge Japanese and mainstream communities, were distributed to the Japanese masses. A striking characteristic of Japanese in Canada in the 1920s, then, was the absence of powerful individuals who acquired unanimous respect beyond their local communities as well as an organized voice more generally.

On special occasions, such as New Year's Day, messages from the Japanese consul, government ministers, and scholars, who spoke only for Imperial Japan, always covered the front page of *Tairiku nippô*, an independent Japanese-Canadian newspaper established in 1907. A small self-appointed Japanese elite did emerge and devoted themselves to acquiring the franchise and building better relations between Japanese and other Canadians through local farmers' or fishermen's unions. An illuminating example was the Christian Yasutarô Yamaga, who expanded his activities in Haney, establishing an agricultural union and a Japanese-language school. Born in Hiroshima in 1886 and unknown in Japan, he was a typical immigrant leader. Although he was not different from other Japanese in that he immigrated to Canada in search of agricultural land, he excelled them in his writing, reading, and analytical skills. His records indicate his great insight into and interest in Canadian history and politics. He made every effort to build a good relationship with local mainstream farmers and was always critical of forming Japanese clusters in Canada.[14] But Japanese leaders such as Yamaga had a limited impact on mainstream politics without the collective power of the franchise. Elites could only express their resentment of racial discrimination and criticize anti-Japanese politicians indirectly through media such as the Japanese ethnic press. It was only natural, then, that the emerging *nisei* saw an "organized lobby for the franchise" as the prime means by which to enhance their status in both the Japanese community and Canada.[15]

The consolidation of ethnic elites often coincided with ideological splits within an ethnic group, which also had significant impacts on their work to promote ethnic consciousness among the masses. Each faction's efforts to represent its ethnic group and to build a solid sphere of power and influence inevitably involved the intensive production of propaganda in the ethnic press and in cultural and educational activities that formed the basis of an "imagined community" and distinguished the group from its competitors. One goal of such competition was to acquire greater influence in Canadian society as the representative voice of a particular ethnic group. Logically, then, the fact that Scots did not need to rely on ethnicity for social and economic upward mobility helps to explain the lack of an obvious internal split among them. In other words, influential Scots competed with others not just within their ethnic boundaries but also in the larger mainstream political sphere. Furthermore, the lack of internal rivalry, which often involved intensive mobilization of the masses around a certain ideology, explains the relative weakness of this group's ethnic consciousness. In fact, in the 1920s and 1930s, Scots rarely reflected the conflict between Highland Catholics and Lowland Presbyterians, which they had carried from their homeland.[16] For example, the minutes of two Catholic associations—the Scottish Catholic Society on Cape Breton Island and St. Andrew's Society of Ottawa—never even mentioned homeland politics, let alone hostility toward the Presbyterian community. Their interests rarely went beyond the preservation of Highland symbols, sports, and events such as Robert Burns Day.[17] At the same time, these associations were locally oriented rather than nation-wide and seldom claimed to represent all Scots in Canada.

Conversely, both Ukrainians and Japanese were severely divided along internal lines—the former between nationalists and communists, the latter between *issei* and *nisei*. Yet differences between the two in the nature of intra-group rivalry made Ukrainians more politically competitive than Japanese during the interwar period.

The first difference simply concerned the origin and timing of conflicts. In terms of origin, while the Ukrainian rivalry was led from Europe with the rise of the Bolsheviks and the failed Ukrainian People's Republic and was imported to Canada, Japanese rivalry began with the emergence of Canadian-born Japanese who did not know Japan, possessed little understanding of loyalty to the emperor, and thus opposed homeland traditions. Ukrainians were divided by incompatible ideologies, while the Japanese rivalry, in contrast, was invented in Canada. *Nisei* identity was a unique case in which Japanese descendants who had been identified with their parents' homeland that they had never known developed a distinctive collective identity. Ukrainian nationalists and communists had to fight intensively to gain their people's support, while Japanese were categorized into *issei* or *nisei* by birth. The *issei-nisei* rivalry thus did not involve recruitment to a camp, which was crucial to the Ukrainian competition.

In terms of timing, it was not until the mid-1930s that *nisei* reached adulthood, started organized political activities, and challenged *issei*. But the conflict among Ukrainians had been intense since the end of World War I and the creation of the Soviet Union. The rivalry gained momentum with the establishment of nation-wide organizations: the communist Ukrainian Labour-Farmer Temple Association (ULFTA) and the nationalist United Hetman Organization (UHO), Ukrainian Self-Reliance League (USRL), Ukrainian National Federation (UNF), and Ukrainian Catholic Brotherhood (UCB). Their ideological organs, such as the nationalist *Ukrainskyi holos* of the USRL, the *Novyi shliakh* of the UNF, and the communist *Ukrainski robitnychi visty,* together with sometimes dozens of local branches, were significant tools in mobilizing the grassroots.[18]

In comparison, the Japanese elite was less politically competitive or ideologically divided throughout the 1920s. Undoubtedly, it was rarely a monolithic group. For example, it produced various pre-World War I co-operatives, including the Fraser River Japanese Fishermen's Cooperative, which focussed on issues such as the fight for workers' rights. At the same time, a group of people became Christians as a demonstration of their assimilation to Canada. *Tairiku nippô,* established by a group of Buddhist individuals, especially resisted the proselytization of Japanese Canadians into Christianity.[19] Yet the individuals who identified with such associations did not face real challenges until the late 1930s, when *nisei* produced their own politically conscious elite, at which point the *issei-nisei* rivalry over representation became intense. While some early *nisei* favoured the idea of a *nisei* organization and launched short-lived newsletters such as *New Age,* more organized activities started with the establishment of the Japanese Canadian Citizens League (JCCL) in 1936 and its organ, *New Canadian,* in late 1938 in pursuit of the franchise and Japanese participation in Canadian political and social life. The real competition between *issei* and *nisei* thus postdated Ukrainian ideological activities and competition, which began several years earlier.

The second difference between Ukrainians and Japanese in terms of internal competitiveness stemmed from relations between the two camps within each group. The two Ukrainian camps sought mutually exclusive goals, while the Japanese rivals were interdependent. Ukrainian nationalists were well aware that communist ideology was at odds with British democratic principles and that its presence among Ukrainians would never benefit them in their pursuit of full participation in Canadian life. Yet *issei* had to rely on *nisei*, who had a birthright to Canadian citizenship, to reinforce their organized activities to resist mounting anti-Japanese sentiment in British Columbia and be accepted in Canadian society.[20] For young *nisei* too, *issei* were important for guidance and deserved respect, for they had built the economic foundation of Japanese life in Canada.

Thus, the respective internal divisions among Ukrainians and Japanese influenced ethnic boundaries differently. While *issei* Japanese regarded *nisei* as a significant part of their ethnic community and vice versa, Ukrainian nationalists tried to alienate rival communists from the Ukrainian ethnic community. In other words, Ukrainian nationalist elite defined ethnic membership in terms of attachment to Ukrainian cultural and linguistic traditions in addition to blood. The intensity of the Ukrainian rivalry is evident from the nationalists' constant criticism of the communists, describing their work as "evil," "dividing our Ukrainian brothers to an extent that no foreigner could,"[21]and "demoralizing" to the people.[22] For the nationalists, Bolshevism was a foreign ideology to which "Ukrainians are by nature and instinct opposed."[23] Thus, they never accepted biological Ukrainians who supported communism as true Ukrainians. *Issei*, on the contrary, defined ethnicity in primordial terms, and saw *nisei* as a symbol of "hope" and the "evolution" of Japanese as "Canadian citizens" and themselves as *nisei*'s collective parents and guides. They thus recognized *nisei* as crucial members of Japanese ethnicity, claiming the CJA to be a province-wide organization in British Columbia, where the majority of the Japanese population resided.[24] In fact, the *issei* elite debated endlessly over how to educate *nisei* as Japanese Canadians in terms of the balance of their Japanese and Canadian identities.[25] The *issei-nisei* rivalry thus rarely developed into hostile name calling, which was common between nationalist and communist Ukrainians.

The nature of the ideological ideals and propaganda that Scots, Ukrainians, and Japanese adopted to engage their peoples' emotions was another factor that created gaps among them. Although not all ethnic leaders chose to evoke nationalist and/or imperialist aspirations (e.g., communist Ukrainians), when they successfully did, they could unite their ethnic communities behind a strong sense of pride in being a special group. Yet the political implications and nuances that imperialism or nationalism exhibited varied among Scots, Ukrainians, and Japanese. Ukrainians were by far the most effective in the use of such ideologies for various reasons.

The situation in Europe provided nationalist Ukrainians with a better basis for constructing the negative collective memories of oppression on which nationalism was best founded. They also possessed a much more pronounced sense of persecution than did Scots, whose history had some parallels. But, while Scottish nationalism, to some degree, had been constructed in comparison with that of the dominant "Anglo-Saxon," Scots regarded the Union of 1707 that had brought the Scottish and English kingdoms together as based on democratic decision making or "semi-independence."[26] Thus, Scottish nationalism rarely became a widespread ideology in Scotland or Canada. Furthermore, as Scots were part of the powerful British Empire, their nationalism often overlapped with British imperialism and could be described as "Scottish imperial localism"[27] rather than as standing in opposition to imperial conquest. In Canada, as Carl Berger pointed out, Scottish imperialism was an integral part of Canadian nationalism and thus defined mainstream Canada.[28] On Canada's diamond jubilee in 1927, *The Scotsman,* an Edinburgh-based national paper, wrote that "Canada may someday be … the greatest nation in the world" but bestows "a token at once of autonomy and of loyalty to the tradition of Imperial co-operation." It treated Canada's anniversary as an event relevant for Scotland, arguing that "the Canadian celebrations, therefore, concern not merely Canada but the whole Empire." It emphasized that the belief that "they (Dominions) have a common root and conform to a common tradition" and was crucial in maintaining their ties with Britain and with each other.[29] Ukrainian nationalism, on the contrary, historically existed in opposition to Austro-Hungarian, Russian, or Polish imperialism rather than overlapping with it. Its primary expression in interwar Canada promoted the cause of freedom for Ukraine from four foreign rulers (Poland, the Soviet Union, Romania, and Czechoslovakia), around which cause nationalists organized the grassroots.[30]

In a similar vein, Ukrainian nationalism differed from Japanese nationalism in terms of both goals and appearance, to the benefit of the Ukrainian nationalist leadership. During the 1920s, Ukrainian nationalists exhibited their national consciousness much more explicitly than did the *issei.* Because of Ukrainians' long history of statelessness and the recent failure of the Ukrainian People's Republic to maintain itself, Ukrainians possessed a cause directly tied to Ukraine's liberation, which encouraged strong emotional identification with the homeland. The concept of nationalism for them meant a search for a separate primordial state. Ukrainian nationalists remained very active on behalf of Ukraine throughout the interwar period; they appealed to Ukrainian Canadians for financial and moral support for their major place of origin, Galicia, in particular, then under the control of Poland.[31] For Ukrainian nationalists, it was an "obligation" to support the native land, and emigration did not free people from such duties.[32] The *issei,* in contrast, originated from a full-fledged nation-state with territory and autonomy, took national identity for granted,[33] believed in the perpetuity of both Japan and its national identity, and did not regard the promotion of "national" consciousness as their task, particularly in the 1920s. Therefore, they drew a clear line between their duty and that of the Legation and Consulates, which represented the Japanese state as a ruling body. They stressed that the CJA should be "a volunteer organization established under Canadian law,"[34] and they tried not to be officially involved in Japanese national ambitions or policies even if the power of consuls over the Japanese-Canadian community could not be avoided. For them, nationalism meant a sense of loyalty to the homeland and racial prosperity.

Yet Japanese Canadians' involvement in homeland politics shifted more dramatically than that of Ukrainian Canadians in the interwar period, affected by the international situation. A turning point was Japan's invasion of China—the Manchurian Incident of 1931 and the establishment of Manchuko, an official colony of Japan, in 1932 —when the attitudes of many *issei* leaders, and to some extent *nisei* elite, toward Japan obviously changed. Both *issei* and *nisei* elites could no longer avoid or try to suppress escalating anti-Japanese feelings in British Columbia, for they were now viewed as part of an expanding Japanese Empire. Since avoiding mention of or keeping distance from Imperial Japan would not change public attitudes toward Japanese, they chose to manipulate the situation by invoking a sense of pride as members of the noble Yamato race among Japanese and strengthening Japanese unity to fight anti-Japanese sentiment in Canada.[35] To some extent, their idea of race overlapped Anglo-Celtic race, which claimed superiority over others. By the end of the 1930s, the CJA, adopting the Japanese government's approach, began increasing its control over Japanese Canadians, restricting their free expression and acting as an organization that represented Japan's political stance. Whether or not these leaders actually supported Japan's imperialist activities is difficult to determine, but their support for Japan's cause was more a means to an end. While Japan's aggression increased throughout the 1930s, the Japanese-Canadian elite rarely changed their attitudes toward the homeland. Immediately after the outbreak of the Sino-Japanese War in 1937, the CJA announced its support for Japan's action and collected donations for its soldiers.[36] Japanese Canadians' enthusiasm for their homeland was obvious when a Japanese official in the Ministry of Foreign Affairs expressed his "gratitude" for their financial support but stressed as well that their patriotism should be demonstrated not only by giving money but also by "promoting better relations between the Japanese and Canadians."[37] The CJA's control over Japanese residents in British Columbia showed some degree of formality; in January 1939, the CJA published guidelines for the mobilization of Japanese Canadians in *Tairiku nippô*. The article, which called the Sino-Japanese War a *seisen* ("holy war"), claimed that Japan's goal was "to liberate the Asian people" and "restore new order in Asia."[38] For this purpose, Japanese Canadians must be "a conscious part of Japanese expansionism" and "respect the honour of the Yamato race, and support its progress, avoiding any insult to the race."[39] At the same time, it recommended that they "promote a correct understanding of Japan among Canadians." Their united effort in Canada, one writer emphasized, would contribute to the "strengthening of the Yamato Race in the world."[40]

In turn, Canada's international politics affected whether or not Ukrainian nationalist and *issei* Japanese elites carried homeland causes into the public sphere. The former, who portrayed Ukrainians as a nation oppressed by the Soviets or Poles in particular, found it easier to support Ukrainian nationalism openly than the Japanese, whose homeland was regarded as the oppressor, could support Japanese nationalism. Homeland nationalism, then, could both increase or decrease the distance between ethnic groups and mainstream Canada. Ukrainians' activities anticipated both British and Canadian involvement in their homeland's affairs. During Ukraine's bid for independence in the wake of World War I, for example, the crystallizing nationalist elite made a number of appeals to the British and Canadian governments. J.W. Arsenych, one of the founders of *Ukrainskyi holos,* a bilingual teacher, and the first Ukrainian lawyer in Canada, for example, wrote to British prime minister Lloyd George on behalf of the rival Ukrainian Canadian Citizens' League, demanding that the Ukrainian nation be liberated from Russian and Polish rule at the Paris Peace Conference.[41] In 1922, delegates from the trial Ukrainian Central Committee of Canada urged Canadian prime minister W.L. Mackenzie King to support their effort "to promote and accelerate the settlement of the political status of Eastern Galicia as an independent state."[42] In this way, Ukrainian nationalists quickly learned how to insert their homeland issues and nationalism into Canadian politics, albeit unsuccessfully. Japanese, in contrast, were much more careful in bringing Japanese issues to the official attention of the Canadian or British government, especially after Japan's colonialism reached its peak in the 1930s. Although *issei* leaders showed their support for Japan in front of their people, confronting such issues formally was something different. Aware that Japan's withdrawal from the League of Nations in 1933 caused friction between Britain and Japan, they rarely tried to discuss Canadian-Japanese foreign relations directly with the Canadian government of the day to gain its sympathies for Japan's imperial pursuits. It was more than obvious that such efforts would be in vain and could even promote further anti-Japanese feeling in Canada.

Both Ukrainian nationalist and Japanese elites were indeed concerned about mainstream reactions to their respective homeland politics since they often affected British Canadians' perceptions of who was loyal and who was disloyal to Canada. Both elites also believed that, insofar as Canada and their respective homelands valued the same goals and political principles, their dual loyalty would never be in conflict. Yet there was a fundamental difference in the international positions of Ukraine and Japan—the former as the oppressed, the latter as the oppressor. This difference affected the distance between the mainstream and each ethnic group, for Ukrainians could at least claim that they shared mainstream political philosophies and ideals.

They stressed the similarities between British and their own values. Ukrainian nationalists did not see their nationalist movement as incompatible with Canadian politics because they believed that it adhered to the British ideals of democracy and freedom. Ukrainians, they said, were "by nature freedom loving"[43] and "one of the most democratic peoples in the world," among them Western European and North American nations.[44] Likewise, they maintained that "the English love freedom. All English history is a history of the struggle for freedom, a history of developing freedom to a higher and higher degree. Ukrainian history is also a history of the struggle for freedom, but the struggle has not always been rewarded with success."[45] In reality, of course, many policies of British imperialism would contradict Ukrainian nationalists' search for independence. Japanese had to try much harder to justify Japan's colonial expansion. Its advance into China, which the CJA elite called a "holy war," was undertaken "to establish eternal peace and a new order in Asia" and "to liberate the Asian people" from other oppressive regimes: "The goal remains distant, but we believe in our victory."[46] This view was actually an echo of the propaganda of homeland leaders; influential military officers and government ministers kept sending messages to the Japanese in North America, maintaining that Japan was "shedding the sacred blood of many imperial soldiers over the Chinese continent for peace and justice."[47] Some *nisei,* who questioned whether or not Japan was an aggressor, also ended up defending its cause. An illuminating example was Yasuharu Kadoguchi, a *nisei* leader who published a series of articles on the question of *nisei* and Japan's war against China. He argued in 1937 that "Japan's aggression against China does not simply intend to conquer China. Its purposes are to build a strong coalition between Japan and China and to contribute to the promotion of world peace and human welfare through establishing peace and stability in the East. To many foreign nations, it simply appears to be an invasion."[48]

Kadogushi's comments, though they did not make any direct connection between Japan's action and British democracy, show his attempt to rescue the image of Japan from which *nisei,* mainly because of their race and parents, could never be detached, especially in the eyes of the mainstream Canadian public. *Nisei*'s duty, then, as Edward C. Banno, provincial secretary of the JCCL argued, was to provide "a correct appraisal of the Far Eastern situation, and then to bring this knowledge to our Canadian friends."[49] Both Japanese and Ukrainian nationalist elites thus used "democracy," explicitly or implicitly, to bridge their communities and mainstream Canadian communities. Yet the Japanese democratic appeal was never accepted by Canadian leaders, as illustrated by the fact that anti-Japanese sentiment in British Columbia often resulted from the growing power of Japan.

Indeed, mainstream British-Canadian leaders, including those of Scottish origin, in general perceived Ukrainian and Japanese homeland politics as something either irrelevant or dangerous for Canada, thereby helping to perpetuate the mainstream/ethnic boundary. Yet there was a difference in the degree of alienation. Ukrainian nationalists' appeal for support for Ukrainian independence received little sympathy from mainstream Canadians since the issue was regarded as outside Canadian jurisdiction if not an immediate menace to the Canadian public. Ukrainian communist ideology and Japanese imperial pursuits, however, were viewed more cautiously. Communist Ukrainians were labelled "a positive danger" that possessed "the firm determination of eventually turning this country [Canada] inside out and upside down."[50] This fear was based partly on the ULFTA's close ties with the Communist Party of Canada and cooperation with related movements in the country, which could expand their influence over other ethnic groups.[51] Japan's growing power also alarmed Canadians, and the concentration of the Japanese population in British Columbia was associated with concerns that Canadian natural resources would be exploited to assist Japan's imperialist expansion.[52] Such a belief was based on the idea that Japanese were sojourners or, even if they settled in Canada, were supporting relatives in Japan financially, taking advantage of the rich natural resources of Canada. As Peter Ward puts it, "once fixed in the west coast mind, the image of an aggressive, militaristic Japan was not to be dislodged."[53] Such anxiety about Japan's expansion, together with racism, was well reflected in Hilda Glynn-Ward's biased 1921 novel, written long before Japan expanded its territory as an imperial power. Her fictional event in which Japanese, who had kept strong ties with the homeland, conquered British Columbia implied that the fear of Japanese expansion did not begin just in the 1930s. The final chapter, entitled "The Future," contains the following: "Within the self-same hour, the Japs, who swarmed like bees in a hive along the west coast of Vancouver Island, overcame by sheer force of numbers the operators in the cable and wireless stations at Alberni, Banfield, Pachena Point and Victoria, and sent their own messages to the outside world—pleasant little messages in which was no sort of mention of Japs and the cataclysmal disturbances in 'Columbia.' Aeroplanes dropped bombs in Victoria and Nanaimo at the same minute that they were dropped in Vancouver."[54] Such sensitivity and caution toward Ukrainian and Japanese homeland politics were the most decisive factors in maintaining interwar ethnic boundaries, which situated both groups outside the mainstream Canadian community.

The British-Canadian elite's definition of race and ethnicity was so powerful that it determined the prevailing ethnoracial hierarchy, which placed Ukrainians above Japanese. Mainstream Canadians, to some extent, attached importance to Ukrainians on several grounds. First, as the following paragraph indicates, Canada initially assessed the value of non-British immigration in economic terms and judged each ethnic group by its suitability for agriculture, thus favouring mostly peasant Ukrainians over Japanese. Second, assimilability to British values and standards also benefited Ukrainians, who were regarded as much closer to Brits because of their European origin. Third, the fact that Ukrainians settled in the Prairies, which needed settlers at the turn of the century, gave them an advantage over Japanese, who lived on the West Coast. These factors gave Ukrainians a sense of significance and a basis for negotiation with mainstream society for full rights in Canada. In other words, mainstream Canadians helped Ukrainians to situate themselves in Canadian society as an ethnic minority, unlike the marginalized position of the Japanese that had no foundation for negotiation.

Most Ukrainians were much-wanted farmers and considered to "have a creditable record" as pioneers.[55] Japanese, on the other hand, were largely unwanted and engaged in a variety of occupations in proximity to Chinese clusters in Vancouver, in fishing villages on the West Coast, and in interior mining camps. While many Japanese did farm, the concentration of the Asian population in Little Tokyo and Chinatown in Vancouver tended to catch greater attention from mainstream British Columbians, who categorized the two peoples as "Asians." These two districts reinforced a stereotype that the Japanese were mainly urban dwellers who would lower the standard of living, creating urban slums.[56] Besides, Japanese could not be racially assimilated and transformed into white Canadians, while Ukrainians—even if less "desirable" than Western or Northern Europeans and without the "possibility of complete assimilation"[57]—were compatible in terms of skin colour. Ukrainians, then, were regarded as potential Canadians and given proper education and guidance, and their economic contribution to prairie agriculture and development was recognized.[58] This hierarchy of economic demand

and racism was well described by mainstream officials and scholars. The *Canada Year Book* for 1927–28, for example, pointed out that "settlers from southern and eastern Europe" were "desirable from the purely economic point of view" though "less readily assimilated" than Western Europeans. "Less assimilable still," it continued, were "those who come to Canada from the Orient."[59] Finally, Ukrainians resided in blocs in the three prairie provinces, which were regarded as "central" to Canadian nation building and economic development and with which the West Coast of marginalized British Columbia in which Japanese concentrated compared poorly. They thus were always identified as the province's problem if not a national one. As W.A. Carrothers, a professor of economics at the University of British Columbia stated, "the problem of Asiatic immigration is a vital one for the Province of British Columbia. The admission of any race that cannot blend satisfactorily is a menace."[60] The double marginality of Japanese, both racially and geographically, plus Japan's imperial expansion and Japanese economic competition with other British Columbians, helped white British Columbia to develop a picture of overwhelmingly evil people. They were economically unnecessary but, "despite restrictive legislation, still swarm over British Columbia's fishing grounds."[61]

The primary concern of the mainstream Canadian elite was building an economically strong and culturally uniform nation-state, making the assimilation of ethnic groups to Canadian ways urgent. Educators and missionaries, particularly British Protestants, were some of the first agents to work for the enlightenment of non-British peoples and to act as guides to Canadian standards and laws. In the interwar period, committed to building a better Canada, scholars and scientific experts joined the effort. Their publications exhibited somewhat contradictory but intertwined tendencies that included ethnic groups in Canada or excluded them from it. On the one hand, they tried to erase the mainstream/ethnic boundary and incorporate non-British peoples into the national scheme. Through careful observation of ethnic clusters and standards of living, they pinpointed what should be done in the interests of "progress" and assimilation. In the process, they expanded the country's knowledge of its ethnic communities and overcame many of the overt prejudices and/or xenophobic tendencies that dominated public discourse at the time.[62] On the other hand, they always drew a clear line between themselves and ethnic groups, acted from a sense of superiority, and were still largely biased. Examples include William G. Smith's *Building the Nation: The Churches' Relation to the Immigrant* (1922), Robert England's *The Central European Immigrant in Canada* (1929) and *The Colonization of Western Canada: A Study of Contemporary Land Settlement* (1936), and

Charles H. Young's *The Ukrainian Canadians: A Study in Assimilation* (1931) and *The Japanese Canadians* (1938).[63]

National projects that investigated the assimilation of ethnic groups into Canada's nation building were officially funded and encouraged, suggesting the importance of such issues during the interwar period. Smith's study of immigrants in Canada's development, funded by the Methodist, Presbyterian, and Congregationalist Churches, presented a standard British Protestant perspective. These denominations assigned to themselves a great responsibility in nation building and thus saw the Canadianization of all immigrants as their most pressing duty.[64] "The task is now quite evident," Smith said, "and to it all genuine Canadians, young and old, are required to give energy."[65] This comment implied that anybody who was British in origin possessed a mission to convert ethnic peoples into Canadians. Awarded a scholarship from the War Memorial Scholarship Fund from the Masonic Order of Saskatchewan to teach in an ethnic community in Saskatchewan in 1922 and 1923, England published his monograph on central European immigrants in Canada based on his experiences and the reports of other scholarship teachers and "experienced nation-builders."[66] These teachers were devoted to the education of ethnic peoples and prepared a number of detailed observations on the positive and negative aspects of the districts in which they lived. Based on these reports, England pointed out low standards of living, lack of cleanness in houses, and intellectual ignorance in Slavic districts, but he admitted that Slavs could be "desirable" citizens should they be provided "with the means of raising the standard of their economic and social life."[67] His 1936 study launched the intriguing notion that ethnic consciousness could be effective in agricultural progress in settlements, promoting cooperation and motivation for development, despite the general belief that ethnic bloc settlements were "subversive of national unity and unprogressive in agriculture."[68]

Young's *The Ukrainian Canadians* and *The Japanese Canadians* (written with W.A. Carrothers and H.A. Innis) were both published under the direction of Helen R.Y. Reid, chairwoman of the Division on Immigration for the Canadian National Committee for Mental Hygiene. Reid stressed the significance of the committee's interest in immigrants' welfare, contending that "Canada cannot have a strong and healthy nation unless its people are mentally as well as physically sound."[69] For her, mental and physical fitness for nation building was to be achieved by improving the standard of living among white immigrants materially and culturally. Thus, living, economic, and health conditions in Ukrainian districts were monitored carefully and compared with national standards, highlighting problems.

For example, though bloc settlement promoted "successful colonization," and thus contributed to nation building, Young believed that large concentrations of Ukrainians "permeated with the atmosphere of the old world" were "inimical to the assimilation of these people."[70] Ukrainian districts were labelled as "notoriously lacking in amenities which might mitigate the incidence of poverty, disease and general hardship."[71] Yet such comments implicitly suggested his conviction that improvements in these fields could make Ukrainians suitable nation builders. Young presented an opposite view of Japanese, recognizing their high standards in fields such as health, living conditions, and culture yet arguing that such good qualities meant nothing in the eyes of mainstream British Columbians because of their racial unassimilability.[72] Their concept of assimilability was simply based on skin colour at the time. Smith, referring to Asian clusters in British Columbia, also saw the assimilation of Asians as problematic. "The problem of the Oriental," he argued, "is intensified by the fact that it is concentrated rather than diffused, British Columbia having to carry the heavy end of the burden."[73] In this way, the goal of nation building—an economically and culturally sound Canada—had much to do with the notion of race.

At the same time, both England and Young contributed to persistent boundaries between mainstream and ethnic communities and produced a static and monolithic image of a single ethnic community. Such categorization, in a sense, was a convenient way to manage and control diverse Canada. England and his teachers were clearly affected by the popular Western colonial terms of the era, especially the dichotomy between civilized and uncivilized. For example, one teacher wrote with respect to the local "Ruthenian" settlement that "we cannot get away from the fact that this 'vast amount' [of ignorance among the non-English] constitutes a serious menace to our own civilization."[74] England himself categorized Mennonites, French, Hungarians, and Germans as "progressive" peoples. The Slavic settlements in which Ukrainians predominated, in contrast, were "not progressive" due to "a great deal of economic and social backwardness" caused by a "lack of education" and primitive "hygiene and sanitation"—the products of bloc settlement, which segregated settlers from outside influences.[75] Ukrainian rural settlements were thus typically portrayed as lagging "a century behind."[76] Young's account of Japanese presented a more modern image of the group, contending that Japanese maintained the average standard of living in both villages and cities. However, Young also thought that their family lifestyle, religion, social cohesiveness, and economic competitiveness created a great gap between them and white Canadians.[77] This dichotomy between mainstream and ethnic groups suggests that close encounters with "peculiar" ethnic customs and habits helped to reassert mainstream Canadians' pre-existing sense of superiority. In some ways, though their primary goal was to promote the assimilation of ethnic groups, commentators such as England, Smith, and Young reinforced ethnic categories and stereotypes of Japanese and Ukrainians by defining them.

The Scottish elite, as the Canadian elite, played a fundamental role in defining the universal and dominant notions of progress and civilization. For some, Scotticization of Canadian values had special meaning, for they believed that it would elevate their status as both Canadians and Scots, attaching noble roots as the founders of world civilization. Watson Kirkconnell, a specialist of ethnic literature, and later president of Acadia University, was a great example. Although he was born in Ontario, he believed in his ethnoracial superiority. He identified Scots as "the most civilized of all," and in terms of education Scots were "three hundred years ahead of English in [the] development of general education."[78]

Both Ukrainian nationalist and *issei* Japanese elites supported the idea of progress and enlightenment, but they differed significantly from mainstream Canadians in that they did not simply regard the adoption of Britishness as "progress." They rather adroitly selected elements to be abandoned from their group's characteristics and others to be adopted from the British system of values. At the same time, their progress meant an increase of power and strength as ethnic groups. In this regard, they were never passive agents who arbitrarily accepted cultural enlightenment or guidance from mainstream dictates; rather, they played an active role in the construction of what it meant to be good Canadians, providing their own definitions of progress. They thus rejected the equation of Canadianization with Anglo-conformity, seeking to maintain their particular ethnic identity and elevating it to something positive that would help their political upward mobility in Canadian society.[79]

Both Ukrainian and Japanese elites also took similar approaches. Quite logically, the removal of activities that generated negative images and education of the masses were top priorities. Customs, attitudes, and behaviour that could retard cultural and/or economic mobility had to be eliminated quickly, and the lists of such traits were endless. Nationalist Ukrainians, for example, pointed to the many "unenlightened" people among them whose children "were running about on their farms without necessary clothing and shoes"[80] or who focussed only on "physical strength and endurance" but lacked cultural sophistication.[81] An *issei* Christian, Yasutarô Yamaga, who advocated Canadianization of *nisei*, argued that the Japanese masses lived in "unsanitary" places or worked on Sundays "when the whites dressed up and went to church."[82] Both Ukrainian physical toughness and Japanese diligence could be positive qualities, but Ukrainian and Japanese elites focussed more on spiritual and philosophical strength. Intellectual, economic, and political development, both groups believed, could be achieved through better education, self-awakening, and orderly life—all elements equated with British success. *Ukrainskyi holos,* for example, often targeted the farmers who constituted the majority of Ukrainians and encouraged "the study of modern farming"[83] for their material well-being. In comparison with the English, the newspaper said in 1924,

> the lack of education is our largest obstacle to life in Canada. Because of the lack of schooling, we can be distinguished neither in all the free professions (doctors, lawyers, politicians) nor in business or industry, nor even in farming. To become successful farmers at present, it is necessary to learn and read about practice, and pursue the market economy, and to study it constantly. The Canadian agricultural department constantly issues extraordinarily valuable research and information for farmers, and the English are making good use of such information, because they receive suitable school training and take advantage of official publications. They thus can avoid economic misfortune. And our farmers? They revert to their familiar shovels and are twenty or thirty years behind.[84]

Learning from British Canadians was particularly encouraged: "Ukrainians have many deficits: Ukrainians lack an intelligentsia, wealthy people, skilled labourers, accountants, and merchants.... And where do Ukrainians learn politics and gain political experience, if not from the people who have the best political experience among all nations in the world? The English are the nation with the longest and best political experience in the world. Living among the English and not learning politics from them is the same as going to school but not learning how to read."[85]

Yasutarô Yamaga attributed Japanese agricultural instability to "selfish" motives. Individual farmers saturated the market with cheaper crops, thereby lowering prices; this practice, he warned, would only lead to farmers' "self-destruction" and "anti-Japanese sentiments."[86] Yamaga therefore recommended that farmers and other workers participate in mainstream cooperatives for "the permanent stability and progress of the Yamato race."[87] Clearly, even a leader such as Yamaga, who encouraged assimilation into Canada, never abandoned the idea that Japanese should keep their racial distinctiveness. The Japanese consul Isago Gomei also entered such debates, emphasizing the necessity of orderliness in 1923: "Harmony or assimilation does not simply mean personal or domestic customs such as speaking English, dressing up in Western clothing, and living in Western houses. It means to be equal with Canadians in social life. The Anglo-Saxon race, namely the English and Americans, is proud of its 'orderly civilization,' which is to build a cohesive social unity that protects individual rights and promotes well-being, thereby preventing disorganized and lawless social life."[88] Thus, for Ukrainian nationalists and *issei* Japanese, progress often meant extracting admired qualities from the British-Canadian tradition without losing the best and most distinctive elements of their own ethnic cultures. Such selectivity undoubtedly created certain dilemmas in terms of how far these ethnic groups should assimilate into mainstream norms. Significantly, race affected this dilemma and the process of selection, determining how Japanese and Ukrainian elites envisioned their ethnic communities and making the former more docile toward the idea of assimilation than the latter. Ukrainian nationalists believed that common culture and language were the main distinguishing characteristics of their ethnicity and as such had to be preserved through people's conscious will and active participation. *Issei* Japanese, on the contrary, always conscious of being racially visible, did not regard these traits as the only elements of their distinctive identity. Such differences in the two groups' understanding of ethnicity were well reflected in their attitudes toward and their debates over cultural and linguistic preservation beyond the first generation.

Native language and culture tied to the specific political goals of the ethnic group preoccupied nationalist Ukrainian and *issei* Japanese leaders—both as the core of their identities and as the means to educate and enlighten their peoples—to slightly different degrees. Undoubtedly, language and culture alone did not define ethnicity, but elites thought that they were the major elements that limited the membership of ethnic groups. Ukrainians remained strong supporters of the Ukrainian language and culture, regarding them as inseparable components of ethnonational identity, arguing that "culture involves the education of people in their mother tongue. Without learning in the mother tongue and without any organization that teaches people in their mother tongue, a nation must perish and blend into other nations. Such educational institutions [that promote the language] can be established with the help of the press, books, schools, and associations. The most powerful cultural organization supports a state. Similarly, nothing can help even the best newspapers, books, schools, and associations when the nation does not have its own independent state."[89]

Notably, for Ukrainian nationalists, language and culture rather than biological traits determined their ethnonational identity, leading to concerns that the growing number of Canadian born might decelerate the spread of national consciousness. Writing in 1935, Ukrainian teacher F.T. Hawryliuk explained the problem: "Besides, they [the older generation] were sure that their children would have Ukrainian blood and a Ukrainian soul and that this strong inheritance would be the same as in their fathers. But it is not so. Physical inheritance alone does not include culture. Moreover, culture itself is based not on 'blood and bones' but on the mind, emotional feeling, custom and habit, a way of thinking and doing, all of which people gain in the process of education.... A sudden change or loss of culture means not only spiritual death but also physical demise."[90] Cultural and linguistic survival in Canada thus was perceived as crucial in the constant "fight" to maintain Ukrainian ethnicity.

In this context, the Ukrainian and Gaelic languages played a similar role because of the repression of the former and the rarity of the latter, providing an illuminating example of how language was preserved as a means of protecting and expressing ethnic distinctiveness. During the 1920s, a sporadic movement for the preservation of Gaelic emerged among some Scottish politicians and scholars, resulting in short-lived Gaelic journals such as *Mosgladh,* launched by the Scottish Catholic Society of Canada in 1922, and *Gaelic Herald,* sponsored by Gaelic scholar James MacNeil in 1925. The movement's supporters saw Gaelic as particularly appealing for its antiquity and rarity, as this comment indicates: "One does not speak Gaelic, one 'has' it. 'Bheil Galig Agaibh?' (Have you the Gaelic?) one is asked. And one goes through Cape Breton Island in bitter regret that one has not, for it is the key to the Highland heart. It is one of the oldest known tongues and excepting only Russian is said to be the most flexible of European languages. It has the wealth of Sanscrit and Greek in native roots and shades of meaning impossible to convey in the less pliant English."[91] Gaelic's difference from English was the key, for Gaelic was seen not only as a language but also as an old symbol that expressed the entire nature of the Highland Scots—"a language of feeling and of sentiment, of ideals and inspiration of a great, free, patriotic and liberty-loving people."[92]

The distinctiveness of the language and its significance in the survival of the ethnic group were also stressed by the Ukrainian elite. Yet, unlike Scots, whose language loss was not necessarily tied to the question of national independence, Ukrainian nationalists politicized linguistic survival more evidently, stressing the originality of their language and its importance in preserving a distinctive culture. As one commentator wrote, quoting a linguist in 1937:

> Professor Hayes defines nationality as "a people who speak the same language, or closely related dialects, cherish common tradition, and constitute, or think they constitute, a distinct cultural society." The world has been convinced that Ukrainian is distinct from any other Slavic language. If the Ukrainian language had been similar to Russian, the Ukase of Ems (1876) would not have been signed by Alexander II, "prohibiting: first, the import to Russia from abroad of books published in the 'Little Russian' language; second, the publishing in Russia of any books in the Little Russian language except historical documents and belles-lettres; third, the use of Ukrainian language on the stage." Russia and Poland have made repeated attempts to destroy our language, knowing well that they could thus win half their battle for Russification or Polonization.[93]

This quotation not only supports Ukrainians' claim to be an independent linguistic group but also stresses the significant role of language in their national survival. At the same time, Ukrainians took a position similar to the Gaelic supporters, distinguishing their language from the dominant one. The article went on to say how the Ukrainian language had a "richness" and "superiority" over Russian because "the Ukrainian language contains a great many Slavic words which cannot even be found in the present Russian language."[94]

For the racially visible Japanese, the loss of their culture and language did not mean the automatic decline of their distinctiveness, so they tended to restrain group markers that might hinder *nisei*'s full participation in Canadian society. *Issei* intensively debated throughout the 1930s whether *nisei* really needed education in their own language—a necessity that Ukrainian nationalists never doubted for their own language. *Nisei,* now seen as a symbol of Japanese Canadians' new era, had to become "Canadians" first. Controversy increasingly focussed on the role played by the Japanese-language school in Vancouver in the education of *nisei. Issei* understood the benefits of teaching their children Japanese, which included "emotional harmony between parents and children" and "understanding of the situation in and nature of the homeland." Yet they also insisted that "our research has proved that the disadvantages overwhelm the benefits."[95] *Issei* believed that "the adjustment to Canadian society at the earliest stage of childhood" and "primary education as Canadian citizens" should be *nisei*'s top priority, and Japanese-language education should not be permitted to cause confusion among the younger generation.[96] This criticism was also directed at the *issei*'s own CJA, said to "contribute to the isolation of the Japanese community from white society spiritually, geographically, economically, educationally, and religiously" by creating its own societies and institutions.[97] Japanese Canadians' future, *issei* argued, lay in *nisei*'s JCCL, which would "overthrow *issei* isolationism" and "make the acquisition of Canadian citizenship the primary goal."[98] However, this thinking does not mean that *issei* Japanese regarded "Japaneseness" as something insignificant. Rather, it was based on the belief that *nisei*'s acquisition of English skills and the loss of the Japanese language alone would never free them from either ethnoracial identification or an obligation to the Japanese-Canadian community and Japan. In other words, *issei* did not regard the acquisition or promotion of language and culture as the primary duty of community members. More significantly, the presence of English speakers among Japanese Canadians was a great demonstration to mainstream society of Canadianization and made it easier for *issei* themselves to remain Japanese.

Ethnic elites and their interactions with mainstream society were most instrumental in the crystallization of Ukrainian and Japanese communities during the interwar period. The emergence of clear internal divisions, changing homeland politics, regional concentration, and an externally imposed ethnoracial hierarchy caused them to constantly redefine their ethnic boundaries. Within this context, Scottish ethnicity was expressed inconsistently and often considered unnecessary. Ukrainian nationalists, who had more advantages and opportunities to engage with mainstream society, were better equipped to consolidate their ethnic community than the marginalized Japanese. Such advantages included the fact that they were farmers, had settled in the prairie provinces, possessed the franchise, and belonged to the white race. All these factors gave Ukrainian nationalists bargaining tools, which the Japanese elite rarely possessed.

Dual Loyalty and Embryonic Multiculturalism

As Frances Swyripa convincingly argues, Ukrainian nationalist elite maintained a fundamental desire to be full-fledged Canadians and simultaneously retain their own ethnic identities.[99] So did *issei* Japanese elite, despite the racism that they faced. The similarities here between the two groups were striking, indicating that the weight that ethnic elites placed on a distinctive identity was never totally ruled by race, national origin, or the existence (or lack) of a state to which they belonged. This idea of dual loyalty was twofold: it focussed first on the promotion of personal pride and a sense of being special among ethnic peoples and second on the progress of Canadian identity. It also became the major vehicle for launching, as the basis of Canadian identity, the notion of multiculturalism over "Anglo-conformity," which justified only the dual loyalty of British Canadians to Canada and their homeland, Britain. This idea was innovative for its era in that it attempted to minimize the binary opposition between mainstream and ethnic identities.

That the idea of dual loyalty primarily concerned a person's inner being or soul was particularly significant because it provided ethnic elites with a solution to the lingering dilemma between their ethnic and Canadian identities and the inferiority complex that stemmed from their ethnic and/or racial backgrounds. Dual loyalty also provided for a concrete definition of what ideal "Canadians" should be. Both Ukrainian and Japanese elites, in their attempt to elevate ethnicity to something valuable, argued that two loyalties not only were compatible but also strengthened each other.[100] Ukrainians stressed the compatibility between their two identities, arguing in 1929 that, "the better Canadian the Ukrainian is, the better Ukrainian he is. Only a conscious, honest, and well-defined person can be a good Ukrainian. Only a conscious, honest, and well-defined person can be a good Canadian. Those who do not have such a nature can be neither good Ukrainians nor good Canadians."[101]

This comment reflected Ukrainian nationalists' rejection of the concept that neither embracing "Anglo-conformity" or remaining "Ukrainian" could create "better"-quality Canadians. It also contained a very inventive concept that hybridity makes a good citizen. *Issei* Japanese, always concerned about the racial complex that Canadian-born *nisei* felt, focussed more on overcoming a sense of inferiority and emphasized the advantages of mixing Japanese and Canadian identities: "Teaching Japanese merits and skills lets [*nisei*] realize in a natural manner that the Japanese can never be inferior to other races and promotes their racial pride. Some critics argue that instilling pride as Japanese hinders them from being Canadian citizens. Yet it is certain that citizens with a firm racial pride and consciousness to fight against discrimination are much better than those who believe in their inferiority because of racism. Therefore, maintaining racial pride and strengths would never prevent them from being good Canadian citizens."[102]

Obviously, dual loyalty or hybridity was deemed beneficial to *nisei*. At least in their own logic, Japanese found a way to be as proud as other Canadians. The fact that both Ukrainians and Japanese thought the same way was perhaps only natural; it allowed members of each group to belong simultaneously to international ethnic and national communities as long as their priorities—Canada first and homeland second—were kept in mind. Both Ukrainian and Japanese elites launched a new model of Canadianness, composed of two complementary parts, and harnessed it to the promotion of confidence and pride in being Canadians of particular ethnic origins.

The second dimension of dual loyalty involved the crystallization of Canadian national identity. It aimed to provide a solution to Canada's dilemma of being a country of immigrants yet adopting Anglo-conformity as its essence and was a first step in the evolution toward ethnic pluralism. Ukrainian nationalist and Japanese elites alike emphasized the possibility that Canada could benefit from their peoples' aspirations for their homelands. In other words, they found their own strengths in cultivating their unique roles in the "imagined boundary zone" that Royden Loewen and Gerald Friesen identify.[103] For the Canadian-oriented USRL and its organ *Ukrainskyi holos* among Ukrainian nationalists, the consistency between loyalties to Canada and to Ukraine was particularly emphasized since Ukrainian national survival and political and cultural contributions to Canada were inseparable goals.[104] In contrast to the Ukraine-oriented UNF, the USRL elite argued that individuals who kept their distance from Canadian politics, "because of their attachment to the Ukrainian nation, are not only making mistakes but also doing damage to their nation [Canada],"[105] because the two loyalties had to be maintained side by side. Such support for dual loyalty was extended to culture when *Ukrainskyi holos* wrote in 1938 that, "in order to facilitate the evolution of very multinational and rich Canadian cultures, we, Ukrainians, must maintain, develop, and create our culture."[106] *Issei* Japanese presented a similar view, asserting that "having the *nisei* study and be proud of their ancestors' land does not contradict the Canadian spirit; rather, it would be a factor that imbues Canadian culture with our merits and virtues."[107] If Ukrainian nationalists tied cultural and linguistic preservation to the enhancement of Canada, Japanese perceived their role in a much larger context beyond the retention of national cultural traditions. *Nisei* themselves embarked on a mission to "build a link between Japanese and Canadian civilizations" because "there are many points in Eastern civilization which are superior to those in Western civilization, and these the Canadian-born Japanese should retain."[108] In this way, they argued that they could contribute to both nations, promoting a mutual understanding between Japanese and other Canadians and building "international brotherhood."[109]

Specifically, ethnic leaders' common goal was to initiate a politicized ethnic pluralism or mosaic that celebrated the sum of the dual loyalties of all ethnic groups but for slightly different reasons. The idea of an ethnic mosaic was also advocated by Scottish elites, to a limited degree. Their notion of ethnic pluralism was first to create a strong dominion of selected races, mainly Western Europeans. Lord Tweedsmuir, a strong advocate of ethnic pluralism, for example, called Scots "the best mixer in the world" who could "mingle freely in an alien society."[110] He thus emphasized the significance of ethnic diversity at a luncheon organized by the Board of Trade in Kitchener in 1936: "Kitchener owes its success to the quality of its citizens. These citizens are drawn from many races, which is fortunate, for every Briton must believe in the supreme value of a racial mixture. What would England be without the Scots, the Welsh, and the Irish? Here you have a very interesting race-mingling, for the bulk of your people are of that fine German stock which has contributed so much to the making of the United States of America, and of more than one British Dominion."[111]

Ukrainian and Japanese leaders echoed the belief in the close relationship between ethnic diversity and strong civilization. However, Ukrainian nationalists were more apt to envision Canada as an ethnically diverse nation than were Japanese because of three major factors: the difference in the ethnic composition of British Columbia and the prairie provinces, race, and the franchise. Because Ukrainians were concentrated in the Prairies, where in 1931 only about 50 percent of the population was British in origin and some 20 percent Eastern European,[112] they could conceptualize themselves as part of a multiethnic society in which they mattered.[113] The size of the Ukrainian population on the Prairies compared with other groups was particularly significant for Ukrainian nationalists since group size and geographical concentration were always seen as bequeathing both the right to and the possibility of political power. *Ukrainskyi holos,* for example, stressed the need for Ukrainian candidates in Canadian elections, particularly in those ridings in Alberta, Saskatchewan, and Manitoba where Ukrainians constituted a majority. Pointing out the lack of interested candidates and voters, it stated that "Canada is a new country populated by people of diverse origins, enough to exercise a power to decide from which nationality politicians can be chosen. Ukrainians have as much right to be chosen as the English, the French, the Jews, or the Germans."[114] Contributors to *Ukrainskyi holos* also offered their own vision of what the future Canadian identity should be. "People in Canada consist of two main cultural groups, Anglo-Saxon and French," wrote F.T. Hawryliuk, one of the founders of the Ukrainian Orthodox Church in Canada, in 1936:

> In addition, there are many other national groups, the more important among them being the Scandinavians, Germans, and Ukrainians. A commonly accepted thought is that, in the distant future, all these cultural elements, having one common goal—the creation of a Canadian nation or Canadian race, which does not exist

> yet—will blend into a whole. This unity will come not through the triumph of one culture over others, as one often sees in European states, but through the mutual appropriation and development of all cultures, selecting what is best, most valuable, and durable from each of these nations. This would be a multicoloured mosaic of Canadian culture and life.... Any cultural group works for its own benefit and obtains such recognition and respect as it deserves.[115]

For Ukrainian nationalists, Canada had to become a nation characterized by the equal representation and recognition of all groups. Ukrainians, as Swyripa points out, "mirrored the 'founding nations'" in the prairie region, which the British and French claimed for all of Canada.[116]

Japanese, overwhelmingly residing in British Columbia, where some 75 percent of the population was still British,[117] were much more limited in terms of imagining Canada as a multiethnic nation. Besides, exclusion from the franchise and racism in British Columbia made Japanese feel psychologically distant from the mainstream society, which delayed evolution of the notion of the mosaic among them. As Kay Anderson has shown in the Chinese case, Asian communities in British Columbia were Canada's Orient.[118] As anti-Japanese sentiment escalated and became common in public discourse in British Columbia in the 1930s, discussion of the problem continued to dominate the Japanese press. *Tairiku nippô,* for example, referring to the prohibition of fishing by Japanese in many fishing villages in the province, advocated uniting all Japanese into a collective force: "The franchise has not been a big deal for the fishers till very recently. Yet now we need to secure the right to fish in any BC fishing villages to make our living. For this purpose, unity for the lobby for the franchise is imperative."[119] Such a comment indicates that Japanese believed in their own collective power, but their imagination rarely went beyond their own group or British Columbia. They usually did not have a clear sense of the distinction between white immigrants who were also treated as inferior and the dominant British. Even when Japanese recognized the diversity that existed within white society, they tended to believe that European immigrants rarely faced discrimination. The CJA president entertained a homogeneous image of white Canada when he said that, "in the case of European groups, by the time they reach the second generation, all problems with respect to politics, occupation, and ethnicity will disappear naturally and completely."[120] Obviously, he did not see Canada as a country in which all ethnic groups, including those sharing the same privileged skin colour, could and would maintain their identities.

Despite these differences at home, dual loyalty was also advocated and encouraged by Ukrainians and Japanese outside Canada, providing the Canadian diaspora with a greater mission than simply the establishment of ethnic pluralism in Canada. Emergence of the mosaic in Canada thus also needs to be conceptualized in a transnational context. Ukrainian nationalists all over Eastern Europe regarded their Canadian counterparts as part of international émigré circles devoted to the cause of Ukrainian independence, while Japan's leaders saw their people in Canada as an outpost of the country's international expansion. Great emphasis thus was attached to the roles that overseas Ukrainians and Japanese could play in Canadian politics. O.I. Bochkovsky, a Ukrainian scholar from Czechoslovakia who specialized in the Ukrainian question and visited Canada at the invitation of the USRL in 1936, provides a good example. His series of articles on Ukrainian Canadians that appeared in *Ukrainskyi holos* preached how a strong sense of loyalty to Canada strengthened the Ukrainian nation:

> Ukrainian Canadians regard themselves not as visitors but as co-hosts of Canada. They have the potential to become a "third nation" of Canada and to create a variation of the Ukrainian nation—the overseas type. This is not only their selfish interest. It is also in the interest of the Ukrainian nation in general, especially when Ukraine is oppressed, because in Canada our countrymen have the opportunity and the rights to be a factor in the state. They do not demand the secession of their nation. On the contrary, as Canadian governor general Tweedsmuir evidently noted, "you will all be better Canadians for being also good Ukrainians."[121]

That the notion that Ukrainians in Canada be a "third nation" came from outside the country suggests that their recognition was considered beneficial to the world-wide Ukrainian community. They were expected to create an outpost to the pressure for Ukrainian independence since Ukrainians in the homeland, oppressed by foreign powers, were limited in such an endeavour. Likewise, the role that *nisei* Japanese could play was assigned, to some degree, by their homeland elites. Inazô Nitobe, a specialist in agriculture and law who served as undersecretary general of the League of Nations between 1919 and 1926 and lectured in North America to promote understanding of the Japanese, stressed *nisei*'s strength at a meeting of the CJA in 1933: "*Nisei* can be both Canadians and Japanese. How lucky they are.... They are able to take advantage of these dual characteristics, by getting acquainted with other Canadians, inspiring in them the Japanese spirit, and building goodwill between Japan and Canada. This is a privilege unique to the *nisei*.... I hope that all of you will keep your affection both to your parents' country, Japan, and to your native land, Canada, and contribute to the promotion of friendship between the two countries."[122]

Nitobe's speech not only aimed to eradicate a sense of inferiority among *nisei* but also reflected his conviction that *nisei* could bridge the growing gap between Western nations and Japan, especially after the Manchurian Incident of 1931.[123] Kenzô Ikago, who worked for the Department of Agriculture in Japan and served as a delegate for Japan's new colony in China, Manchuko, also sent a message to the gathering. He argued that "the *nisei*'s greatest duty as Canadian citizens" was to introduce to Canadians the Japanese spirit and qualities and to contribute to the development of the Canadian nation.[124] In such ways, Ukrainian nationalists and Japanese in Canada were always regarded as part of international ethnic communities and assigned great responsibilities by both overseas elites and themselves, playing a role in the construction of ethnic pluralism in Canada.

Ethnic pluralism thus became the major political principle among Ukrainian nationalists and, to a lesser degree, among Japanese. For Scots, whose dual loyalty had coincided with legitimate Canadian identity for a long time and thus was not divided, ethnic pluralism as a theory to bridge the conflicting loyalties seemed unnecessary. Canada was always an integral part of the world-wide British Empire, and Scottishness never contradicted Canadian identity. Yet some leaders, including Lord Tweedsmuir, believed that limited ethnic pluralism among Western Europeans would strengthen Canada. Through ethnic pluralism, Ukrainian nationalists and Japanese found a vehicle to enhance their personal and ethnic pride as Canadians, just as Scots had always seen their special role in their dual loyalty. In this process, the ties with their homelands provided new missions for the two groups. Yet Ukrainian nationalists were the strongest advocates of ethnic pluralism because factors such as the size of their group, the franchise, and their pursuit of democracy allowed them to establish a foundation for political negotiation to gain a better position in Canada. Ethnic pluralism or a mosaic never became a dominant idea in Canada until the late 1960s, yet it was the major vision of what Canada should be among ethnic groups as far apart as Ukrainians and Japanese.

Homeland Myths and Symbols and the Canadian Mosaic

Although ethnic elites relied on propaganda and ideological concepts such as ethnic pluralism and democracy to promote ethnic consciousness in Canada, Anthony D. Smith's historical myths and symbolic figures and cultural traditions—much more flexible and easily manipulated for political purposes—constituted other components that shaped their identities.

Interwar Canada witnessed three kinds of myths and symbols, sometimes coexisting in harmony and sometimes competing with each other. First, there were British myths, symbols, and cultural traditions, including Scottish ones that had dominated Canadian identity since the colonial era. Second, there were ethnic myths, symbols, and cultural traditions, invented in and transplanted from the homeland, that played a significant role in the promotion of ethnic consciousness in Canada. All three elites—Scottish, Ukrainian, and Japanese—valued them for the emotional appeal that they had among their peoples. Third, there were Canadian-made ethnic myths, symbols, and cultural traditions that were limited in effect but began to emerge in specific regions or localities. All three categories of myth or symbol making existed independently, and ethnic leaders manipulated them for recognition of their ethnicity in Canada.

Ukrainians and Japanese, and certainly Scots, all saw the British monarch as the most powerful and all-encompassing Canadian icon during this period. For Scots, it was both a national and an international symbol that consolidated unity in Canada and the British Empire under the most powerful common symbol. Lord Tweedsmuir, for example, in his address "The Meaning of Our Monarch," celebrated the crown as fundamental to Canadian identity and unity: "Why has kingship this peculiar prestige with us? Let me suggest one or two reasons. In the first place it focuses the historic consciousness of the nation. It is the mystical, indivisible centre of national union. It is the point around which coheres the nation's sense of a continuing personality. It gives us of today a feeling of partnership with the old makers of Britain when we realise that they too served the Throne, and the same Throne."[125]

Intriguingly, ethnic elites shared such enthusiasm. In a sense, the crown indeed functioned as a unifying Canadian symbol. The visit of King George VI and Queen Elizabeth to Canada in 1939 provided the best platform for Ukrainian and Japanese elites as outsiders to show their allegiance to the British monarch. The occasion symbolically served as an opportunity for them to demonstrate that they could be loyal to Britain without losing their ethnic identity. For example, both Ukrainians and Japanese welcomed the king and queen with great enthusiasm, hoisting Union Jack flags and assembling floats that featured ethnic symbols such as Mount Fuji for the Japanese and Cossacks for the Ukrainian nationalists.[126] Yet the two groups saw different political implications in the monarchy as the universal Canadian symbol. For Ukrainians, the king and queen were symbols of the "freedom," "justice," and "equality" that had created "the tolerance shown to the heterogeneous people of this country" and provided land for "the oppressed and suffering people" of Ukraine.[127] The royal couple were thus viewed as a symbol of the cosmopolitan British Empire, in which many ethnic groups coexisted. For Japanese, George VI and his wife represented the "goodwill between the British and Japanese Empires," which, by the late 1930s, had become crucial to Japanese Canadians, who were facing an anti-Japanese movement because of the rise of their homeland as a colonial power. The royal couple were also used to justify loyalty to Imperial Japan when an *issei* Japanese maintained that "to be loyal to the king of Canada, where we reside, just as being loyal to Japan's royal family, is our pride."[128] In this way, Ukrainian and Japanese elites politicized and attached different messages to the British monarchy that British Canadians, including Scots, did not necessarily think were relevant.

Despite support for the British monarch as a uniting figure, all three groups possessed their own symbols and historical myths rooted in their respective homelands. Scots provide a good example here because of the symbolic character of their ethnicity and parallels with Ukrainians due to somewhat similar situations in Europe. First, both groups sought to protect their distinctiveness against neighbouring dominant peoples in their homelands. The Scots traditionally distinguished themselves from the English to gain "a sense of the country's worthiness to be a partner in a Union."[129] In a similar manner, the Ukrainians demonstrated their difference particularly from the Russians, with whom they tended to be identified. For this goal, their respective ancestors, whether Highland Scots or medieval Kievan Rus' and the Cossack state under Bohdan Khmelnytsky (1595–1657),[130] were used to show their distinctive ethnic origins. Ukrainians claimed to be "the closest descendants of the inhabitants of Rus'," whom the Russians also claimed as ancestors,[131] while Scots emphasized their Highland as opposed to their Lowland roots for the former's peculiar language, religion, and distance from England. Second, influenced by late-eighteenth-century Romanticism in literature, both groups chose poets as their national heroes. Robert Burns (1759–96) and Taras Shevchenko (1814–61) were intertwined with the national consciousness of their respective peoples.

Japanese behaved somewhat differently because of little influence from other cultures, the lack of a survival mentality, and the absence of internationally enshrined figures in literature. The emperor, the most powerful national symbol of modern Japan, served as the foremost icon. Invented as a descendant of the ancient Sun Goddess, who gave birth to the Japanese in the Shinto tradition, and the eternal head of the Yamato race, whose ancestry could be traced back to ancient times,[132] he stood at the core of the Japanese "myth of common descent." Imported to Canada, all these historic myths and symbolic figures enhanced a sense of being special among the three groups in Canada. The fact that even the politically influential Scots valued them supports the theory of Anthony D. Smith that attributes ethnicity to a sense of being a distinguished race or "chosen people"[133] and emphasizes the role of the homeland as a "sacred" place that invokes past memories in ethnic community formation.[134]

Although both Scottish and Ukrainian elites used homeland myths and symbols to bolster their political ambitions in Canada, Scots Canadianized the symbols more enthusiastically. Paradoxically, their claim that they were a chosen people who built Canada made the boundary between Canadian and Scottish myths and symbols indiscernible. For example, Burns, bagpipes, and the Highland Regiment constituted Canadian identity. The overlap of Canadianness and Scottishness proved their superiority over others, highlighting Scots' impact on the creation of universal cultural traditions and democratic principles that Canada inherited and enjoyed. In this context, as a symbol of democracy and liberty, Burns could become a "Canadian" hero whose work "brought to modern political conceptions those accepted tenets which are the very fabric of the systems of self-government by which our race holds dominion and authority from sea to sea."[135] Ukrainian nationalists also saw Shevchenko as a symbol of democracy and freedom, and thus he too embodied Canadian values.[136] Yet it was even more critical for them to keep him as a "Ukrainian" hero and "as the greatest son of Ukraine" who brought "light and justice" to all Ukrainians[137] since their state-building goals remained unachieved. Ukrainians thus maintained ethnic boundaries in defining their hero, while Scots tried to make Burns as universally Canadian as possible. The two men reflected different messages: Ukrainians were safeguarding ethnic distinctiveness, and Scots were defining Canada.

Japanese elites took a completely different approach to homeland myths and symbols, rarely preaching the "myth of common descent" in their press or in public prior to the late 1920s. Japanese Canadians did not enshrine any homeland literary heroes or heroines equivalent to Shevchenko for Ukrainians and Burns for Scots. At the same time, Japanese identity was self-evident among *issei.* Furthermore, they were aware that promotion of their symbols would give other Canadians the wrong impression that they were disloyal to Canada. Yet a sense of pride rooted in membership in the Yamato race and loyalty to the emperor were intertwined with messages from *issei* and homeland leaders and displayed in public on special occasions.

Daijôsai of Hirohito in November 1928 was the most significant homeland event that connected Japanese people in both Canada and Japan, celebrating the same national figure, roots, and history. It is a religious ceremony with roots in eighth-century Japan in which "the newly crowned emperor offers the first harvests to God while he himself consumes them."[138] As "the only major event that occurs in an emperor's lifetime," it held particular significance for the Japanese elite.[139] *Tairiku nippô* carried various reports on *daijôsai* in October 1928, including four series of articles written by homeland scholars. These detailed accounts of the event provided Japanese Canadians with an opportunity to relearn their history and traditions.

Hidematsu Wada, a prominent historian, authored the first series, *Godaiten ni tsuite* ("About the Ceremony"), which explained the origin and history of *daijôsai* in nine articles.[140] A major characteristic of his articles was their focus on the historical continuity of this event from the ancient era. Such a long history was significant as it elevated the Yamato race to the level of the British, whose ancient roots were admired by Canadians. *Daijôsai,* in fact, discontinued frequently; the modern ceremony revived only after the Meiji era.[141] According to Wada, however, its significance lay in the fact that "its meaning had been consistent since the ancient era," and it was "an old ceremony that was begun by the Sun Goddess," whose descendants included Hirohito.[142]

The second series published articles by Takaya Nakamura, also a historian, who taught at the University of Tokyo. His articles, which explained the process of the ceremony and stressed its "sacred" nature, promoted the idea that Japan was "a godly nation" that inherently possessed "religious origin." At the same time, Japan emerged as an "ethnic nation" that "possessed a single root" whose head was the emperor. "To know one's own country," he continued, would "enhance national consciousness and spirit."[143] What is obvious from his comments is that the "myth of descent" gained significance on this occasion as a popular story that might attract readers' interests.

The third and fourth series, written respectively by Masatake Tôgô and Masanao Sekine, two other prominent specialists in Japanese culture, provided information on the place, ritual, ornaments, and process of *daijôsai,* focussing on the "holiness" of the ceremony.[144]

Tairiku nippô thus focussed on the historical interpretation of *daijôsai,* yet it also tried to tie Japan's long roots to its contemporary strength as a nation. It added a militaristic touch that was incorporated into the ceremony in Japan. For example, one article introduced the story that a newly built ship called the *Nachi,* the largest Japanese auxiliary vessel built by 30,000 people over four years, would be unveiled on the day of *daijôsai.*[145]

Another good example is the celebration of Crown Prince Akihito's birth in 1933, when the Consulate organized a ceremony involving most of the Japanese associations in British Columbia, including the CJA, the Japanese-language school, and the commercial and fishermen's cooperatives. It was a unique event that showcased Japanese allegiance to the emperor, opening and closing with Japan's national anthem and drinking a toast to the royal family. *Tairiku nippô* proposed that "participants in the ceremony could be in casual outfits yet should not appear disloyal to the emperor" and that "all Japanese hoist both British and Japanese national flags to pay their respects."[146] On other occasions, the emperor's messages were manipulated by the consul in the interests of his influence over Japanese Canadians. "When I was appointed as consul," he said in a speech to the Japanese-language school board, "I was told by the emperor to promote the goodwill between Japan and Canada and for the Japanese in Canada." He added that King George VI had signed his appointment as consul for the Canadian side, implying that he had been chosen by the will of the two monarchs,[147] which would give him double authority and legitimacy as both a Japanese and a Canadian delegate. The emperor, as a source of Japanese moral teachings, was also incorporated into education of *nisei*. Emphasizing the need to instill a "Japanese spirit" in *nisei*, Kenzô Ikago, the Japanese minister of agriculture, quoted the Meiji emperor and argued that things such as loyalty, trust, and compassion can be found in "the teachings of the ancestral emperors."[148]

The supremacy of the emperor as a symbol gained more influence in the late 1930s as Japan's imperial activities accelerated in Asia, making it critical for Japanese in Canada to unite against escalating anti-Japanese sentiment in British Columbia. At this point, rhetoric about the emperor and the Yamato race came to dominate public discourse. Consul Hirokichi Nemichi, celebrating the anniversary of the start of the Sino-Japanese War in 1937, noted how a "glorious tradition, kept for 2,600 years, had built the distinctive moral values that Imperial Japan, as the best moral state in the world, maintained under successive emperors, without defiling anyone or being defiled by anyone."[149] This type of national pride was supported by the CJA when President Eikichi Kagetsu stated that, "needless to say, our country is a nation-state, formed around the emperor, that possesses a profound sense of nationhood. We must be united, abandon selfishness, be economical, respect God's achievements, and contribute to the advancement of the imperial power with a spirit of perseverance.... Since the Manchurian Incident, anti-Japanese sentiment intensified. We, however, patiently resisted this sentiment against humanity, showing the real value of the Yamato race, by enlightening the white race, working hard, and never breaking the Canadian law. It has been a very difficult two years for the Japanese in Canada, overcoming all hardships."[150] The fact that this *issei* leader shared the homeland's enthusiasm for Japan's imperial ventures is suggestive: his kind saw the Yamato race and the emperor as key factors in the promotion of a sense of community and solidarity after Japan's invasion of China. Such a concept of the Japanese as a family with a long history helped to boost a sense of pride among Japanese Canadians, who were more marginalized in Canada than ever.

Despite ethnic elites' constant manipulation of their own myths and symbols, Canada's British-dominated ethnic hierarchy affected how influential these homeland traditions could be to the formation of a Canadian identity. In the 1930s, a few individuals put forward the idea of a mosaic as Canada's potential national identity, in which cultural elements such as literature, music, and handicrafts—but neither loyalty to the homeland nor homeland politics—could be preserved.[151] This notion was best defined in the works of men such as Watson Kirkconnell, John Murray Gibbon, and Robert England. Kirkconnell, as a literary critic and translator of several European languages, including Ukrainian, had a special interest in ethnic poetry and fiction. Gibbon was a publicist for the Canadian Pacific Railway who organized folk festivals, such as the New Canadian Festival in Winnipeg in 1930, to celebrate immigrants' cultural traditions in Canada as part of the promotion of immigration to western Canada.[152] England, through his association with ethnic settlements on the Prairies, became fascinated by old exotic cultures and traditions as he grew more familiar with them, contending that Canada should not "destroy those indigenous natural colours that enrich the national character" in the process of Canadianization.[153]

Scottish symbols and heroes, including Robert Burns, were obviously most cherished by these mainstream commentators and politicians, themselves often Scottish in origin, and understood to be part of Canadian identity. Burns, according to Lord Tweedsmuir, was an ideal Scot who accepted "no spur democracy" and "was equally interested in the history and the welfare of the wider unit, the British Empire."[154] On official and unofficial occasions, Scottish bagpipes, dances, and Highland tartans were integral components of public events, creating an antecedent for the Canadian mosaic. However, the Ukrainian hero, Taras Shevchenko, was viewed with ambivalence—accepted as a poet who fought for freedom and democracy in general but neglected as a symbol of the fight for Ukraine's liberation. Gibbon, in his book *Canadian Mosaic: The Making of a Northern Nation,* appreciated the broad impact of both Ukrainian poetry and Shevchenko as its greatest creator: "The Ukrainians have been described by Professor Seignobos, of the Sorbonne, as 'a race of poets, musicians, artists, who have fixed for all time their national history in the songs of the people which no centuries of oppression could silence—the Ukrainians became the first singers of Europe; the celebrated Russian music is the music of the Ukraine, and it is a Ukrainian, Gogol, who has opened the way to the Russian romancers of genius. Their greatest poet, Taras Shevchenko, wrote the songs they love best to sing."[155] Shevchenko and his songs were detached from the concrete campaign for Ukraine's independence but valued as a symbol of the survival of the oppressed.[156] Gibbon believed in the quality of Ukrainian literature and placed it high in his cultural hierarchy. He quoted the praise of Stephen Rudnitzky, former professor and director of the Ukrainian Scientific Research Institute of Geography and Cartography, that "the worth of Ukrainian culture appears, in its most beautiful and its highest form, in the unwritten literature of the people.... But the national genius of the Ukrainians has risen to the greatest height in their popular poetry."[157] Gibbon then contemplated this literature's potential for the Canadian mosaic, concluding that "those new flowers ... will surely add a richness and colour to the present somewhat monotonous Canadian literary garden."[158] He also drew a comparison with Scots, equating Robert Burns Day to "the annual celebration held in March in honour of the memory of Taras Shevchenko."[159] Kirkconnell also emphasized the necessity of paying attention to Ukrainian cultural works and creativity, stating in his collection of Canadian poetry that, "unheeded by the Anglo-Canadian, they [Ukrainians] have tenaciously cultivated their handcrafts, music, ballet, drama, fiction, and poetry."[160] Such comments indicated that Ukrainians were granted participation in the building of Canada's new cultural identity.

The Japanese symbol of the emperor, in contrast, was regarded as both politically dangerous as the reigning head of Imperial Japan and culturally irrelevant to the Canadian mosaic. In fact, both Gibbon and Kirkconnell excluded Japanese from their list of cultural groups—the "cosmopolitan" West usually did not include non-Europeans. Intriguingly, Charles Young's *The Japanese Canadians* did not even mention the group's traditional culture and literature. For these commentators, non-Europeans did not possess the world-class literature and traditional cultures that could contribute to the enrichment of the Canadian mosaic.

Meanwhile, Ukrainian, Japanese, and Scottish elites began inventing their own new historical myths based on specific regions and localities in Canada—Nova Scotia for Scots, the Prairies for Ukrainians, and small BC fishing villages such as Steveston and Powell Street in Vancouver for Japanese. The emergence of such new myths pointed to a growing sense of attachment to a particular place for Ukrainians and Japanese, while Scots found a more practical use of region. Such myths showed similarities in their emphasis on "first" arrivals and pioneering and in the development of a collective memory around settlement, the significance of the land, and their imprint on it. Frances Swyripa has shown the different and similar patterns in which European immigrants, including Ukrainians, commemorated the firsts and assessed their impacts on western Canada.[161] The question here, then, is whether or not other groups—Scots and Japanese—that did not settle on the Prairies as farmers had developed similar myths and collective memories. The production of these Canadian-made myths associated with a place suggests that geographical boundaries reinforced ethnic communities.[162]

First, the Scots' attempt to promote Scottishness in Nova Scotia was more deliberate and official than were the Japanese identification with British Columbia or the Ukrainian identification with Alberta, Saskatchewan, and Manitoba. The artificiality of the Scottish geopolitical boundary is obvious since historically Scots were not always numerically predominant in the province's population[163] and since only 17 percent of all Scots lived in the Maritimes in 1931.[164] At the same time, Scots constituted the first case in which ethnicity officially became a provincial identity—something that Ukrainians and Japanese never achieved. Ian McKay convincingly attributes this interwar Scottish movement in Nova Scotia to Angus L. Macdonald, who became premier in 1933. Because of his enthusiasm for the Scottish tradition and his conviction of its effectiveness as a tourist attraction, McKay argues, he promoted "Scottishness" as the "brand-name of the province." The project was large scale and went beyond his own entertainment or recreational search for his roots.[165] The premier's obsession with the Scottish past and traditions was a key factor in making collective Scottish identity more predominant and powerful in the province. His commemoration of the *Hector,* a ship that brought a large group of Highland immigrants to Pictou in 1773, provides an illuminating example of his project. The *Hector* had already gained symbolic status when Nova Scotia commemorated its 150th anniversary in 1923,[166] but Macdonald further promoted its relevance to the province. He depicted it as the ship that brought important founding fathers of Canada: "The arrival of the *Hector* is one of the outstanding days in Nova Scotian history," and "the history of this Province and this Dominion would have to be written differently if there had been no *Hector* and no Pictou County."[167] In reality, these immigrants were not the first Scots who came to Canada, yet, as the Scottish Catholic Society of Canada pointed out, they had a great impact in that they spearheaded large-scale Highland Scottish immigration to Nova Scotia's small community.[168] Such comments stressed not only the crucial role that Scots played in province building but also the significance of Nova Scotia to Canada.

The premier was not the only one who pushed the Scottishness of Nova Scotia. Lord Tweedsmuir, for example, in his 1937 address in Halifax said that

> I am happy to find myself at last in Nova Scotia, for to any Scotsman with a memory of history it is a classic land. We have old

> connections.... But there are two characteristics which you especially share with Scotland. You are a mixed people, for you have in you elements drawn from France, from all parts of Britain, and from the great Republic to the south of you, and, if I may say so, from these sources you have managed to draw the most tough and stalwart elements. But you have made of this mixture a new type. A Nova Scotian, whatever his ultimate origin, is always recognizable as a Nova Scotian.... I thought that today I might say a few words on this question of racial unity—I mean that power which some peoples have of welding diverse elements into a single national type.[169]

Clearly, Lord Tweedsmuir pushed the premier's ambition further, arguing that Nova Scotia was Scottish in origin but also strengthened by many other peoples. Taking Nova Scotia as an example, he presented a notion of what an ideal diverse nation could be.

Ukrainians also nurtured a sense of region, associating their ethnic boundaries with the three prairie provinces.[170] Unofficially, the fusion between Ukrainianness and the prairie region was documented both by Ukrainians themselves and by mainstream Canadians. Ukrainians' attachment to the Prairies was obvious when a newspaper such as *Zakhidni visty* stressed the hard work of Ukrainian farmers on the Prairies that made "the Ukrainian name deserve distinction and respect."[171] The claim that Ukrainians built western Canada appeared in the 1930s in *Ukrainskyi holos,* which promoted a sense of possession of the region. Bochkovsky, for example, wrote that "our people in Canada were not only able to gain land but also maintained it.... I was convinced of this, driving through the vast prairie in Manitoba, Saskatchewan, and Alberta ... along 'our' land."[172] Mainstream Canadians did not always agree that Ukrainians were builders of the west yet admitted their success in colonizing the prairie land.[173] In contrast, Japanese rarely saw British Columbia as "their" province, both because their population was small and because they tended to reside on the province's western edge, geographically close to their homeland. Mainstream Canadians identified British Columbia with Japanese only in negative terms concerning their high birth rate, competitiveness in the labour market, and strong ties with Japan, while all problems were created or dramatized by white Canadians in British Columbia.[174]

Second, the three groups differed on the relationship between these Canadian-based ethnic myths and Canadian nation building. While Japanese and Ukrainians exaggerated their hardships and sacrifices and contributions to their specific regions in the context of Canadian nation building, the Scottish myths were launched predominantly from Nova Scotia but were more pan-Canadian in content.[175] For Scots, their founding myth in Nova Scotia overlapped with that of Canada. The greatness and contributions of the "Celtic race" were emphasized specifically in James MacNeil's Sydney-based newsletter the *Gaelic Herald:* "These moral and inspiring ideals [of the Celt] gave grandeur and beauty to the life and work of the Celt since he first set foot on Canadian soil. The life work of the early Gael or Celt immortalizes the pioneers of this great dominion who courageously braved the wilds of Canada under intolerable hardships, privation and sacrifice, felled the majestic forests, cleared the land, tilled the soil, built its grand system of highways, railways and canals, established its numerous educational and cultural institutions, evolved its government system based on equality, freedom, and justice."[176]

The sense of being a select people, tied to the myth of Canadian nation building, echoed Scots' strong influence in the British Empire more widely. The same article continued that "Canadians may well be proud of the role they [Scots] have played in the building of a happy and prosperous country. Let us rejoice in the magnificence and splendor of their great achievements and the glorious harvest they have garnered for future generations in this great Dominion and far-flung British Empire."[177]

The same rhetoric of "pioneer saga" and participation in nation building put forward by Ukrainians was more regionally confined and did not exhibit the sense of supremacy that Scots had.[178] The following represents the typical myth that Ukrainians developed during the interwar period:

> Ukrainian immigrants settled down some forty to eighty miles from the railway. They cleared the land of forests, drained swampy land, and cleared the land of rocks. Ukrainian immigrants did not come to Canada with great resources, but they established themselves on homesteads, and needed to seek work outside the place where they lived, in order to keep the family together and make money for the purchase of plows, wagons, oxen, and horses. Immigrants could not choose jobs, as there were not many of them; the construction of new railways and the maintenance of old lines were the main source of work. For long years, Ukrainians nearly monopolized the jobs on the railways in western Canada. We can say boldly that every mile of railway in western Canada was bedewed with the sweat and blood of Ukrainian labourers. The strength of Ukrainians constructed a fine railway network.... When the Canadian people acquire a sense of justice and gratitude in the future, they will build monuments to the Ukrainian pioneers in

> Canada just as eastern Canada erects monuments of their Cartier, Champlain, and Frontenac.... Ukrainians, to a large degree, built western Canada. They endured the hardest of pioneer lives and helped open up western Canada. May gratitude and respect be offered to them by the residents of western Canada, if not from the entire country.[179]

This passage clearly shows how Ukrainians combined struggle and lack of appreciation with their desire to be recognized as nation builders and full-fledged Canadian citizens. The fact that they contributed to western Canada's economy through homesteading, railway construction, and farming—which could be achieved only by the physical strength of a "peasant race"—gave them a sense of pride and significance.[180] Ukrainians depicted themselves as "Sons of the Land" who could easily cultivate and become attached to the land, and they argued that they naturally possessed "the qualities of colonizers" who opened up the prairie region.[181]

The Japanese-Canadian myth was also regionally focussed, concentrating on urban and rural communities on the West Coast. Yet, unlike Ukrainian elites, Japanese leaders rarely tied their pioneer myths to Canadian nation building, perhaps because they developed around the fishing village of Steveston and Powell Street in Vancouver—whose inhabitants were not farmers who actually worked on the land. The sense of struggle was expressed through fishing stories and the prejudice that Japanese encountered in the new land. In 1935, on the thirty-fifth anniversary of the establishment of the Fraser River Japanese Fishermen's Cooperative, *Tairiku nippô* stated that,

> in the turbid waters of the Fraser River, in the wind blowing through the Georgia Valley, and in the suntan on their faces, the power that only fishermen possess pulsates silently like an artery. Two thousand Japanese Canadians! This number exceeds that of Vancouver. Why and how could this wonderful progress be made? Who is responsible for the flourishing of the Japanese community in Steveston today? Every Japanese who lived in Steveston is.... Yet on this foreign land of Canada, until the Japanese achieved this success, there were numerous hardships and instances of prejudice; it was a life of endurance.... Imagine the brave people in the past who fished for salmon, sailing boats on the turbid waters of the Fraser River![182]

This romantic portrayal of Japanese pioneers clearly embraces their pride as an island race as well as their roots on the Fraser River. This sort of myth was similar to the ones that Ukrainians created on the Prairies in tone but differed in its distance from nation building. At the commemoration ceremony, the Japanese consul stressed that Canadian Japanese "should stop remittance back home and build an economic base with firm roots on this land."[183] He did not, however, claim a Japanese contribution to Canada's national economic development. The fiftieth anniversary of the City of Vancouver in 1936, which received unprecedented enthusiasm from the Japanese community, best illustrated this limited sense of their community. Although Japanese attached special meaning to that year, indicating their growing sense of being part of Vancouver, the festival was generally limited to Powell Street. Featuring everything Japanese—including kimono parades, folk dances, Japanese drums, and *koto* (a musical instrument)—the occasion was named the Japanese Festival by local Japanese. Primarily, it was a gala that demonstrated Japanese commercial development on Powell Street, both to the group itself and to mainstream Canadians.[184] To mark the occasion, *Tairiku nippô* gathered five early immigrants for a roundtable discussion on the hardships and experiences of the past. They portrayed life on Powell Street as that of a self-contained Japanese society, focussing on pioneer economic, social, and political activities, and never politicized or expanded them in a nation-building context.[185]

That Ukrainians, more than Japanese, envisioned Canada as a diverse but united "imagined community" was reflected on special occasions. The diamond jubilee of Canadian Confederation in 1927 provides a good example of how the two ethnic elites showcased their dual loyalties, vision of Canada, and regional identity all at once through their myths and cultural symbols. Both the Ukrainian-language press and its Japanese counterpart published a history of Canada distributed from Ottawa that covered mainstream landmark events from Jacques Cartier's arrival on the St. Lawrence in 1534 to the passing of the British North America Act in 1867 and the subsequent births of the various provinces.[186] While both groups were kept from this official version of "Canadian" collective memory, Ukrainians perhaps exhibited a slightly better sense of participation in it. *Ukrainskyi holos* stressed a sense of loyalty to Canada:

> Today, being a Canadian citizen is an honour, and those who deem it an honour owe gratitude to all those people who contributed to the building of Canada, as it is. Ukrainians in Canada belong to the youngest of its citizens, but exactly for that reason we can sense the great significance of the work of the Fathers of Confederation, who created Canada, and their successors who continued and

> perfected their work. Therefore, while Ukrainians participate in the anniversary holiday of Canada, they do this not superficially, through moral obligation, but with a sincere heart, as peoples who, with complete integrity, appreciate the goodwill of Canada.[187]

For them, the anniversary was an occasion on which all diverse ethnic groups demonstrated their sense of appreciation to Canada, exhibiting the mosaic character of the country. Looking at Winnipeg specifically, the Ukrainian newspaper praised the participation of "patriotic clubs and separate national groups" representing French, Icelanders, Italians, Poles, and others who entered floats in the city and lamented the absence of a Ukrainian one.[188] Yet Ukrainians still "distinguished" themselves with Ukrainian choirs, singers, and dancers in Ukrainian costume,[189] publicly displaying their heritage as part of the landmark event. Japanese also showcased their culture in Vancouver, with a float from one of the labour associations, folk dances, and fireworks, though they did not make any official remarks on the anniversary.[190] Unlike Ukrainians, who were always conscious of celebrating Canada's birthday, Japanese tended to focus on an ethnic festival rather than situate their events in the larger Canadian vision.

~

Interwar Canada was characterized by the crystallization of distinct Ukrainian and Japanese communities that had first emerged in the late nineteenth and early twentieth centuries and the revival of Scottish ethnicity, both instrumentally and symbolically. Political causes in both the homeland and Canada as well as homeland myths and symbols played significant roles in the reinforcement of ethnic boundaries. Mainstream and ethnic identities rarely merged, except for Scots, whose ethnic boundaries were fluid and often needed to be artificially redefined. Ukrainian nationalists and *issei* Japanese, in particular, sought full recognition in Canadian society without having to abandon their ethnic identities and loyalty to their respective homelands. Such a desire to maintain a dual loyalty became a major force in the rise of the idea of the Canadian mosaic. Overall, Ukrainian nationalists, with all their prerequisites—the franchise, intensive ideological rivalry, lack of an official and overriding voice from their homeland, and statelessness—strengthened their boundaries. They also did so more than mainstream Scots, who defined Canada to a great degree, and marginalized Japanese, who had few means of participation, given their race, Japanese imperialism, and concentration in British Columbia. Ukrainian nationalists, therefore, envisioned Canada as multiethnic more enthusiastically and earlier than did others.

CHAPTER 3

Increasing Tensions and the Wartime Mosaic

The outbreak of World War II posed dilemmas for both mainstream Canadians and ethnic elites in terms of how they envisioned Canada and dealt with ethnic groups' homeland issues. Mainstream British-Canadian politicians and academics faced difficulties in balancing democratic principles with deep-rooted suspicions of and prejudices against certain ethnic groups. They reconfirmed the supremacy of the political, legal, and cultural traditions—particularly democracy and liberalism—that Canada had inherited from Britain. Paradoxically, however, the ideals for which they were fighting overseas raised questions about how to deal with ethnic minorities in Canada. On the one hand, Canada had to denounce racism, now identified with Nazi Germany, at every opportunity; at the same time, the presence of "enemy aliens"—particularly Japanese—within its territory was seen unfavourably. On the other hand, Ukrainian and Japanese elites faced their own dilemma of conflicting loyalties between Canada and their homelands, now more acute than ever. Both communities pledged their allegiance to Canada and Britain, yet they rarely abandoned homeland politics even if they conflicted with Canada's war effort.

The war era was thus a period filled with contradictions and political manoeuvring. In this chapter, I argue that, at one level, the war reinforced the existing ethnic and racial hierarchy to the point of broadening the gap between suspect ethnic groups and their acceptance as participants in Canadian nation building. All three groups had different fates during this period. Scots were ethnically invisible as part of the wartime leadership, Ukrainians were increasingly incorporated into or expected to contribute to Canada's war effort, and Japanese were excluded. Yet, at another level, the escalating tensions between potentially problematic ethnic groups and Canada urged the Canadian public to contemplate the roles that ethnic groups could play in the country and how they should be treated. Both Ukrainian and Japanese elites seized the opportunity that this rethinking presented. Ukrainian nationalists demanded equal rights and the broad acceptance of ethnic pluralism in Canada, while *nisei* Japanese denounced racism and internment and renewed the call for the franchise in the name of democracy. In this sense, both ethnic groups took a critical step in the pursuit of full partnership in Canadian society.

Reinforcing the Ethnic Hierarchy: Mainstream Canada

During World War II, the situation among Ukrainians and Japanese in Canada was always affected by international events compounded by political considerations of the Canadian government, while Scots were integral to wartime policy making. The decision of Parliament under Prime Minister W.L. Mackenzie King, himself of Scottish origin, to join Britain in the war against Nazi Germany in September 1939, following Adolf Hitler's advance into Poland, made Germany and its allied Axis countries Canada's enemies. On the home front, Canadians were categorized into loyal and disloyal groups based on alleged formal or informal ties with such foreign powers—Germany after 1939, Italy after 1940, the Soviet Union between 1939 and 1941, and Japan after 1941.[1]

Ukrainians' loyalty was assessed according to the ideological line between nationalists and communists, and, as the international situation affecting the two groups shifted, so did their status in Canadian society. The Nazi-Soviet Non-Aggression Pact of 1939, as well as general suspicion of communism, automatically made communist Ukrainians disloyal and challenged the Ukrainian Labour-Farmer Temple Association (ULFTA) leadership. Their organized activities and newspaper, *Narodna hazeta* (renamed from *Ukrainski robitnychi visti* in 1937), were banned in 1940; several leaders were interned between 1940 and 1942; and their community halls were confiscated and sold to other Ukrainian associations.[2] The position of communist Ukrainians improved after Germany's invasion of the Soviet Union, which made Canada the latter's ally and upset nationalist Ukrainians.[3] Before the war, the leaders of the right-wing Ukrainian National Federation (UNF) had hoped that Hitler would help redraw national territories in Europe and give Ukrainians sovereignty. They were thus particularly vulnerable after the outbreak of hostilities to accusations of being pro-German and often came under suspicion.

The loyalty of Japanese was viewed collectively and monolithically in that no distinction was made between Japanese-born *issei* and Canadian-born *nisei*. The Anti-Comintern Pact between Germany and Japan signed in 1936 and the latter's participation in the Rome-Berlin Axis in 1940 were initial factors in labelling Japanese unreliable. The start of the Pacific War in December 1941 officially made them enemy aliens. In the following year, the federal government announced the evacuation of 22,000 Japanese residents from the West Coast, their relocation to camps (e.g., Tashme, Greenwood, Kaslo, New Denver, and Slocan) in the BC interior or to farming communities outside the province, and the confiscation of their property.[4] The evacuation was undertaken gradually rather than all at once, starting with males, so that the separation of family members and the removal of community leaders became a major problem. Also in 1942, the Canadian Japanese Association (CJA) was dissolved; the *issei*'s organ, *Tairiku nippô*, was banned; and both the Consulate in Vancouver and the Legation in Ottawa were closed, leaving Japanese with neither the organized *issei*'s voice nor official representatives from Japan.

Such measures were similar to those that the federal government imposed on Ukrainians from the Austro-Hungarian Empire during World War I in that it assessed people's loyalty simply by their national origin. In both cases, its policy was based largely on ethnoracial discrimination. Yet the fundamental difference concerned the scale of internment. Although not all Ukrainians were interned during World War I, the policies against Japanese during World War II, by which the entire community was removed from the West Coast, destroyed their foundation. The old Japanese elite, who lost their long-nurtured role as a bridge between mainstream and Japanese Canadians in fishing villages, in urban centres, and on farms, could not function in the same way as before. It was during this period that the Japanese-Canadian leadership changed. New leaders were ethnic activists more determined to fight against racism and injustice.

While mainstream Canadian policy makers, which included ethnic Scots, thus viewed both Ukrainians and Japanese with caution and suspicion when World War II began, pre-existing factors made them treat the former with greater flexibility and openness. First, there was the critical fact that Ukrainian nationalists lacked a sovereign homeland and did not identify with Soviet Ukraine, whereas Japanese in Canada were regarded as part of a now dangerous imperial power. Second, over the previous two decades, Ukrainians had acquired increasingly political as well as economic importance in Canada, unlike Japanese, and a certain level of trust had developed between them and a handful of well-placed mainstream Canadians. Third, the concentration of the Japanese population in British Columbia, within reach of Japan, intensified anti-Japanese sentiment, while Ukrainians, residing mainly in remote central provinces, rarely raised such fears.

These differences were evident in the attitudes of not only mainstream politicians but also academics with close associations with governments at both provincial and federal levels. These individuals played a critical role in the mobilization of public opinion regarding Ukrainians and Japanese. Watson Kirkconnell, then a professor of English at McMaster University, and George W. Simpson, a professor of history at the University of Saskatchewan, were two of the influential figures who provided background information on Ukrainians both to the public and to the Department of National War Services established in 1940. An advocate of the Canadian mosaic since the 1930s, Kirkconnell had written extensively and favourably about Ukrainians. Yet, as the war progressed, his focus moved to questions about the loyalty of nationalist Ukrainians in Canada, a key theme in his books *Canada, Europe, and Hitler* (1939), *The Ukrainian Canadians and the War* (1940), and *Our Ukrainian Loyalists* (1943). Simpson had a close relationship with the Ukrainian Self-Reliance League (USRL) and played a central role in the establishment of the Ukrainian Canadian Committee (UCC) in 1940 to facilitate Ukrainians' war effort.[5] Having strong personal connections with nationalist Ukrainian organizations such as the UNF, Kirkconnell, in particular, tried to justify alleged strong ties with Nazi Germany. He argued that Ukrainians were only trying to take advantage of Nazi Germany's eastern expansion, which might destroy the Soviet Union and help to establish a sovereign Ukraine. The UNF, according to Kirkconnell, did not support "the Nazi régime and its political ideals" but saw it just as a means to an end.[6] Similarly, after investigating the issue, Simpson concluded that "it is a conjunction or coincidence in international affairs which at the present time links Hitler's ambition for power with Ukrainian aspirations for national independence. Such a situation is by no means unusual or novel."[7]

Nor were Japanese without advocates. In fact, prior to Pearl Harbor, Mackenzie King took a very sympathetic approach to Japanese: "The decision of the Japanese government to ally itself with Germany and Italy, under certain conditions, has undoubtedly greatly increased tension in the whole Pacific area.... Partly, perhaps, as a result of growing tension in the far east, we recently witnessed an unfortunate recrudescence of anti-oriental feeling in British Columbia. This campaign was characterized by wholly unsubstantiated and irresponsible charges and accusations against our fellow nationals and other residents of British Columbia who are of Japanese racial origin."[8]

As this remark suggests, the Japanese problem was initially identified only with British Columbia and not yet perceived as a national one. Other individuals, such as Henry F. Angus, a professor of economics at the University of British Columbia,[9] and members of the Co-operative Commonwealth

Federation (CCF) also advocated tolerance toward Japanese, particularly the Canadian born. Yet their moderate voices were overwhelmed by anti-Asian politicians from British Columbia, including Liberal MPs such as Ian A. Mackenzie and Thomas Reid and Independent MP A.W. Neil.[10] Mackenzie, who happened to be an expert in Gaelic and Scottish literature, served first as minister of national defence and then as minister of pensions and national health, and he spearheaded the anti-Japanese movement in Parliament. Through his influential position in the governments in Ottawa and British Columbia, he exercised power and was involved in the creation of anti-Japanese policies during the war, including internment.[11]

One of the striking differences in activities and rhetoric among these diverse individuals was their characterization of the Ukrainian and Japanese groups. The mainstream elite rarely treated all Ukrainians in the same way, recognizing internal diversity among them, yet they categorized all Japanese in Canada as a single dangerous ethnic community. Kirkconnell, for example, devoted a series of publications to stressing the difference between Ukrainian nationalists and communists. For him, the former represented genuine Ukrainians and loyal Canadians, who "were so organized, not primarily as Ukrainians but as Canadian citizens in support of the war effort," and whose "support has been loyally and generously given."[12] Conversely, he was anticommunist, attributing all signs of suspicious activities to the latter and their "rural constituencies," which were "closely identified with the Ukrainian Labour-Farmer Temple Association, a small but vigorously organized Communist group, which is far from representative of the Ukrainians as a whole."[13] The ULFTA, he said, was "not even Ukrainian," since "authentic Ukrainians are apparently an actual minority within the alleged total of 20,000 members."[14] Clearly, ideology rather than common ethnic descent based on blood played a great role in the assessment of Ukrainian loyalty. This distinction was rarely made for the Japanese even if mainstream elite were aware of the growing number of *nisei* and naturalized *issei* among them. In fact, A.W. Neil did recognize these differences, explaining, in a lengthy address to the House of Commons in 1942 regarding his work to restrict Japanese rights, that "there are three classes of Japanese we must deal with. There are the Japanese nationals, those born in Japan and never naturalized in Canada; they are Japanese nationals. Then there is the man born in Japan and naturalized in Canada. He is called a naturalized Japanese or a Canadian. Then there is the Japanese who was born in Canada, who can call himself a Japanese-Canadian if he likes. The government orders with regard to seizing the boats and the sale of gas and explosives applied to all three classes. That was all right."[15] Clearly, this remark represented both racism and the strong conviction that Japanese loyalty to the homeland would remain, no matter what an individual's legal status. In this way, the mainstream elite played a role in redrawing Ukrainian and Japanese boundaries, determining who made up the membership of the two ethnic communities, regardless of how Ukrainians and Japanese themselves perceived their identities.

Another Japanese/Ukrainian difference concerned mainstream Canadians' expectations regarding participation in the war effort. The fact that these Canadians anticipated Ukrainians' full support for the war while denying Japanese such opportunities particularly served to increase the distance between the two groups. In many ways, the federal government often evaluated loyalty and participation in Canada's war effort according to the ethnic group rather than the individual, thereby reinforcing ethnic boundaries. The high expectations of the federal government for Ukrainians collectively to participate in the war effort was well illustrated by its involvement in the establishment of the UCC, which brought nationalist Ukrainians together and encouraged closer supervision of the masses. For example, Tracy Philipps, the government's own advisor in European affairs, worked behind the scene on behalf of the Department of National War Services and the Department of External Affairs to create the UCC as a unified umbrella organization that would shift Ukrainian Canadians' focus from Ukraine to Canada.[16] The obsession with good "group" performance became obvious when Canadians criticized Ukrainian bloc settlements, especially the Vegreville colony in Alberta, for failing to cast majority votes for conscription in the national plebiscite of 1942.[17] In contrast, the Japanese were collectively denied participation in the war. Mackenzie and other MPs from British Columbia promoted anti-Japanese sentiment in Parliament, insisting that Japanese not have the right to enlist in the Canadian military. Although Mackenzie King initially took a moderate approach to Japanese, he announced his decision to exempt them from enlistment in January 1941, before Pearl Harbor, to show that the opinion of mainstream British Columbians weighed more than that of Japanese. Such measures, together with the internment after Pearl Harbor that segregated the Japanese community from the rest of Canada, were undertaken, to some extent, to unite the rest of the country behind the war effort.

Conflicting and Unconflicting Loyalties: Between Homelands and Canada

World War II highlighted the tensions in the dual loyalty that Ukrainian and Japanese elites—nationalists and *issei* in particular—had cultivated since the interwar period. Scots were the only group among the three whose dual loyalty was never in conflict, and the war served to strengthen it by reminding them of the value of British ideals and the need to pursue them. Naturally, Scottish elite thus focussed on Canada's unity and cooperation with Britain. For example, the Scottish-dominant Presbyterian Church called for full support beyond one nation for the British Empire, arguing that the war was for universal Protestant virtues. *The Presbyterian Records,* for example, Protestantized terms such as "freedom" and "liberty" in 1942: "the English Puritans, the Dutch Calvinists, the Scottish Covenanters and the Pilgrim Fathers, asserted their claim against the state; it was a claim to worship and serve God as conscience should direct. They had no belief in liberty, as they showed when they themselves had power; but the claim which they successfully asserted carried within itself the claim to liberty, and by fidelity to God they initiated liberty among men. They became unwittingly the pioneers of freedom."[18]

In such an effort, the church was not without its own agenda. *The Presbyterian Records* called for donations, relating the denomination's religious survival to the war cause. An article entitled "To the Task: The Call of 1942," which called Winston Churchill the "greatest leader of our time," argued that "since we have so valiantly and self-sacrificingly responded to the call of the Empire shall we not as eagerly respond to the call of Christ's Kingdom to come to the Lord against the mighty, to stand for the integrity and the expansion of the Church which God has made the medium of world enlightenment and inspiration?"[19]

Intriguingly, Presbyterian elites, in their war effort, tried to de-Scotticize their church, thereby blurring the distinction between Canadianness and Scottishness: "We are striving to become a truly Canadian Church.... If we were to remain self-consciously Scottish, our scope would be limited. We would appeal then only to Scots in the Dominion. But our people come from all the tribes and nations of Europe. We are English and French, Scots and Scandinavians, Russians and Germans, Poles and Finns. All of us are Canadians. We are the true British Commonwealth of Nations."[20]

For Ukrainian nationalists and *issei* Japanese, the gap between mainstream Canadians' and their respective causes for the war was much greater. Both elites pledged their first loyalty to Canada and Britain, expressing full support for the Allies. Yet, as Bohdan Kordan has shown, Ukrainian nationalists within as well as outside Canada regarded the wartime turmoil as a great opportunity to liberate Ukrainian territories from foreign rule and establish a unified, independent Ukrainian state.[21] The expectation in certain circles of the role that Nazi Germany might play in this quest was obviously incompatible with Canada's war aims. *Issei* were also torn between their support for Japan's campaign to become a world power and participation in Canada's war effort. Nonetheless, there were also major differences that helped to consolidate a sense of community among Ukrainian nationalists that was missing among Japanese.

The first difference was that, since ethnic communities are often built on causes closely tied to their homelands psychologically and physically, the absence of such a cause can weaken community bonds. The homeland remained a core of Ukrainian nationalist propaganda and a unifying force throughout the war regardless of the difficulties that it presented, while to Japanese the homeland was no longer perceived as politically advantageous. In this light, Ukrainian nationalists renewed their sense of community in pursuit of independence for Ukraine, but the Japanese elite, especially once they became enemy aliens, could no longer use Japan's imperial messages to mobilize their people.

The need for Ukrainians to grab the chance created by the war to fulfill their goal of nationhood was stressed, for example, in *Ukrainskyi holos* in an article entitled "All Ukrainians—Together!" It implied that such a chance was rare and would not last long: "Here we need to act quickly. Ukrainians have to be independent, free, and self-reliant. This has been our long-term goal."[22] Such a message might conflict with Canada's interests, especially given the Allies' guarantees to Poland and cooperation with the Soviet Union after 1941. Yet political contradictions were relatively easy to hide in the name of a united war effort for Canada.

For Japanese, the conflict in their dual loyalty was much more obvious. Between September 1939 and December 1941, prior to Japan's attack on Pearl Harbor, the Japanese elite emphasized homeland issues to unite their people. *Issei,* in particular, had never lost their loyalty to Imperial Japan and publicly expressed it until right before Pearl Harbor. Such sentiments were expressed well by Eikichi Kagetsu, president of the CJA in 1940: "Now, our Imperial Japan has advanced above the world's powers and stands in a superior position. Today, we, residing abroad, are able to look upon the gallant figure of Japan, thanks to its imperial virtues and the nation's consistent efforts to pressure the traditional Japanese spirit.... The road to progress for our race is still far. The mission that the young generation carries on its shoulders on this road is of great significance. Yet behind our efforts, there is a great motherland and the world's best national spirit."[23]

Understandably, this sort of open celebration of Japan rarely surfaced in public after December 1941 as the Japanese elite deliberately hid any emotional attachment to Japan. At a regular meeting organized by the *issei* who looked after Japanese internees in the Slocan camp, for example, the discussion went as follows: "They [the British Columbia Security

Commission (BCSC)] complained about some people waving the Rising Sun when a group of internees set out. It would be better to conceal the Rising Sun in our mind."[24] Both because Japanese symbols became increasingly "dangerous" and because *issei* lost their organized voice, the homeland was rarely incorporated into Japanese propaganda. *Nisei* often took a very ambivalent and low-key approach to the war between Japan and Canada. The *New Canadian,* for example, wrote that, "if we are honest, we shall never say that we hate the Japanese or that we hate Japan. And if we stand for Canada, we need not be ashamed of being a 'Jap.'"[25] Clearly, Japan no longer served to promote a sense of pride and unity among Japanese and became, instead, a source of tension.

The second difference between Ukrainians and Japanese concerned the role of organizational activities and the press, crucial to incorporating all Ukrainians and Japanese in Canada into "imagined communities." Ukrainian nationalists, supported and spurred by mainstream Canadian leaders, began to overcome internal rivalries and increasingly unite, at least at an organizational level. This unity was considered particularly significant as it strengthened the power of the Ukrainian nationalist elite as the voice of the grassroots.[26] The great achievement was the establishment of the UCC in 1940, bringing together the USRL, the UNF, the Brotherhood of Ukrainian Catholics of Canada, the United Hetman Organization (UHO), and the League of Ukrainian Labour Organizations. Its first national congress in 1943 served as a demonstration of Ukrainian unity behind two goals: Allied victory and Ukrainian independence. The publicity that the congress attracted and such a grand gesture in support of Canada's war effort were very effective in helping the UCC leadership promote the role that Ukrainians should play in the war.

Issei Japanese, on the contrary, lost such a means to mobilize their people as *Tairiku nippô* was banned and organized activities were restricted. They published some articles in the *nisei* organ, the *New Canadian,* which became bilingual and ran throughout the war, but censorship limited its contents to official information that *issei* needed to know. Japanese associations were often under the close scrutiny of government agencies, such as the BCSC, which carried out the evacuation. In fact, Japanese leaders came into the crisis with limited organization and few leaders who could unite them in the emergency. For example, when the evacuation began, the BCSC appointed *issei* Etsuji Morii, who had experience in working with the Royal Canadian Mounted Police (RCMP), to carry out its orders. He was considered notorious among his people, who did not regard him as their representative, and in his new position of authority was completely opposed by other Japanese leaders.[27] What was happening among Japanese leaders was the transformation of their roles. They could no longer simply function as old-style intermediaries between mainstream Canadians and their fellow Japanese. Rather, Japanese needed much more politically active individuals as their representatives. Japanese were divided into three organizations: the *issei*'s Naturalized Japanese Canadian Association, the *nisei*'s Japanese Canadian Citizens Council (JCCC), and an independent group of *nisei* who resisted the government orders for evacuation.[28] None of these organizations could take effective leadership in the camps, however.[29] In fact, as their leaders went to different camps, organizational activities became increasingly difficult. For example, the JCCC saw its own demise:

> We may take the stand that we have been taking up till now, that is, to co-operate with the Commission even against great opposition from many quarters and do what we can do to help the Japanese community carry out the evacuation as safely and as comfortably as possible. It probably will mean the slow starvation or strangulation of the Council because sooner or later the male Council members at least will be picked off one by one. The other way of settling this question is to hand in our permits [to leave for the camps] in a wholesale manner and break up the Council at once.[30]

Outside British Columbia, some *nisei* Japanese organized in Toronto in 1943 as the Japanese Canadian Committee for Democracy (JCCD). The war thus created a critical difference between Ukrainian nationalists and Japanese at an organizational level, uniting the former around a centralized umbrella association and leading to a division of power among the latter.

The third difference between Ukrainians and Japanese concerned the intensity of internal rivalry within their groups. As the war progressed, the nationalist/communist rivalry intensified among Ukrainians over both homeland issues and the representation of Ukrainians in Canada, providing momentum to each faction's activities on behalf of mobilization of the masses. The *issei-nisei* relationship among Japanese, in contrast, became much more interdependent than it had been during the interwar period since *issei* and *nisei* alike faced evacuation and camp life.

Among Ukrainians, the conflict between the UNF and the ULFTA was particularly severe as the latter attacked the former for Fascist propaganda and Nazi connections and the former criticized the Soviet Union and communism.[31] The two groups exchanged shots in their respective organs, the UNF's *Novyi shliakh* and the communists' *Ukrainske zhyttia* and *Ukrainske slovo*.[32] The first UCC congress, which publicly proclaimed nationalists' loyalty to Canada, also demonstrated to communist Ukrainians the size of the nationalist community and its good relations with mainstream Canada. This sense of community and its size were exaggerated in the congress's official proceedings: "The hearts, the feelings, and the thoughts of those present transcended the external manifestations of the Congress—they embraced the many thousands of Ukrainians in Canada."[33]

Similarly, among Japanese, the war increased the antagonism between *issei* and *nisei,* which surfaced over a number of issues such as loyalty to Japan, representation of evacuees, and the preferred response to evacuation orders. One illuminating example involved how to demonstrate Japanese loyalty to Canada. *Nisei,* who regarded purchase of the government's Victory Bonds as the most visible way to show their "group" dedication to the war effort, criticized an *issei* group for making direct donations to Canadian soldiers, as the *New Canadian* stated: "Differences in training and heritage have unfortunately left the average *issei* quite unable to grasp Canadian psychology. And viewed from the standpoint of a Canadian, the attitude of many of the first generation, though undoubtedly sincere and well-intentioned, is incredibly naïve and unrealistic."[34] Clearly, *nisei* were more aware that the federal government tended to judge loyalty in terms of the ethnic group rather than individuals.

Yet these differences were not as far-reaching and profound as those dividing their Ukrainian counterparts. In fact, to a certain degree, the lack of an organized voice among *issei* after 1942 gave *nisei* the power and opportunity to speak for the community, particularly at the beginning of the evacuation.[35] As both *issei* and *nisei* were facing the crisis that threatened their community life, and as *issei* lost effective leadership, intense competition seemed counterproductive. The JCCC often worked with the CJA to carry out the BCSC's orders of confiscation and evacuation, held joint meetings, and eventually took over the CJA's responsibilities.[36] While effective leadership of *nisei* rarely lasted in the camps or later on the farms, to which many Japanese were moved, some voices anticipated the *nisei* era that followed. For example, a letter from an *issei* Japanese, sent to the *New Canadian* from a sugar beet farm in Manitoba, noted how a *nisei* had already been acting as a local representative, adding that "everything belongs to the *nisei*'s era. We should only follow them."[37] Another letter from an *issei* in Ontario foresaw *nisei*'s success as sugar beet farmers, building a good relationship with white society and winning its trust because of their fluent English.[38] These comments suggest that a shift of power from *issei* to *nisei* was obvious at the new places if not all at once on a national scale.

While both Ukrainian and Japanese leaders strove to maintain ethnic identity, they also wanted to demonstrate loyalty to Canada, using propaganda and rhetoric that targeted mainstream Canadians as well as their own peoples. USRL circles and *nisei* Japanese, both Canadian oriented and adherents of liberal democracy to distinguish themselves from their rivals, exhibited similar attitudes toward the war. As soon as the war broke out, both the USRL and the JCCL officially declared their full support for Canada. The USRL announced that the association "at no time wavered in its loyalty and devotion to the British Crown or to Canada."[39] Similarly, the JCCL maintained that, "since Canada is at war, and we call ourselves Canadians, we are anxious to do our share to help Canada; and there should be no doubt in our minds as to this issue."[40] Furthermore, both the USRL and *nisei* Japanese contended that their ethnic backgrounds would never affect their Canadianism. This position is evident from the USRL's message to its members: "As we live in Canada, try to be good Canadian citizens. As Canadian citizens, you should not place the interests of a second state higher than those of Canada, and you should not have an obligation to those other countries higher than to Canada.... Even if the Ukrainian state should become independent, the obligations of Ukrainian Canadians toward Canada must be placed first.... And because an independent Ukrainian state does not exist, there is no difficulty for Ukrainians in Canada to sustain their loyalty to Canada over other loyalties."[41]

Ukrainskyi holos frequently expressed a sense of belonging to Canada in statements such as the following: "As Canadian citizens, we want Canada to have fewer guests and more real citizens. As Canadians of Ukrainian descent, we want Canada to have fewer guests of Ukrainian origin. We want Ukrainians in Canada to be the best of citizens."[42] The *nisei* Japanese, though well aware of their dilemma, expressed similar thoughts: "He [a *nisei*] realizes that his destiny lies primarily in Canada, the land of his birth and education."[43] The war was viewed as a great chance for Japanese to destroy any suspicions about where they stood. "Indeed," the *New Canadian* wrote after the attack on Pearl Harbor, "the war has not lessened our contribution as a group to the Canadian nation; it has imposed upon us a greater task for the future."[44]

Both Japanese and Ukrainians also demonstrated their loyalty by enlisting and/or participating in Victory Loan drives and Red Cross collections. Yet establishing Ukrainian support for the war effort was much easier, especially after Pearl Harbor, when Japanese participation was greatly restricted. The war thus broadened the gap between the two groups in terms of their distance from mainstream society. At the UCC's first congress in

1943, Vice-President W. Kossar provided concrete evidence of the Ukrainian contribution. He estimated that 35,000 Ukrainians had enlisted to date, representing about 14 percent of the entire Canadian forces, and he claimed that Ukrainians were taking a major role in the Victory Loan drives in Alberta, for example, where 71,863 Ukrainians had purchased Victory Bonds.[45] George E. Dragan, who was the first Ukrainian to sit in the Saskatchewan legislature, also stressed the good record of collecting money among his people in Saskatchewan.[46] The call to contribute to the Red Cross and Victory Loans also appeared frequently in *Ukrainskyi holos,* which urged readers to participate in these collective endeavours to support Canada.[47]

Japanese also tried to emphasize their role in the war and throughout 1941 devoted much energy to the Victory Loan campaign, to some extent reading the international situation and anticipating a war between Canada and Japan. Contributions to the war effort, particularly from *issei,* were frequently announced in the *New Canadian* to prove the immigrant generation's loyalty to Canada. For example, Bunjiro Uyeda, a businessman who owned Yamato Silks Limited on Granville Street in Vancouver, gained fame for his large donations to the National Defence Fund.[48] Besides the amount of money collected, the Victory Loan drives were regarded as important to showcase *issei*'s stance in the event of war between Canada and Japan. The *New Canadian* depicted the Japanese headquarters of the Victory Loan campaign: "Decked in Union Jack bunting and gay in red, white and blue, this sign [of the Victory Loan] above the offices of the Canadian Japanese Association in Vancouver tells its own story."[49] After the internment and the confiscation of Japanese property, participating in such campaigns was neither expected nor easy, yet Japanese tried since it was the only possible way left to prove their loyalty to Canada. Financially contributing to the war effort might make some sympathizers if not overturn anti-Japanese wartime policies. The *New Canadian* implied that demonstrating that Japanese were doing what they could was more important than the amount of money raised, admitting that "recent drastic economic changes" hurt potential donations.[50] The propagandistic value of such collective efforts was well illustrated by the president of the CJA when he reminded the BCSC that since Canada's entry into war with Germany his association had tried "its best to aid in the defense of Canada."[51]

Although Scots had no need to highlight their loyalty during the war, some of them nonetheless emphasized the particularly "Scottish" contributions to the conflict. In part, such manifestations reflected resistance to the weakening ties between Canada and Scotland, which increasingly made Scots just mainstream Canadians. For some people, especially in Nova Scotia, Scottish origin still provided a sense of pride and distinctiveness, and the war offered an opportunity for Canada and Scotland to bond against a common enemy in Nazism and Fascism. A good example of the ethnicization of the war effort emerged from the reaction of Scottish associations in the province to the appeal for donations made by the Association of Highland Societies in Edinburgh to supply Highland regiments with comfort kits.[52] Angus L. Macdonald, who served as minister of defence for naval services between 1940 and 1945, stressed supporting the Scottish cause: "I realize quite fully, of course, that there are many appeals to the charity in these times. But I think, nevertheless, that this appeal from the country of our origin stands in a position somewhat different from other general appeals."[53] At his behest, organizations from the North British Society in Halifax to the Antigonish Highland Society and the St. Andrew's Society of New Glasgow raised funds for this cause.[54] It was presented as the obligation of "persons of Scottish blood," assigned a special mission in preserving the long-treasured "Scottish" ideals of democracy and liberalism.[55]

Bridging the Gap: Democracy and Ethnic Rights

Ukrainian and Japanese elites, aware of the tensions in their dual loyalty to Canada and their respective homelands, regarded democratic ideals as the best way to overcome such contradictions. The Allies framed the war as a struggle for democracy against Nazism and Fascism and defined democracy broadly as standing in opposition to totalitarian regimes. The Atlantic Charter signed in 1941 by Franklin Roosevelt and Winston Churchill became the model for democratic principles, which included the sovereignty of nations, a ban on the use of force, and the abolition of territorial expansionism. While mainstream Canadians tended to view democracy narrowly, following those principles, Ukrainian nationalists and *nisei* Japanese expected Canada to be consistent in upholding the ideals for which both groups had given their support through concrete activities such as enlistment or buying Victory Bonds. They exaggerated mainstream wartime propaganda and incorporated their own definitions of democracy into the mainstream vision. For Ukrainian nationalists, democracy meant being able to participate fully in Canadian politics and life generally and to liberate Ukraine. For *issei* and *nisei* Japanese, it meant an end to long-term racism as well as the difficulties that they faced as enemy aliens during the war. Ironically, the entire wartime treatment of Japanese placed them at the centre of mainstream politicians' attention and thus provided them with a chance to be heard.

In this process, nationalist Ukrainians and *nisei* Japanese led a campaign for a new Canada that was strongly tied to democracy and ethnic pluralism. Not surprisingly, both groups had much broader definitions of democracy than did mainstream Canadians, who identified it with the British parliamentary and legal systems or the provisions of the Atlantic Charter at best. Yet the question of whether homeland politics could realistically be incorporated into Canadian democracy separated Ukrainian nationalist and *nisei* Japanese elites. Ukrainian nationalists regarded the liberation of Ukraine as an integral part of the war for democracy and as part of Canadian ethnic politics, whereas *nisei* Japanese withdrew comments on Imperial Japan and focussed on their rights in Canada. In other words, the former sought democracy beyond Canada, while the latter did so domestically. The outbreak of the Pacific War had made Japan's foreign policy actions no longer justifiable as a movement toward democracy in Asia, while the war in Europe provided Ukrainian nationalists with ideal grounds for their support of Ukrainian independence. That this goal was in line with the Allies' principle of democracy, at least in theory, made Ukrainians more active on behalf of their homeland.

The war thus accelerated Ukrainian nationalists' lobby for a sovereign state that had begun during the interwar years, putting the two facets of their dual loyalty in greater harmony than ever. The nationalists expected the Allies to assist Ukrainians in their campaign for independence in Europe on the grounds that the liberation of Ukraine would limit the size of the territory under communist rule and eventually contribute to expansion of the democratic world. At the same time, struggle for the liberation of Ukraine coincided with Canada's wartime propaganda on behalf of democracy and thus had to be assisted by Canadian policy makers. Democracy as defined by *Ukrainskyi holos* was a principle "best described as a national right and in terms in which people govern or have a decisive voice in the state."[56] Ukrainian nationalist leaders tried to pressure the Canadian government on behalf of their agenda, but once the Soviet Union became an ally security concerns and diplomatic issues ensured that they would be unsuccessful.[57] For example, Anthony Hlynka brought the issue of Ukrainian independence to the House of Commons in 1942 and explained why it mattered to Canada and the world: "In view of this increasingly dangerous threat [communism], the allies should, therefore, take it upon themselves to become the guardians of sovereign ideals and sovereign nations.... Above all, a Ukrainian independent state in Eastern Europe would be important to the British Commonwealth of nations and the United States as a balance of power. I venture to suggest that in the not distant future the British people and the principles for which they stand will be more closely associated with the Ukrainians than they have ever been before."[58]

Meanwhile, developments in Europe alarmed Ukrainian nationalists in Canada for seeming to increase communist power. A series of events occurred in 1943 that expanded the power of the Soviet Union. German armies suffered the first serious defeat by the Soviet Union in Stalingrad. The Soviet Union also cut off ties with the Polish government in exile, which reopened the question of the borders of future Poland and the autonomy of Ukraine. The UCC presented a memorandum to Mackenzie King in 1943 asking for Allied support for redrawing the boundaries of autonomous Ukrainian territory after the war. Nevertheless, conscious that the Soviet Union remained Canada's ally, the UCC simply interpreted democracy as the self-determination of nations: "The Atlantic Charter clearly and unmistakably lays down as a principle the right of a people to determine their political destiny," and this was "the basis of their [the Allies'] present war objective." Making such an appeal, according to the memorandum, was "a duty which they [Ukrainian Canadians] owe to Canada," for democracy needed to receive "the greatest support from all Canadian citizens."[59]

Nisei Japanese, in contrast, abandoned their interwar justification that Japan's imperial aims were to liberate Asia. Yet the war and internment gave them a different cause, fuelling their demand to be treated as equal Canadian citizens and already nurturing the ideal of human rights. They stressed the definition of democracy as a principle that guarantees the basic rights of citizens, which, in their view, should be based on "the preservation of an unwritten code of British justice, irrespective of race, color or creed."[60]

Such a definition was stretched to include enemy aliens, particularly *nisei,* who were supposed to possess the birthright to be Canadian. The JCCL, for example, contested the government's policy to ban Japanese from enlisting on behalf of their understanding of democracy, which guaranteed "the duty and privilege of every citizen of a democratic country to defend the land of his birth."[61] For *nisei,* a comparison between Nazi racism and the treatment that they received in Canada appeared to be the best ammunition in their fight for recognition. In June 1941, six months before Pearl Harbor, the *New Canadian* foresaw war between Canada and Japan and argued that "as a Japanese racial minority in British Columbia we recognize the shortcomings of our Canadian democracy. But for the same reason we recognize just what Hitler and his doctrine of racial persecution would mean to us were it to gain even temporary ascendancy. If we have not always enjoyed the full benefits of democratic freedom and equality in our native and adopted land, we have not come to believe thereby that these are only empty phrases."[62] Clearly, such an argument was never taken into account at the start of the Pacific War.

Although the majority of *nisei* Japanese, except for a few militant individuals, obeyed the evacuation order to prove their loyalty, they never accepted internment and property confiscation and kept criticizing such policies as racist and undemocratic. That they never portrayed themselves as passive victims is clear from their demand that the BCSC protect their fundamental rights and dignity, securing in turn the physical and psychological well-being of evacuees and evacuation as family units. As the war moved toward the end, the *New Canadian* anticipated changes in public opinion in 1944: "Notwithstanding the almost fanatical prejudice of some of the members [of Parliament] from British Columbia, we cannot yet believe that the Canadian people think their 'good interests' are to be served best by the adoption of the same tactics of racial persecution so significant in the ideology of the enemy with whom we are at war. On the contrary, we have seen and experienced so many instances of genuine democratic belief among the Canadian people that we still look forward to the future with confidence."[63] The *nisei* elite, concerned with the disillusionment felt by Japanese Canadians over establishing a better life and pursuing their rights in Canada, looked ahead and encouraged their people to retain their confidence in democracy.[64] As it unfolded, *nisei* would have an impact on the development of Canadian democracy itself.

Despite their different agendas, Ukrainians and Japanese contributed to a similar panethnic definition of democracy that both guaranteed everybody full rights and equal privileges as citizens and accommodated ethnic pluralism, interpreted to include non-British and non-French peoples. The war prompted both Ukrainian nationalists and *nisei* Japanese to contemplate interethnic cooperation and the role that they could play as part of a united force. The messages that they sent to their respective peoples were strikingly similar in terms of the marriage of the notions of democracy, citizenship, and ethnic rights and the strategies that they used to make their appeal. For example, a Ukrainian delegate to the first UCC congress in 1943 anticipated postwar Canada to be completely different from the interwar notion of Anglo-conformity:

> In my humble estimation, the root of this problem [discrimination] lies in the fact that we still have in our midst that first school of thought, which believes in building the Canadian nation on the pattern of British traditions only. If the French would have seen their cultural stripe woven into the Canadian way of life, if all other ethnical groups would have seen their finer qualities forming part of the Canadian culture, they would have felt that this culture to

> which they have contributed and which is now their own is being challenged and they would have raised their voices in a unanimity that would have been commendable to our great nation.... In building a strong, united nation, we should place on the shoulders of each and every individual the responsibilities and the obligations of a citizen of a democratic country.[65]

Nisei Japanese developed a similar concept just after Canada entered the war with Germany, yet they added a racial dimension to Ukrainians' ethnic pluralism. Equal partnership with the British, which they thought the French already enjoyed, was stressed as the most significant element in the building of Canada. The war years marked the first time that *nisei* Japanese clearly claimed that Asians could also be part of Canada, as the *New Canadian* noted just before Pearl Harbor in 1941:

> Fully as vital to Canada today and in the future … must be the establishment of unity between races; and dominating Anglo-French Canadian relations in the east have their counterpart in Occidental-Oriental relations in the west. If we … Canadians of Oriental origin can play our part in the welding of national unity in British Columbia, we shall have made a contribution to this nation equal to in principle if not in degree to the work of French Canadian leaders, headed by the Hon. Ernest Lapointe, whose stand on the question of military conscription last year is said to have saved Confederation in Canada.[66]

Such an optimistic vision of Canada was toned down, of course, after the evacuation, but it recovered toward the end of the war, when *nisei* and their organ anticipated drastic changes in postwar Canada. The *New Canadian* discussed what both Canada and Japanese Canadians had learned in terms of the evils of racism and how the lessons could be used to build a new Canadian citizenship in which "no exceptions" could be made because of "race or national origin."[67] "Despite all the things that have been said and done since Pearl Harbor," said a Dominion Day editorial in 1944,

> and despite all the things which becloud the horizon, this Dominion Day serves as an appropriate time to re-affirm here the fundamental purpose for the existence of this newspaper. That purpose, simply, is to lift a voice and fight to establish the right and privilege of every citizen of the Dominion, irrespective of his racial origin[,] to walk with equal dignity, freedom, and service among his fellow Canadians. Over five years ago *The New Canadian* dedicated itself

> to a particular phase of that purpose. It was to seek the fulfillment of the democratic aspirations of a particular Japanese Canadian minority, which formed a small, but important part in Canada's all important problem of establishing a nationhood and citizenship of enduring value.... We point, today, to the substantial evidence of a large and powerful reservoir of genuine goodwill and democratic conviction in Canada, which is opposed to the emotional prejudice and blind bigotry of some Canadians.[68]

In the circumstances, Dominion Day was seized on as an appropriate occasion to proclaim a new Canadianism. Clearly, the wartime evacuation and the rise of democratic discourses urged Japanese to demand full participation in Canada.

The Wartime Mosaic

The embryonic interwar notion of Canada as a mosaic and its component ethnic myths and symbols proved to be significant to both mainstream and ethnic elites during the war, even though they conceptualized and manipulated the idea very differently. Major interwar mainstream advocates of a mosaic kept developing the concept during the war, moving beyond simply celebrating ethnic groups' cultural traditions such as music, folk art, artifacts, and dance as potential components of a Canadian identity. As Ivana Caccia has shown, they now placed more emphasis on the rhetoric of unity in diversity, in recognition of the need to mobilize the country's diverse population behind the war effort.[69] Their wartime mosaic also exercised more control over ethnic groups, investigating and censoring their newspapers and cultural activities. In a sense, it became a vehicle to understand ethnic groups' ideologies and test their loyalties to reduce tensions between them and mainstream society. For Ukrainian nationalist and Japanese elites, the mosaic had the same meaning as it had before the war, providing the logic to remain loyal to both Canada and the homeland. Yet, at the same time, they saw cultural events as particularly useful during the war to build a better relationship with mainstream Canadians and help to integrate ethnic groups into the war effort more directly. Meanwhile, Ukrainian nationalist and Scottish elites used their homeland cultures and myths to promote a sense of unity among their peoples, tying them to the goal of Ukrainian independence for the one and renewed pride as a dominant race for the other.

The rhetoric of unity became common among mainstream advocates of the prewar mosaic. For example, John Murray Gibbon noted how, "in the Army, Navy, and Air Force, and in munition plants, Canadians of many racial origins are beginning to understand each other better through working together."[70] In Kirkconnell's words, "we are all minorities but all Canadians, entering each with his own capacities … into the richness of the national amalgam."[71] Such an idealistic vision of wartime Canada also became intertwined with a Scottish sense of superiority, as this address to the Highland Society of Antigonish in 1940 illustrates: "Perhaps when this terrible struggle is over, the distracted people of war-torn Europe will seek … in millions a heaven amongst us to start life anew. To blend these diverse peoples into a Canadian Nation will be Canada's task for the future. And for us of Highland blood what part shall we play? To pour into that leaven that will be Canada, the idealism, the loyalty, the courage, the manly independence of the Highland Scot, that, I believe[,] is the high destiny of the Celtic race."[72] While such comments completely ignored the tensions between mainstream Canadians and ethnic groups, especially enemy aliens, they were considered effective in terms of promoting national consciousness.

At the same time, ethnic groups' cultural activities were brought under scrutiny and official and unofficial censorship, which politicized them and contributed to tensions. Kirkconnell, for example, used his language skills to study a number of ethnic newspapers and literary works to determine whether the group was politically dangerous and should be watched carefully.[73] Among Ukrainians, he greatly preferred nationalists to communists, whose cultural activities he viewed as being dangerous to Canada.[74] The politics behind their concerts and dances "were the icing on the educational cake, but the cake itself was filled with political arsenic," which sought to launch revolutionary activities by the working class and "destroy both Christianity" and the "British form of government."[75] Yet scrutinizing ethnic cultures went too far at times and caused unexpected tensions. Scots' sense of ethnic pride and confidence was challenged when Gaelic was banned in telegraph communications and on the Canadian Broadcasting Corporation (CBC), following general guidelines for the treatment of foreign-language exchanges. An angry Scottish Catholic Society in Cape Breton wrote to Angus L. Macdonald: "The fact that this innocent Scottish Custom was ruthlessly interrupted for no sensible reason at all … hurt every true Cape Breton Scot deeply, for his language is one of his greatest pride [sic], and that this language should be treated as a foreign language implied that he was a foreigner. He, whose ancestors were pioneers in the formation of a glorious new nation based on democratic ideals."[76] Scottish elite believed that Gaelic, as a mainstream tradition, should not be treated in the same way as ethnic languages. The censorship issue even reached the prime minister when Reverend A.W.R. Mackenzie, a founder of the Gaelic College in Cape Breton, reminded him that "Highland Scottish

Gaelic has now a high ranking position with the other two main languages of Canada; namely English and French, in that it has a College at St. Ann's, Cape Breton," which focussed on the preservation of Gaelic.[77]

For Ukrainian nationalist and Japanese elites, the public presentation of their artifacts, dances, and costumes appeared to be a valuable method of showing to mainstream society the politically innocuous side of ethnicity.[78] The war made celebratory occasions such as folk art and music festivals special as homeland politics, ideologies, and loyalty issues had always been highlighted since the outbreak of the war. Referring to Gibbon's recommendation to the Royal Society of Canada to publish a collection of ethnic literature, Ukrainian nationalists repeated the point that Ukrainian cultural works could appeal to mainstream Canadians at that critical time, arguing in 1943 that "we have often appeared before our Anglo-Saxon friends with our beautiful folk songs, our spirited dances, and our colorful national costumes. With the exception of our songs, it is highly improbable that any of our artistic attainments will be accepted by our English compatriots. Through our music and songs, however, we have practically unlimited possibilities for the enrichment of Canadian culture."[79]

Nisei Japanese, aware of the deteriorating relationship between Japan and the Allies, focussed on the potential of their folk culture to create bridges to mainstream Canadians. Although occasions on which they could display their heritage declined after Pearl Harbor, *nisei* kept participating in folk culture festivals in British Columbia until they received their evacuation orders. In 1940, they clearly placed strong emphasis on such events. The *New Canadian* appreciated the Vancouver Folk Festival Society for organizing the annual event despite the war, "to bring to public attention something of the beauty and charm of the cultural sources."[80] Thus, folk cultures, as opposed to the discrimination and suspicion that Japanese were increasingly facing, symbolized peace. The significance of this kind of festival as a meeting place, particularly during the war, was well illustrated by the *New Canadian*, which reported on the Drama Festival in Vancouver in 1942:

> In the face of the grim realities of abnormal war conditions, the participation of two *Nisei* drama groups in the annual Greater Vancouver Young People's Drama Festival augurs well for the future. On the one hand, the Festival officials have raised no barriers against the entry of the *Nisei* groups, but have given them every encouragement, furnishing for us all but another example of the fair mindedness and tolerance of the goodly portion of our fellow citizens. On the other hand, the *Nisei* themselves must receive credit

> for the fine spirit they have shown in their willingness to keep up and not abandon the splendid record and reputation they have so deservedly earned in past years, and for their faith in the fairness of both the Festival officials and their audiences. In these days and times we cannot stress too much the need for continued contacts and co-operation by the *Nisei* with our fellow Canadians. For it is true, now as never before, that we must work among and with the great body of Canadian citizens in order to disprove the charges of disloyalty and disaffection that are often times laid against our door, and to secure their willing admission to our claim to an honourable place in Canadian society.[81]

As this passage indicates, the festive occasion was politicized. The emphasis that *nisei* attached to holding the Folk Festival during the war suggests that opportunities for mingling were declining considerably and that the distance between Japanese and mainstream society was broadening. The *New Canadian* thus urged *nisei* to "take advantage of this opportunity" by participating in the event and proving their loyalty to and cooperation with mainstream Canadians.[82]

Not surprisingly, Ukrainian nationalist and *nisei* Japanese leaders identified with the mainstream wartime mosaic, claiming that it marked the recognition of ethnic groups. That both elites cited the same interpretation, even though such a concept was supported by only a handful of mainstream leaders, points to how much impact the notion of mosaic had on ethnic elites' thinking. Such leaders frequently quoted interwar advocates of the Canadian mosaic such as Kirkconnell and Gibbon to stir up patriotism for Canada, and thus enthusiasm for the war, among their peoples as well as to urge mainstream leaders to include ethnic groups in the war effort. Both Ukrainian and Japanese elites, then, agreed with each other, indirectly using mainstream leaders as media. As Frances Swyripa argues, Ukrainian nationalist leaders went beyond celebration of the cultural mosaic, politicizing the cultural mosaic that mainstream leaders, particularly Lord Tweedsmuir, advocated.[83] C.H. Andrusyshen, secretary of the UCC and later a professor in the Slavic department at the University of Saskatchewan, pointed out at the first UCC congress that "Dr. Gibbon thinks, and rightly so, that the successful completion of such an anthology [of literature] will assist the Canadians in understanding each other thoroughly, and so will help to consolidate their varied cultural attainments into a single Canadian mosaic."[84] Another speaker repeated Kirkconnell's comments: "A Canadian of Ukrainian extraction is a better Canadian if he realizes that the stock from which he comes has a fine past, incorporated in literature, music, handicraft and religious faith."[85] Anthony Hlynka quoted Lord Tweedsmuir on two separate occasions in the House of Commons.[86] In 1940, he urged the government to trust and recognize Ukrainians during the war, reading Tweedsmuir's entire 1936 speech, which stressed the value of Ukrainian handicrafts and folk songs as components of Canadian identity and argued that "the strongest nations are those that are made up of different racial elements." Hlynka expanded on this concept in the wartime context, arguing that all ethnic peoples could work together to make a strong Canada, united by principles such as "liberty" and "justice," and thus their participation was essential.[87] In 1943, Hlynka again quoted Tweedsmuir, this time to envision what postwar Canada should be. Now that Ukrainians had proven their loyalty, joining the country's armed forces, he argued, Canada had to produce a citizenship that brought the various ethnic groups "into our one common Canadian mosaic."[88]

Nisei Japanese belatedly picked up the concept of the mosaic in the late 1930s and, with the outbreak of war, began engaging with the idea so that their people would realize that they could become part of Canadian unity. Although Kirkconnell's *Canadians All* devoted only one paragraph to "the Asiatic Canadians," briefly mentioning the participation of *nisei* in the annual Vancouver Drama Festival, the *New Canadian* praised the book as an example of how mainstream society valued wartime unity among various ethnic groups. It stressed Kirkconnell's expectation that the cooperation of all ethnic groups would make a stronger Canada, implying that the tensions within the country would result in the opposite.[89] For Japanese, Kirkconnell was highly respected, as he was a rare voice that expected them to join Canada—albeit only in terms of cultural festivals.

Meanwhile, ethnic groups' myths and symbols, components of the mosaic, were modified in the wartime context to strengthen a sense of ethnic community. Ukrainian nationalists and Scots in particular related their homeland myths and heroes to Canada's war effort, thereby encouraging their respective people to simultaneously do their part and be proud of the heritage that was part of their identity. Only Japanese did not cultivate wartime symbols, at least publicly, since the emperor and the Yamato Race around which Imperial Japan promoted wartime ultranationalism represented totalitarianism in the eyes of Canadians. The absence of such historical myths among Japanese led *nisei* to seriously question who they were.

Both Ukrainian nationalists and Scots regarded the democracy for which Canada was fighting as something inherent in their peoples and histories. This concept attached high value to their characterization as "free-loving" peoples with a great mission in the contemporary war. Historically well trained in and inspired by democratic principles, both groups believed that they could guide Canadians in the creation of a better world. The Cossacks, founders of a Ukrainian state in 1648, for example, became forerunners of democracy. As *Ukrainskyi holos* argued:

> The Ukrainian nation has been democratic from time immemorial. It was democratically governed already from the very beginning of its history, when the "viche" was a key part of their way of life, and not only enacted the law, but also called in and discharged the prince. Democracy was the foundation for the Cossacks, who did not allow any power of heredity, if appointed at the top, and selected every official in the same way, that is only at the time that official was needed. In the name of democracy, in the name of sovereignty, the entire real struggle for the liberation of the Ukrainian nation was carried out. The same right which the Ukrainian people heard from them is the right to govern themselves, the right of democracy. Therefore, their entire struggle is the struggle for democracy. The Ukrainian people strove for democracy between the first and second world wars and fought against Poland and Russia.[90]

Clearly, this passage contains a number of messages. It implies that Ukrainians were fighting for democracy long before it became a principle of the Allies and thus were most effective in Canada's war effort.[91] It also looked toward the future, implying that it was high time for Ukrainians to achieve the goal and return their nation to democracy.

Scots also saw the war as their fight for democracy, which represented the traditional Scottish political system that had dominated the world with the expansion of the British Empire. As Ian McKay argues, Scottish elites and Ukrainian nationalists acted similarly in that they found democratic systems in their histories.[92] Robert Burns became "one of the foremost of democrats,"[93] whose legacy Angus L. Macdonald explained in an address to the Ottawa Gaelic Society in 1944:

> "We shall drain our dearest veins, but they shall be free," said Burns, and no people have had a fiercer passion for freedom and democracy than the people of Scotland. That passion has its roots in the sturdy independence of Scottish character, and in the clan system of Scotland, which was in itself a great democracy.... The Clansmen did not preach democracy. What they did was to practice Government of the people by the people. When you say that "A man's a man for a' that," you imply that he has an essential dignity; that he has certain rights, foremost of which is the right to independence. It

> has been the ceaseless struggle of Scotsmen to maintain the rights of the common men. That being so, need we wonder that today, when these rights are threatened by the most ruthless of tyrants, Scotsmen are fighting with all their traditional courage and gallantry.[94]

Clearly, much like that of Ukrainian nationalists, the message is that the historical roots of Scots as democratic people gave them a special responsibility to lead Canada's war and build a peaceful world. In 1942, Macdonald underlined why it was necessary to listen to and celebrate Scottish history and songs during the war at the Gaelic Mod in Cape Breton, maintaining that doing so helped to "renew the tie with Scotland" and "strengthen and rekindle the fires of our patriotism."[95] The impact of Scots on Canada was also noted by T.C. Davis, high commissioner for Canada in Australia, in anticipating the great role that Canada could play in the postwar world: "People have marveled at Canada's contribution to this war. Thanks largely to the influence of the Scots, a young vigorous nation is emerging with an ultimate destination of a world power."[96]

The other common ideal that both Ukrainian nationalists and Scottish elites could appeal to was the Christian tradition. Speaking of postwar reconstruction as president of the UCC, Basil Kushnir, a native of Ukraine, theologist, and Ukrainian Catholic priest who later became archbishop major of the Ukrainian Catholic Church, contended that "the senseless cries about the supremacy of race and nation will die, too, and in their stead will appear appeals for Christian democracy voiced by people of good faith, respect, virtue and justice."[97] As a member of the Catholic world, he could also use Christianity to generalize his narrowly defined notion of democracy that focussed on the independence of Ukraine. The Scottish-dominant Presbyterian Church, to some extent, shared such a view. A message posted in the *Presbyterian Record* in 1943, for example, theorized a link among democracy, a united war effort, and the Christian faith: "For Christianity, exalting individual liberty, binds men together in common devotion to the great worthy goal of righteousness and unselfish service. In the unity of this willing obedience to the call of the Spirit of God there is national strength. Christian Democracy is strong. Therefore in our war effort throughout Canada and the Empire we must keep before us always this unity, through Christian living, as an absolute necessity."[98] In reality, such unity based on religious faith was a myth. Non-Christian people such as Japanese were excluded from the Canadian war effort even after their conversion. Racial and national origins remained top criteria in judging their fitness for the nation.

The war also made both Scots and Ukrainian nationalists highlight the hardships in their histories. The endurance of their peoples gained particular significance both because it proved their readiness for the challenges of the war and because it promoted ethnic consciousness based on memories of persecution. The landmark fights for their great causes in the past overlapped with the ideals of the contemporary war. Scots praised the Jacobite Uprising of 1745 in which Scottish Highland chieftains tried to make Charles Edward Stuart the legitimate successor to the British throne. For example, it was depicted as "the world's last outburst of chivalry," which showed clansmen's "loyalty," "devotion," and "idealism."[99] Scots believed that such Scottish qualities were both inherited and exercised by Canadians, enabling them to distinguish themselves in the war effort.[100] Among Ukrainian nationalists, Bohdan Khmelnytsky—who had "created on the basis of Ukrainian tradition a free and independent Cossack state"[101]—represented their ability to fight for sovereignty. "The history of the Ukrainian Cossacks," *Ukrainskyi holos* wrote, "is a history of the several-hundred-year pursuit of the Ukrainian people for liberty and a history of their struggle for liberty."[102] Their long struggle in the past proved that they could overcome the "extreme tragedy of slavery and death" inflicted by the Soviet regime.[103] For each group, the failure of independence or uprising was compensated for by spiritual strength and revival. Burns and Shevchenko, once again, functioned as icons of the national spirit that had survived. Scottish culture, once "in danger of extinction" after the failure of the 1745 uprising, was rescued by Burns, "with his true Scottish patriotism," while Ukraine's "greatest" disaster in national survival in 1917 was saved by Shevchenko, who promoted the "national and political consciousness of the Ukrainian people."[104]

World War II imposed a test of loyalty on Ukrainian and Japanese elites. While both groups had to face the same dilemma of balancing between Canada and their respective homelands, the war created clear gaps between the two groups that made for a stronger sense of ethnic community among Ukrainians. First, Ukrainian nationalists, to a greater or lesser degree, were incorporated into Canada's war effort and thus consolidated their position in defining the ethnic group, as opposed to the enemy alien status imposed on Japanese, which dismantled their organized activities and way of life. Second, Ukrainian nationalists could renew their ethnic consciousness around their long-term goal of Ukrainian independence as Axis expansion in Europe and the ideals of the Allies gave some hope for their cause. Japanese, on the contrary, could no longer support Imperial Japan after the outbreak of the Pacific War. Third, while Ukrainian nationalists maintained homeland myths and symbols, Japanese had to abandon them at least in public. In this regard, Scots, as participants in the war who helped to shape wartime policies and public opinion, belonged to a different category. They certainly kept their pride as chosen people, yet their ethnicity was defined always by choice and was thus fluid. However, though the war reinforced the existing ethnic hierarchy in Canada, democracy bridged the gap. All three groups made an effort to define a new identity for Canada based on the democratic principles for which the Allies and Canada fought during the war.

CHAPTER 4

Democratic and Multicultural Citizenship

The postwar period was a turning point in the evolution of Canadian and ethnic identities. Major changes in the attitudes of mainstream Canadian political leaders toward ethnic groups occurred in conjunction with international events such as the end of World War II (1945), signing of the Universal Declaration of Human Rights (1948), and start of the Cold War (1946), as well as domestic developments such as the Canadian Citizenship Act (1947) and removal of various discriminatory laws at national and provincial levels. Within this context, Canada tried to redefine its identity around the notions of democracy and freedom, particularly as part of the world reaction to the terrible consequences of racism in Nazi Germany and the growing power of Soviet-led communism. Ethnic leaders were actively involved in the consolidation of Canadian democracy and citizenship during this period, both in their pride for having contributed to Canada's victory and in their expectations for growing signs of tolerance in postwar Canada. For the first time, Ukrainians and Japanese were officially recognized as Canadians, and mainstream and ethnic visions of Canada overlapped in the name of democracy. As historians such as Patricia Roy and Stephanie Bangarth have shown, racial minorities became a more integral part of Canadian citizenship as mainstream Canadians began to support their right.[1]

In this chapter, I analyze how Canadian identity was reconstructed around the new postwar political discourses of human rights, democracy, and freedom in the first decade after 1945, focussing on the roles that Ukrainian and Japanese elites played. As Franca Iacovetta has shown, Canada, as part of the Western world, pushed democratic principles, educating and Canadianizing postwar immigrants.[2] In this process, prewar ethnic elites were driving forces in the creation and expansion of pan-Canadian identity, bridging the gap between mainstream and ethnic visions of Canadian democracy. They adroitly adopted evolving mainstream principles of human rights, democracy, and freedom in their efforts to pressure the federal government to act on behalf of their specific political goals. For Ukrainian nationalists, the goal was reclaiming Ukrainian territory from Soviet communist control in the homeland and protection of Ukrainian cultural and linguistic rights in Canada. For Ukrainian communists, the goal was the establishment of world peace alongside the protection of proletarian rights and the promotion of ethnic equality.[3] Both *issei* and *nisei* Japanese sought compensation for wartime property losses and, especially important to *nisei,* basic citizenship rights.

Yet a closer look at the interplay between mainstream and ethnic visions of Canada reveals that, despite changes in mainstream attitudes toward and policies for ethnic groups, conflict persisted. The tension between Canadian and ethnic leaders, however, shifted slightly in nature. Before the war, it was based largely on ethnoracial discrimination. In the postwar era, it had more to do with different priorities. High-level government leaders and policy makers still possessed a limited vision of democracy, designed to protect Canada's interests and international reputation, and thus took a cautious approach to ethnic issues considered beyond Canada's duties or contrary to its policies.

Ethnic leaders were not always consistent in their activities. The 1950s witnessed a general decline in ethnic activism, though differences could be seen among the above three groups in terms of how they maintained a sense of ethnic community. Nationalist Ukrainians, who had a continuing cause in the liberation of their homeland from foreign and communist rule, remained the most active, while Japanese and communist Ukrainians began losing momentum for organized activity. Nationalist Ukrainians were thus the best equipped to push their interpretation of ethnic pluralism and claim group rights, regarding ethnicity as a crucial category with which to identify themselves. Throughout these years, both Ukrainians and Japanese still possessed political agendas that were incompatible with the accepted vision of Canada.

Toward a New Canada: Canadian Democracy and Citizenship

After World War II, democracy and freedom became main principles in Canada for both mainstream and ethnic elites. For mainstream leaders, democracy and Canada's new status as an autonomous nation had to be promoted side by side so that the country would not lose a self-image that appealed to both Canadians and people abroad. Internationally, democracy was the means by which Canada would express its opposition to communism and confirm its role in the construction of a peaceful postwar order and in the new United Nations. Domestically, democracy was to provide a sense of pride and unity among the people of Canada, erasing the ethnic tensions that had characterized much of the war on the home front. Within this context, Ukrainian and Japanese elites welcomed Canada's growing power in the world and celebrated the introduction of citizenship. The first development provided great grounds for maintaining their loyalty to their respective homelands as world citizens, while the second marked a step forward to their full recognition as Canadians, which they thought they certainly deserved after their participation in Canada's war effort. At the same time, in redefining Canadian identity and redrawing the boundary of the national community, ideological conflicts within the Ukrainian and Japanese groups over the meaning and desirability of Canadian citizenship resumed.

From an international perspective, democratic discourse gained momentum in Canada after the war for two purposes: to promote people's pride as citizens of a peaceful and free nation in the non-communist West, and to demonstrate that Canada was a full-fledged world power.[4] As the comments of Secretary of State Paul Martin near the end of 1954 illustrate, mainstream Canadian leaders were primarily interested in Canada's new role as peacekeeper and its attendant international responsibilities:

> The nations which, between the wars, had pinned their hopes on the League of Nations had done so without being willing to use collective force to deter aggression. This led to the Second World War from which we learned that peace was the responsibility of all and that strength was needed to deter and, if need be, to resist aggression. Canada's growing strength, which had been shown during the war in the effort of the fighting services and in our increased productive capacity, was also reflected in the development and strengthening of the external affairs service, both at home and abroad. Thus, at the end of hostilities, Canada stood prepared to participate in the challenging task of international co-operation.[5]

The Canadian Citizenship Council (renamed from the Canadian Council of Education for Citizenship), established in 1940 as a non-profit federation of more than fifteen national and provincial educational groups with a particular focus on citizenship,[6] also provides a great example of how postwar Canada perceived its role in the world. To promote awareness, the council published several pamphlets, including *The Democratic Way* (which appeared as a series), *Canada as a Democracy,* and *Freedom of Association,* as well as its periodical, *Canadian Items.* In outlining what Canada could do in the world, an article in the last publication argued that "the responsibilities of Canadian Citizenship do not stop at our boundaries. As a people who are a participating member of the United Nations Organizations, we have obligations as United Nations Citizens."[7] This role, strongly tied to citizenship and Canada's new status as a full-fledged nation, was obviously a response in part to the spreading communist ideology and its menace to Canada. The council made it clear elsewhere that Canada would never be willing to tolerate anyone communist, referring to "a man, misguided or otherwise, who scorns the 'untidiness of democracy' and subscribes to and works for a totalitarian regime, often giving first and devoted allegiance to a foreign power."[8]

Ukrainian and Japanese elites, whatever their ideological stance, welcomed Canada's new muscle as an independent power and anticipated the major role that the country could play in the reconstruction of world peace. Underlying this attitude was the expectation of better relations between Canada and their homelands; for Japanese, and Ukrainian communists especially, Canada's peaceful ties with Japan and the Soviet Union, respectively, had to be maintained. Japanese, because of the persecution that they had experienced during the war, stressed the necessity of their active work for the cause of internationalism. Canadian *nisei,* wrote the *New Canadian* in 1950, "are gradually becoming aware of the great need to promote, and one day achieve, a kind of citizenship which knows no national boundaries. In their JCCA organization, they are finding the opportunity to contribute in some measure by their active interest in the promotion of the important principles contained in the United Nations Charter and the United Nations Universal Declaration of Human Rights. For peace in the world must come through learning to live at peace with each other in the neighbourhoods of the world."[9]

Similar support for world peace was expressed by communist Ukrainians, who reorganized as the Association of United Ukrainian Canadians (AUUC) in 1945, as they faced a new challenge created by ideological polarization in the world. They celebrated the end of the war, declaring that, "together with all good Canadians, we rejoice that the dread nightmare of atomic war is receding from the world."[10] They also encouraged both Canada and the AUUC to take a leading role in the construction of a better place to live in light of the "new hopes arising for the possibility of completely eliminating the danger of war and for peaceful co-existence and fraternity among the nations in the world."[11] Obviously, communist Ukrainians tried to minimize the political gap between Canada and the Soviet Union.

Nationalist Ukrainians valued Canada's increasing profile and responsibility in world affairs for a slightly different reason: namely, the common enemy that they shared with other non-communist Canadians. In essence, they expected Western countries to unite in putting pressure on the Soviet Union and ultimately bringing about its downfall. Addressing the fifth national congress of the Ukrainian Canadian Committee (UCC) in 1956, former Alberta MP John Decore explained the Canadian role: "After the war, two worlds were created. The other world caused so much menace to the Western world that Canada had spent half its budget on security to watch the Soviet Union very closely. In such situations, one nation cannot pursue an independent cause. Although Canada does not belong to the great powers in terms of population, it can play a distinguished role in international politics."[12] Canada's new role in such politics thus was greeted with high expectations from Ukrainian and Japanese ethnic groups.

With the position that Canada should take in the world confirmed, both mainstream and ethnic leaders turned to the creation of a strong basis for citizenship and democracy domestically.[13] Mainstream leaders emphasized Canadians' democratic roots and a sense of mission, associating democracy and freedom with their vision of a new Canada, yet they simultaneously reinforced the legal and political traditions that were the legacy of old Canada. For example, though it certainly did not exhibit any of the prewar discrimination and hostility aimed at ethnic groups, the Canadian Citizenship Council valued the British parliamentary and legal systems and underlying philosophy that Canada had inherited. Democracy and freedom were also often identified with Britain and its history. In 1949, *Citizenship Items* noted how the British Bill of Rights passed in 1689 ensured "many of the basic freedoms" that contemporary society accepted.[14] The first pamphlet in the series, *The Democratic Way*, emphasized the fairness of the British legal tradition compared with justice in a "totalitarian system," stating that "British democracy over many hundreds of years has worked out a system by which no man may be arrested without evidence and without knowing the charge brought against him."[15] Focussing on freedom of conscience, the third pamphlet in the series maintained that "modern democratic Britain, like nineteenth-century Britain which was in [the] process of becoming democratic, is a community where free associations flourish."[16] Britain also symbolized freedom of faith, as reflected in "the Church of Scotland Act passed by the British Parliament in 1921. This act recognizes the church's right to alter its confession of faith and to unite with another church without losing its identity, and at the same time guards against any inference from the act prejudicial to any other church in Scotland."[17] That the roots of democracy and freedom were always associated with Britain reconfirmed the deeply felt belief that the British political system had nurtured and promoted fundamental values that had made Canada a better place in the past and would do so in the future.

Yet mainstream leaders also believed that Canadians, as a nation, should move on from Britain. With implementation of the Citizenship Act of 1947, people in Canada were no longer British subjects, placing new emphasis on cultivating their pride as a distinctive and strong people, which inevitably focussed on the promotion of a sense of togetherness beyond the ethnic group. Attitudes toward ethnic minorities were thus dramatically transformed from the interwar period. Moreover, not only did the war make racism taboo, but the Cold War also led to the unprecedented recognition of some ethnic groups. Anticommunist Ukrainian nationalists, in particular, were increasingly portrayed as representatives of a loyal ethnic group that participated in Canada's growth as a nation and had contributed to its war effort. At the fourth congress of the UCC in 1953, for example, Prime Minister Louis St. Laurent acknowledged the Ukrainian war effort, stating that the commitment that the UCC had made "towards winning the war ... is a splendid example of the steady growth in unity that is being achieved throughout our nation."[18] The issue of unity seemed imperative as Canada received new postwar immigrants. Presenting the citizenship bill to the House of Commons in 1945, Paul Martin stressed its necessity as a means to national unity:

> Our "new Canadians" bring to this country much that is rich and good, and in Canada they find a new way of life and new hope for the future. They should all be made to feel that they, like the rest of us, are Canadians, citizens of a great country, guardians of proud traditions and trustees of all that is best in life for generations of Canadians yet to be. For the national unity of Canada and for the future and greatness of this country it is felt to be of the utmost importance that all of us, new Canadians or old, have a consciousness of a common purpose and common interests as Canadians: that all of us be able to say with pride and say with meaning: "I am a Canadian citizen."[19]

Established mainly for the education of new citizens, the Canadian Citizenship Council provides a clear example of the goals to "stimulate in the minds of all Canadians a greater appreciation of the meaning and implications of democracy as a way of life" and "to strengthen and revitalize throughout Canada the ideals of democratic citizenship."[20] From the council's perspective, the Citizenship Act of 1947 symbolized the rise of a new Canadianism and an effort to mobilize both new and old citizens, together with postwar immigrants, to become one nation.[21] As a result, it was "increasingly important to awaken in Canadians, and prospective Canadians, a pride in the development, institutions and life in our country, an understanding of the nature, privileges and obligations of citizenship, an appreciation of the positive and dynamic implications and possibilities of democracy, and the threat of other ideologies to our free, democratic way of life."[22]

Yet this comment failed to suggest that the council had a concrete vision of what Canada should be and on what model its peoples should be educated. This ambiguity with respect to Canadian identity often surfaced when the council attempted to justify and seek a niche for itself in practical terms. Executive Director J.P. Kidd, in response to the general concern raised in a council executive meeting about the council's lack of vision and ineffectiveness in guiding Canadians, tried to avoid dealing with the fundamental issue of Canadian identity and focussed on the roles and directions that the council should take: "I feel that we should give a great deal more attention to the structure of the Council, not only from the standpoint of a constitution, but also in order to make it a live and useful organism. We need to work out, improve working relationships and affiliations with other organizations; we need to find ways of getting more effective national representation; and we need to develop a number of technical and working sub-committees to deal with various aspects of the Council's work."[23] The roles and responsibilities of Canadian citizens also remained undefined. For example, the council contended that it should "mould Canadian public sentiment and opinion in such a way as to increase the consciousness on the part of every Canadian of being Canadian,"[24] without providing any concrete idea of what that meant or entailed. Undoubtedly, integration was its key concept, though statements such as "the integration of the various organized ethnic groups into the group-life of our Canadian communities" never clarified to what extent postwar integration differed from prewar assimilation.[25]

Yet such new interests in a more inclusive democratic Canada were by no means imposed by Anglo-Canadians. Ukrainian and Japanese elites played active roles in the consolidation of the pan-Canadian identity as a democratic and free nation. Focussing on both Chinese and Japanese, Patricia Roy argues that "the plight of Japanese Canadians was a major stimulus to the development of a human rights movement in Canada."[26] The introduction of citizenship was widely celebrated since they saw it as recognition of their people as full-fledged citizens who possessed rights and duties equal to those of other Canadians, a status earned through their long-term contribution to Canada's nation building and recent performance in its war effort. Paul Yuzyk, a former president of the Ukrainian National Youth Federation and in the early 1950s a professor at the University of Manitoba, explained how special Canadian citizenship was to Ukrainian Canadians in a report to the Ukrainian section of the international service of the CBC. "Each year," he said, "May 15 is designated as Citizenship Day to bring to the minds of Canadian citizens and those to be admitted to citizenship the importance of their inheritance of freedom and democratic rights as well as responsibilities." Those Canadians and prospective Canadians included "a considerable number of Ukrainians, who had escaped from under the Soviet tyranny and who now were happy to live in a country of freedom."[27] Ukrainians in Canada, Yuzyk stressed in another CBC report, thus had extra motivation to assume the rights and responsibilities that they enjoyed as citizens under the Canadian democratic system, particularly by participating in federal and provincial elections.[28] Although regarding Canadian citizenship as key to seeking support for Ukrainian causes, the Ukrainian Self-Reliance League (USRL) encouraged its members to fulfill their duties as Canadian citizens first: "It can be argued that the access of the USRL and its members and associates to Canadian and Ukrainian affairs in Canada and in Europe always lies in and builds on the basis of Canadian citizenship. The USRL argues that it is the only real approach which Canadians of Ukrainian origin have to every matter of our life. Maintaining such a stance, Ukrainians would not end up in an unfavourable result, going beyond Canada's sphere [of interests]. Any sensible person who comes to Canada must consider becoming a host and citizen here."[29] While Ukrainian nationalists had always embraced and defended the idea of their dual loyalty to Ukraine and Canada, the establishment of Canadian citizenship, and the rhetoric surrounding it, facilitated and legitimized a renewed sense of duty to both countries.

A similar hope for what Canadian citizenship could do for ethnic equality and rights can also be seen in the case of Japanese. For a community and individuals who had long been marginalized, becoming Canadian citizens was of utmost significance. The *New Canadian,* for example, expressed *nisei*'s sense of appreciation, regarding the achievement as something for which they had worked diligently: "Those of us who were born in Canada or have been granted naturalization papers are now qualified to call ourselves Canadian citizens; we are also British subjects.... The experience of the war years ha[s] taught us much about citizenship rights and fundamental liberties, because these things were endangered and at times denied especially where Japanese Canadians were concerned. But those of us who did not lose faith in Canada—in our belief that the Canadian way of life is fundamentally sound—are finding our faith vindicated."[30] For Japanese, the Citizenship Act symbolized the end of an era since it was followed by the long-awaited federal franchise in June 1948, the provincial franchise in British Columbia in March 1949, and the end of the ban on Japanese migration back to the West

Coast in April 1949. The *New Canadian* called 1949 "the best year," stating that "no other period from the latter part of the last century when Japanese immigrants first entered Canada is prominent with as much progress in the attainment of equal opportunities and full citizenship as 1949."[31]

In redefining Canada's national boundaries around democracy, freedom, and citizenship, ethnic elites were once again divided internally—between nationalists and communists among Ukrainians and, to a lesser degree, between *issei* and *nisei* among Japanese. Each faction sought status and recognition as the representative of its ethnic group and greater influence in Canadian politics, whether for sidelined Ukrainian communists in the Cold War or for Ukrainian nationalists and Japanese after the doubts concerning their loyalty that they faced during World War II. Lingering internal cleavages and competition among rival elites, in fact, were crucial factors in how Ukrainians and Japanese defined Canadian democracy as they debated who were the better Canadians and labelled their opponents antidemocratic.

Not surprisingly, the rivalry among Ukrainians crystallized around the conflicting ideologies of communism and nationalism. Each camp maintained that it was the real defender of democracy and thus that its sympathizers would make more loyal Canadians. Representing the nationalist perspective, *Ukrainskyi holos* made a link among the Ukrainian national character, the Ukrainian thirst for independence, and democracy: "The Ukrainian people are well known for their democratic way of thinking. Ukrainian democracy is not a fake. It is a particular democracy—the democracy of a freedom-loving nation. When Ukrainians fight for independence, they fight for freedom 'for all and for themselves' ... and do not deliberately seize foreign countries.... Ukrainian democracy—this is an idea of a great nation. The Ukrainian democratic idea can stand for the salvation of the entire world."[32] Communism was the negation of these values and resulting Ukrainian mission as well as harmful to Canadian democracy. The USRL confirmed its stance against communism at its national congress in 1946: "This congress condemns the activities of the Communist Party of Canada, activities hostile to the interests of this country and its democratic institutions. It especially struggles against the activities of this party among our people as harmful and hostile to our cultural interests in Canada and calls for our citizens to stay away from involvement in them by all means."[33]

Ukrainian communists also cited the need to preserve democracy, but on their own terms, which rejected narrow and/or excessive nationalism in favour of the communist vision of equality among people. Referring in particular to the often intensely anticommunist Ukrainian refugees who had entered Canada after the war, the AUUC argued "that this type of 'selective immigration' is contrary to Canada's democratic traditions and in so far as it serves as a mask to cover the bringing over to Canada of the pro-Nazi remnants in Europe it is subversive and fraught with dangers to Canadian democracy and security."[34] Ukrainian communists held that they, together with all like-minded Slavs, were the best citizens of Canada, who also kept pride in their homelands and imported from them "strong traditions of democracy" and "a militant defense of their rights and mutual aid."[35] The Cold War, which intensified competition among nationalist and communist Ukrainians in Canada, helped to define membership in the Canadian nation.

Competition between *issei* and *nisei* Japanese was less intense, even though *nisei* tried to distinguish themselves from the undemocratic or imperial image often attached to the past society of *issei.* The *nisei* organ, the *New Canadian,* developed a new way of interpreting prewar and wartime anti-Japanese sentiment, attributing it to the lack of democracy within Japanese ranks rather than to racial or economic factors. In short, "the Japanese Canadians were treated as dangerous people and had to face 'internment, control, and confiscation of property'" because of *issei*'s unwillingness to adopt "Canadian democracy."[36] The adoption of democracy was therefore urgent "for the further development of the Japanese race in Canada."[37] In promoting these arguments, *nisei* were speaking in particular about their own community, specifically the power that *issei* had been exercising over *nisei* and the lack of openness of the Japanese community toward the outside society. In this way, democracy became a symbol of *nisei,* who gained power in the Japanese-Canadian community that formed after the war.

Tying Ethnic Causes to Canadian Democracy and Citizenship

Although democracy defined pan-Canadian identity, mainstream and ethnic elites differed considerably over what Canadian democratic principles and citizenship rights should include. On the one hand, mainstream Canadianism rarely embraced the specific interests of either Ukrainian or Japanese elites. Their agendas were taken into consideration only when directly related to or affecting Canada's image as an international power, its economic interests, or its national unity. Ukrainian and Japanese leaders, on the other hand, strove to add their peculiar interests and perspectives to the definition of Canadian democracy and citizens' rights. Defining the principle in their own terms left, in turn, a positive imprint on Canada's identity.

Well aware of the rhetoric that mainstream Canadians were using, Ukrainians and Japanese strove to bridge the disparity, thus revealing the extent to which ethnic agendas helped to shape Canadian democratic identity.

There was, of course, the continuation of long-term missions such as the liberation of Ukraine for Ukrainian nationalists and gaining the franchise for Japanese. Yet the end of the war also produced new agendas, which imposed their own unity of purpose. For Ukrainian nationalists, Canada's acceptance of Ukrainian refugees from Nazi camps all over Europe was imperative, an initiative opposed by their rival communists, who focussed on the peace movement instead. Both *issei* and *nisei* Japanese shared common goals and expected the most dramatic changes, concentrating on compensation for wartime property losses, removal of restrictive laws, and cancellation of the deportation of those who had been forced to agree on repatriation to Japan at the end of the war. The propaganda that Ukrainians and Japanese launched to appeal to the public affected both the formation of a new Canadian identity and the renewal of their particular ethnic consciousness. That not only Ukrainian nationalists and communists but also *issei* and *nisei* Japanese adopted the same strategy, language, and logic in these negotiations indicates how all elites searched for and quickly selected the most useful political discourses to mobilize their peoples behind their ethnic causes and to challenge mainstream politics.

The years immediately after the war can be characterized as the most active period for both Ukrainian and Japanese leaders, for the end of the war left them with high expectations. For *issei* and *nisei* Japanese, it was the right time to be compensated for discriminatory wartime policies. A volunteer *nisei* organization, the Japanese Canadian Committee for Democracy (JCCD), and a joint mainstream-Japanese association, the Co-operative Committee on Japanese Canadians (CCJC), established in Toronto in 1943, undertook nation-wide research on Japanese wartime losses and the resettlement orders issued by the federal government. The immediate issue for them was to stop the deportations. Following the repatriation survey administered by T.B. Pickersgill, commissioner of Japanese placement, which had asked Japanese whether they preferred to live east of the Rockies or return to Japan, 43 percent, voluntarily or not, agreed to repatriation by August 1945.[38] In 1947, the JCCD evolved into a nation-wide *nisei* association, the National Japanese Canadian Citizens Association (NJCCA), and worked in close cooperation with the CCJC. Besides these large-scale associations, some Japanese evacuees, often frustrated with their representatives, organized into local groups such as the Toronto Claimants Committee, which took a more militant approach toward the federal government.[39] The postwar era was also significant for Ukrainian nationalists since it appeared to be the last chance for redrawing Ukrainian boundaries in Europe and securing an independent Ukrainian state. Moreover, the issue of Ukrainian refugees in camps in Germany and Austria, who refused to go back to their Soviet-controlled homeland, became the UCC's primary focus, both for the refugees' own salvation and to strengthen the existing Ukrainian community in Canada both physically and psychologically. The end of the war thus galvanized ethnic leaders into political action, thereby promoting a sense of unity and purpose among their peoples.

In pursuing their goals, ethnic elites adopted various strategies. Both Ukrainian nationalist and Japanese leaders challenged Canadian politicians, pointing out contradictions between Canada's stated democratic principles and its actual policies. Their lobby was directed not only at promoting public awareness of such contradictions but also at expanding the definition of democracy and citizenship rights. Both elites thought that citizenship should guarantee all citizens' demands, insofar as they did not harm Canada's interests. In their minds, the geographical and political boundaries of Canada did not necessarily determine the boundaries or priorities of citizens.

For Ukrainian nationalists, the fact that World War II, repeatedly referred to as a war for democracy, brought more power to the Soviet Union constituted a major contradiction and needed to be challenged. *Ukrainskyi holos,* for example, stressed that the fight was far from over: "Democracy did not win in the Second World War; rather, it lost. The end of the war left much less democracy in the world than before the war. And where democracy remains, it is threatened very much, just as it was before the war. In many countries in the world, it remains only an empty phrase and seems like a betrayal to democracy, or leans toward the politics of the greatest enemy of democracy, the Communist Party, which was a prototype of a totalitarian party, an antidemocratic organization."[40] Criticizing the lack of support from Western nations, including Canada, for the liberation of Ukraine, another article in the same newspaper reminded readers that "no country can claim a better reason than Canada or the United States that they entered the war for the liberation of oppressed nations." Therefore, it continued, "democratic countries can and must stress, based on moral principles, that they recognize the right of oppressed nations for autonomous life and that their sympathy is definitely on the side of those who desire freedom."[41] Speaking about the Ukrainian question, the Ukrainian Catholic priest and president of the UCC, Basil Kushnir, encouraged Ukrainians in Canada, as "freedom-loving" Canadians, to fight against "the menace of communism.... Our Canadian faith in democracy and people's rights cannot be indifferent. We must cultivate it with our personal and collective efforts for the benefit of us all."[42] The UCC always spearheaded the lobby for Ukraine's independence, submitting various memoranda to

Canadian authorities. Its report on Canada's foreign policy submitted to the federal government in 1956, for example, urged Canada's active involvement, as a democratic country, in world affairs.[43]

The opening of Canada's doors to Ukrainian refugees in Europe just after the war was also discussed in terms of democracy and humanitarianism.[44] "In the name of humanity," the UCC said in a brief presented to Mackenzie King, "we appeal to the Government of Canada to do whatever may be possible to prevent such deportations [of Ukrainian refugees] to the Soviet territories."[45] Anthony Hlynka also urged the Canadian government to act against the "forceful repatriation of displaced persons" from refugee camps to Soviet territory, citing Winston Churchill's speech in the British House of Commons on 16 August 1945: "Yes, democracy is on trial. No atheistic philosophy of force, torture and extermination shall ever restore the God-given democratic right to humanity unless the surviving democracies write a new chapter of history founded on Christian principles."[46] Hlynka, somewhat frustrated by the government's slow response to the Ukrainian refugee issue, repeatedly challenged immigration policies in Canada. For him, if Canada was to be democratic and humanitarian, the federal government should "give first consideration to stateless or displaced persons," both because they were "unfortunate" and because they were "democratic-minded people who had to move on into Western Europe when totalitarianism was advancing."[47] He further nuanced his high expectations for postwar Canada to distinguish itself in the area of humanitarianism, contending "that Canada was not the first nation to make that move" and offer refuge.[48] In his memoirs, Hlynka stressed the significance of his initiatives, including establishment of the Resettlement Fund to support displaced persons, thirteen speeches in the House of Commons on the Ukrainian refugee issue between 1945 and 1949, and visits to the refugee camps in Europe.[49] Similar frustration was also expressed by Japanese, who were protesting deportation from Canada. Now that the war was over, the federal government was urged to adopt a democratic solution. "The forcible deportation without clear justification," the *New Canadian* argued, "should not be allowed in a country professing to be a democracy, and for attempting such a plan, the government lays itself open to serious criticism."[50] The *New Canadian*'s tone was more determined than ever, seizing this great opportunity to pressure the federal government: "We must continue the fight [against deportation] because we believe in the justice of our cause, and because we firmly believe that there is in Canada a thing called democracy."[51] The government's treatment of Japanese in Canada was implicitly identified with methods used by the Nazi regime. For example, the CCJC claimed that "the war was fought to destroy the hateful doctrine of racialism which is the basis of the Nazi system everywhere." Therefore, it continued, "it is of vital importance to Canadian democracy at home and our reputation abroad that we deal justly with the Japanese-Canadians in our land."[52]

Japanese soon picked up one of Mackenzie King's statements in the House of Commons in 1944—"It is a fact that no person of Japanese race born in Canada has been charged with any act of sabotage or disloyalty during the years of war"[53]—and frequently repeated it as if it were official evidence of Japanese loyalty. Now that Japanese loyalty had been "officially" recognized, they claimed, lingering discrimination against them must be a sign of persistent racism. The *New Canadian* repeatedly quoted a phrase from the Nuremburg Trials: namely, that the "deportation of civilian populations on racial grounds" was "one of the crimes against humanity."[54] In a similar vein, a CCJC pamphlet cited the United Nations Charter, which vowed to "encourage and promote respect for human rights and for the fundamental freedoms for all without distinction as to race, sex, language, or religion."[55] When Muriel Kitagawa, a writer and activist, addressed the National Council of Women in 1948, she informed her audience that "23,000 Japanese Canadians [who] were displaced persons within our country" represented "an unfortunate page in Canadian history."[56] The CCJC also emphasized Canada's responsibility to Japanese: "On humanitarian grounds the exile [of Japanese] cannot be permitted if Canada is to be worthy of a place in the United Nations and if Canadian Citizenship is to have any meaning whatsoever."[57]

Clearly, such references and comparisons were carefully chosen, in effect asking Canada to honour the principles that it professed to uphold. The *New Canadian* also pointed out the implicit contradiction in the concept of Canadian citizenship, for it appeared to value the concerns of British Columbians and other Canadians who wanted to keep Japanese out of the province or elsewhere more than those of Japanese:

> When the government introduced the Canadian Citizenship bill last year, it also had up its sleeves orders-in-council which were contrary to the spirit of that bill and which would have denied normal citizenship privileges to one racial group of Canadians. This situation led to much heated discussion in the House of Commons. A similar situation seems to be building up in the current session. As indicated in the throne speech, the government intends to give special attention to the study of individual rights in Canada. Yet at the same time it proposes to continue its control over the move-

> ment of Japanese Canadians and to determine for them where they may and may not live.[58]

During the 1950s, frustrations were also expressed over Canada's immigration policy, which still restricted the entry of Japanese, including deported *nisei,* into Canada. Jack Pickersgill, Minister of Citizenship and Immigration from 1954 to 1957, whose brother had administered the repatriation survey, was regarded as a major voice in racially discriminatory immigration policies and became a focus of criticism among Japanese. The *New Canadian,* for example, criticized his comment that no racial restrictions would be removed from Canada's immigration policies.[59] *Tairiku jihô,* which replaced the prewar *Tairiku nippô* in 1951, pointed out that, even though "racial equality" was "commonsense in the world" and "declared in the well-known Atlantic Charter," Canada's immigration policy and Pickersgill's comments "tended to be retrogressive."[60] Canada as a democratic nation in the postwar free world, the Japanese elite believed, could not contradict or ignore its principles.

The second strategy that Ukrainian and Japanese elites adopted was to assign themselves specific missions that would not only see their own goals achieved but also help both Canada and the rest of the world to establish a more complete or genuine democracy. A fine example is the memorandum that the UCC sent to the Paris Peace Conference of 1946 (which guaranteed nations such as Italy, Romania, Hungary, Bulgaria, and Finland sovereignty) opposing the Soviet delegation from Ukraine as well as Soviet control over Ukrainian territory. The denunciation of Soviet power, the document stated, "contributes its utmost to the cause of freedom, democracy and peace in the world."[61] Given the growing threat of the Soviet Union and its military power, nationalist Ukrainians believed that their role was to constantly warn the West of the dangers. At the fifth congress of the UCC in 1956, for example, S.W. Sawchuk, its first vice-president (representing the USRL), noted that communists survived in Canada under the guise of "Ukrainian ethnonational activities and public manifestations of Ukrainian national culture" and "without publicizing the existence and menace of communism in the English-speaking world." He also noted that "communism is detrimental and threatening not only to us but also to the entire world."[62] For nationalist Ukrainians, it was essential to remind both their own people and other Canadians that Canada could benefit from assisting in the collapse of the Soviet Union. Canadians were thus encouraged to "be informed about the Ukrainian question not just for sentimental purposes."[63] In contrast, communist Ukrainians tried to bridge the ideological gap between Canada and the Soviet Union. For example, their support for Slavic unity and the flourishing of the Soviet Union was "in concert with the loftiest ideals of the democratic and peace-loving people in Canada," and they constituted "an additional force to the struggle for the peace, national independence and democratic progress of Canada."[64] Emphasizing the benefits of Canadian-Soviet friendship, communists criticized the overwhelming power of the United States over the world in the postwar era as "chauvinist savagery." They also praised Slavic solidarity or the Union of Soviet Socialist Republics (USSR), in contrast, for its "peace and respect for the independence and equality of all the nations on the earth."[65]

Japanese also equated their community agenda with the evolution of Canadian democracy. Immediately upon conclusion of the war, the CCJC stressed how the Japanese cause and actions would make a better Canada: "For over a period of three years the people of Japanese origin in Canada had been deprived of and removed from all the natural benefits belonging to trusted citizens of this country. As in the process of assimilation of any group, linguistic and cultural differences, lack of citizenship rights and the fact that they were of oriental origin, all contributed to a certain sense of insecurity and fear of the white population and of government action, even before evacuation took place.... In their struggle to defend their rights they have furthered the cause of democracy in our land."[66]

In this context, Japanese individual compensation claims and the establishment of a royal commission to investigate their property losses in July 1947[67] were regarded as a landmark "contribution to the principles of democracy, for it will reveal starkly that Canada is not free from the germs of racial intolerance, and that there is a constant need for vigilance against this evil."[68] The Japanese sense of accomplishment is well illustrated by the booklet *They Made Democracy Work: The Story of the Co-operative Committee on Japanese Canadians*, published by the CCJC and NJCCA. It attributed the success of some claimants for property compensation, though very limited, to the work of CCJC members, including non-Japanese Canadians, emphasizing bottom-up forces:

> Thus, after eight years, the issues which led to the forming of the Co-operative Committee on Japanese Canadians have been settled. The committee was not solely responsible for this settlement, but it did play a leading part. It was the instrument by which thousands of Canadians who wanted to see justice done were able to influence government policy.... The particular crisis that called the Co-operative Committee into being has now passed, but there will

> always be fronts on which our civil liberties are threatened. Perhaps this story of what one group was able to do will encourage other groups working on these other fronts. Here is one clear-cut example of how individual citizens, by banding together, managed to change the course of events in a very significant way. They made democracy work because they cared enough about it to make it work. What they did can be repeated.[69]

Clearly, for the Japanese, Canadian democracy was not defined solely by mainstream leaders but constantly reconstructed and redefined with crucial input from the specific Japanese experience. The royal commission and compensation were the first real recognition of the Japanese recently treated as enemy aliens and traditionally kept outside the mainstream community.

Mainstream leaders, however, did not necessarily take into account the demands or arguments and agendas of ethnic groups, imposing instead their own criteria to select what deserved attention. Not surprisingly, they were never concerned about anything that was not directly related to their definition of Canadian interests or that was beyond their control, choosing to focus on Canada's image in the world and foreign relations, particularly with the Soviet Union, and unity among Canadian citizens. In this sense, traditional mainstream/ethnic boundaries persisted. Yet some changes could be seen in the priorities of the mainstream elite in Canada's policy making. Factors such as race and ethnic representation in provincial legislatures and the House of Commons, which had shaped Canadian policies regarding ethnic affairs for a long time, became subordinated to other immediate Canadian concerns.

First, the presence of Ukrainians in the federal and some provincial governments, as well as their more general "participation" in the mainstream political structure, did not always determine whether or not Canada took the Ukrainian agenda into account. The Japanese demand for property compensation, for example, received more attention from mainstream Canadian leaders than did Ukrainian nationalists' call for Ukraine's independence, even though Japanese did not have their own representatives in any provincial legislature or Ottawa. Ukrainians, in contrast, had MPs such as Anthony Hlynka, who brought up the independence of Ukraine and the opening of Canada's doors to refugees in the House of Commons both during and after the war. Yet, despite his numerous speeches on refugees, the Canadian government saw the issue as something beyond national politics.[70] For Mackenzie King, peaceful relations between Canada and the Soviet Union were more important than the demands of Ukrainian activists or how they viewed his government.[71] Given the great military power of the Soviet Union, and the threat that it posed to all Canadians, Ukrainian criticism of government inaction mattered less. In addition, Ukrainian independence, which would have entailed the violent dismantling of the Soviet Empire, did not affect the Canadian masses, and for this reason, as well as Cold War concerns, the Canadian government made no effective intervention on behalf of Ukrainian sovereignty.[72]

Compensation for Japanese property, which had been sold to other Canadians at below market value during the war, in contrast, was treated as an issue that required action in response to the compensation movement that Japanese spearheaded. The government response gained momentum, as Ann Sunahara points out, partly because the "virtually friendless" Japanese of 1942–43 had "some determined friends" in 1945, particularly members of the Co-operative Commonwealth Federation (CCF), who, before the outbreak of war, had frequently expressed pro-Japanese sentiments.[73] Some sympathetic organizations in and outside British Columbia, which had obviously overcome wartime racism, also appeared in support of Japanese.[74] This support from the general voting public undoubtedly affected the attitudes of Canadian officials. Moreover, while such voices helped the Japanese cause, the fact that Japanese property losses occurred in Canada's jurisdiction as a result of Canadian policy distinguished the Japanese case from the Ukrainian case and prompted the federal government to act. Establishment of the 1947 royal commission reflected changing government priorities and attitudes toward Japanese. It also marked a shift in the nature of Japanese ethnicity from negative and marginalized to more positive and influential.

Second, race or national origin, a major factor in determining public opinion on ethnic groups before and during the war, could no longer be used as a legitimate reason for discriminatory policies. Of course, racism did not completely disappear from Canada's policy-making process; race remained a category of selection in Canada's immigration act until February 1962. Yet the growing tendency to place priority on Canadian citizenship rather than on colour can be seen in the federal government's attitudes toward the acceptance of Ukrainian refugees and the contemporary deportation of Japanese. While the Canadian government acted very slowly and somewhat reluctantly in both cases, it saw a clear difference between the two cases. Canada would be completely responsible for producing Japanese "refugees," including *nisei*, who deserved Canadian citizenship, while it would not be blamed for Ukrainian refugees. Mackenzie King's statement in 1944 that the "Japanese problem" should be treated not as a BC problem but as a national matter illustrated how central this issue became to Canada.[75] As Japanese associations and mainstream sympathizers enthusiastically championed Japanese rights to remain in Canada, deportation of Japanese attracted more official and public attention. The CCJC led the publicity campaign, publishing pamphlets such as *A Challenge to Patriotism and Statesmanship* and *From Citizens to Refugees—It's Happening Here!*[76] Despite attempts by anti-Japanese politicians such as Ian Mackenzie and Minister of Labour Humphrey Mitchell to prove the legality of the deportation orders in council, by the end of 1946 Ottawa had abandoned the enforcement of deportation mainly "on humanitarian grounds."[77]

Ukrainian displaced persons, initially moved to work in German agriculture or war industry and now living in refugee camps, had nothing to do with the Canadian government.[78] The desire to avoid a conflict of interest with the Soviet Union, which regarded the refugees as its "citizens" who should return to Soviet territory, and concern about the potential danger of an influx of Nazi collaborators, made the Canadian government "indifferent" to this issue.[79] Responding to Hlynka's request in the House of Commons to speak on the Ukrainian refugee issue, King stated somewhat obscurely that "the subject to which the hon. member has referred is one which relates to Europe. I am not in a position to say whether the representations made are wholly correct. I would suppose in that respect that my hon. friend is in the same position as I am. I can assure him however that the government has watched this whole Ukrainian situation most carefully and, so far as it is within our power to control matters, we have sought to see that the course taken would be such as would protect their interests."[80] Two years later King was more specific. "Canada is not obliged," he said, "as a result of membership in the United Nations or under the constitution of the international refugee organization, to accept any specific number of refugees or displaced persons," though he added that it would have "a moral obligation" to do so.[81] While Canada eventually took 34,000 Ukrainian refugees after 1947, the decision was based on the nation's labour requirements rather than on humanitarian or democratic ideals.[82]

That the federal government prioritized its reputation and the goal of a united nation over humanitarian concerns was well reflected by the royal commission on the Japanese property issue since its establishment was due more to pressure from both Japanese elites and mainstream human rights supporters than to government initiative. The commission, as such, served more as an official demonstration of dealing with the Japanese problem fairly. As a result, a fundamental barrier surfaced between Japanese and mainstream political circles regarding the commission's purpose. One gap in understanding appeared over the issue of limited eligibility for compensation and general procedures for assessing property losses. The commission set up regulations as narrowly as possible in terms of who qualified for compensation, limiting eligibility to cases in which the custodian of enemy and evacuee property did not take care of the property in a satisfactory manner and it was sold at below market value. In addition, these facts had to be legally proven for the owner to be compensated.[83] The CCJC, led by mainstream legal consultants Andrew Brewin and J.R. Cartwright, and the NJCCA agreed to the regulation in order not to jeopardize relations with the government and to secure any possible compensation.[84] But such an approach frustrated some claimants, who organized the independent Toronto Claimants' Committee, which rejected any settlement unless the properties were fairly assessed and compensated. Its declaration that it represented Japanese evacuees' voice and would continue to fight for full compensation well illustrated that the Japanese elite rarely saw the federal government's investigation as meeting their demands.[85]

The distance between mainstream and ethnic elites was also obvious in the activities of the Canadian Citizenship Council, which claimed to be "non-denominational" and "non-party."[86] It took either a very cautious approach or no decisive action with respect to ethnic issues. This hesitancy is explained by the fact that the persistence of mainstream/ethnic boundaries was not limited to the political level, which required detailed and official procedures to alter existing laws to accommodate ethnic groups. The council undoubtedly had an interest in Canada's acceptance of postwar refugees from Europe, but it showed more concern for the assimilation of immigrants to Canadian norms than for amending immigration policy. In 1955, it summarized its postwar priorities and activities as follows: "For the first time in thirty-five years, Canada was embarking on what approached mass immigration. Genuine sympathy for the Displaced Persons, a desire that they be helped to fit into life in Canada quickly, and some anxiety about the possibility of the communists getting to them first sparked an interest and concern on the part of organizations and individuals all across the country. Some national focus, some advice and assistance, and educational and other materials were needed, as was a further awakening of citizens to the coming of these new people."[87]

The fact that the council's interests were confined to Canada's boundaries is understandable. Yet, despite its lofty ideals "to provide the setting, the machinery and the opportunity" for ethnic and other organizations "to work together,"[88] its minutes suggest very limited cooperation on refugee issues with ethnic associations such as the UCC, though there are sporadic references to the education of Jews.[89] In a similar vein, the council rarely supported anything that served specifically Japanese causes. For example, when its executive committee was approached by the CJCC about the publication of a monograph on the Japanese compensation movement, members "felt that it was a controversial subject" that demanded "careful thought and careful perusal of the manuscript ... before a decision was reached."[90] In other words, ethnically specific concerns and activism did not figure in the council's immediate agenda or, perhaps more precisely, were treated with extreme caution.

Toward Multiculturalism

Ukrainian and Japanese elites regarded Canadian democracy and citizenship as a step toward ethnic pluralism. Yet the facts that the integration of Ukrainian nationalists into Canadian politics was well under way by the late 1950s and that they were long-term supporters of the survival of anything Ukrainian distinguished them from their rival communists and Japanese in terms of how they perceived Canada's multiethnic nature. In other words, Ukrainian nationalists had already reached the stage where they regarded democracy and citizenship as something that embraced and guaranteed their collective right to preserve their ethnic identity in Canada. Although communist Ukrainians also valued ethnic diversity as part of Canada's identity, they preferred to attach symbolic values to culture and language to attract more people to their ideological point of view and organization. For their part, Japanese paid more attention to group members' individual rights and integration into Canadian society without discrimination and without losing their ethnic identity. In this sense, then, nationalist Ukrainians were better equipped and programmed to launch a form of multiculturalism that would not only guarantee their individual rights to sustain who they were but also secure their ethnicity at an official level.

Consequently, nationalist Ukrainians concentrated on the preservation of language and culture as the foundation of a multicultural Canadian identity, always focussing on their own language and culture as the key to their own national survival. Nationalists thus urged Canadian federal and provincial governments to recognize them as a group equal to the British and French and propagandized among both Ukrainians and the Canadian public. For example, it was important to encourage their people, the younger generation in particular, to take pride in things Ukrainian. *Ukrainskyi holos* stressed that Ukrainians were no different from the French: "There is no need to be ashamed of your mother tongue. One's mother tongue should be used proudly by all those who honour their national group. The Ukrainian mother tongue is among all of us, a testimony to a nation's culture.... The French in Canada everywhere use their own language among their own people. Let us speak Ukrainian among ourselves: on the street, in the streetcar, in the theatre, on the train, in the restaurant."[91] According to the national convention of the USRL in 1946, Ukrainian language and culture also deserved special status in Canada: "Ukrainians as a cultural nation in a free autonomous country have full rights to look to the future with hope for the expansion of our unique culture, with hope that it will be reflected in the new Canadian culture."[92] The speaker then mentioned that "the philosophy of moral obligation is just under construction. Canada is building Canadian identity, made up of nations with diverse cultures, including, among others, the Ukrainian nation.... It depends only on the strength of one's national culture, whether it possesses something worth contributing. Canada is only different from other states in that it has more sovereignty of the people, more freedom, and more peoples for the diffusion of an ideal culture."[93]

Although the culturally diverse nature of Canada was not a new theme by the late 1940s, Ukrainian nationalists were promoting the idea as the essence of a unique Canadian identity tied to serving their goal of linguistic and cultural survival. State support of the Ukrainian language was also frequently discussed by the UCC and *Ukrainskyi holos,* including its reintroduction into state schools after some four decades as a sign of the importance of Ukrainians. When the Alberta government announced the introduction of teaching of the Ukrainian language at the high school level in 1959, *Ukrainskyi holos* called it "comforting news" for the Ukrainian "institutions and individuals which made every effort to ensure that the instruction of Ukrainian language was territorially broadened."[94] Michael Luchkovich, an educator and the first Ukrainian MP, applauded "a fine gesture towards the Ukrainians because of their heroic struggle for freedom, and being a nation that the world forgot."[95] Full recognition of the Ukrainian language, however, remained for the future. Meanwhile, following the Alberta triumph, *Ukrainskyi holos* called for the expansion of Ukrainian linguistic rights in Manitoba schools:

> The resolutions about instruction in languages other than English, Ukrainian in particular, do not meet the expectations of the Ukrainian community. The [Manitoba Royal] Commission recommends the introduction of French or German in the first grade in the schools provided that there are qualified teachers for them. The report further states: when there are qualified teachers, it is possible to teach another language, including Ukrainian, but this has to be in addition to French or German.... Such a solution to this question relegates Ukrainian language to secondary place, and no one could

> agree with this. Ukrainian citizens in Manitoba now must endeavour to ensure that in Manitoba regions populated by considerable numbers of Ukrainians, the Ukrainian language has the same status as French and German.[96]

Obviously, for Ukrainian nationalists, linguistic and cultural equality was an integral part of democracy and multiculturalism. They were the first group of people after the French to claim their collective rights in Canada.

Communist Ukrainians also championed ethnic pluralism by this time but for more practical reasons than did their nationalist rivals. They were guided by the principle of national communism, which adopted a nation's traditional way of life, culture, and language, to facilitate the expansion of communism among the grassroots in the Soviet territories.[97] They thus stressed the significance of Ukrainian culture and language among the younger generation. Juxtaposing Canada's multiculturalism against the American melting pot, seen as a symbol of chauvinism, the *Ukrainian Canadian* criticized American imperialism and the menace that it posed to Canada: "Canadian culture, under attack by United States imperialist cosmopolitanism and obscurantism, which seeks to deny and destroy it, feels the onslaught in this field as well, in the so-called 'melting-pot' steamroller policy—the other side of the coin of racism and discrimination—which is applied in the U.S. and prescribed by Wall Street for Canada too."[98]

Such comments were intended to warn Ukrainian Canadians that their traditional culture would eventually be absorbed into the dominant North American culture, defined by an expansionist United States. For postwar communist Ukrainians, Canadian multiculturalism represented "mutual aid" and "peace" among different peoples, which communist discipline, they believed, offered to the masses. They also attached their proletarian message to multiculturalism, arguing that it secured for every ethnic group the right to maintain its traditional culture, which the working class could enjoy,[99] as opposed to the materialism that defined "American bourgeois culture."[100] Within this context, communist Ukrainians advertised the greatness of the Soviet Union, which, according to them, had been practising the system that "guaranteed full equality and free, independent development of all nations and nationalities" ever since it had ended "the tsarist policy of force and oppression."[101] Multiculturalism, tied to communist ideals, was particularly significant to communist Ukrainians in Canada, who felt their influence threatened in the West and thus wanted a vehicle besides the conventional appeal to proletarian rights and world peace to attract more followers.

The postwar Japanese elite, preoccupied with restitution for wartime discrimination, understood ethnic pluralism more as something that would secure individual rights for Japanese as Canadian citizens.[102] As during the interwar period, they focussed more on integration than on preservation of collective distinctiveness, evidence that they still saw their group boundaries as both stigma and obstacle. They were also well aware that the purpose of the federal government's policy to disperse the Japanese population throughout Canada was to facilitate its assimilation. Thus, while Japanese community leaders envisioned Canada as a multiethnic nation, they believed that the contributions of diverse peoples came from the individual's commitment and effort to be Canadian. The *New Canadian* expressed this sentiment well: "Canada is the Frenchman, the Englishman, the Irish, the Chinese, the Finnish, the Jew, the German, the Ukrainian, and the Japanese. It is the Roman Catholic, the Presbyterian, the Methodist, the Baptist, the Four Square, the Confucianism [sic], the Buddhist.... True, Niseis [sic] differ in many aspects from other groups: the difference can also be their contribution to the Canadian life. In the final analysis, a true Canadian is one who firmly believes in democratic ideals, recognizes the rights, accepts the obligations and discharges the duties of Canadian Citizenship."[103]

That this statement treated Japanese more as individuals implies that Japanese group boundaries were an externally imposed impediment that one day would have to be overcome. A 1947 article made the connection explicit: "Now they [the Japanese masses] are ready to take further positive strides towards reaching the true maturity of citizenship that comes when they can see themselves, not as a group apart, but simply as Canadians sharing the rights and duties and a common destiny with twelve and a half million fellow Canadians."[104] The fact that Japanese Canadians had always been situated outside Canadian society because of their racial background forced them to act more individually than collectively, always prioritizing their duties and interests as Canadians.

Searching for a Cause

After accelerated activity in the last half of the 1940s in pursuit of postwar settlements peculiar to each ethnic group, Ukrainians and Japanese, to a greater or lesser degree, lost some momentum during the 1950s. This shift reflected both the growing number of Canadian-born generations and the setback experienced in the great expectations held at the end of the war. Ukrainian nationalists, who had maintained the same political goals since the interwar period, kept their sense of community alive and relatively active. The influx of new nationalist immigrants also regenerated the national consciousness of the existing Ukrainian-Canadian community. Even so, with the admission of Ukrainian refugees to Canada and the consolidation of Soviet power across Ukraine, making independence appear remote, their activities calmed down for a while. Yet their communist rivals and Japanese elites tended to lose more influence as ethnic community leaders.

The start of the Cold War made Canadians more sceptical than ever of the Soviet Union, while the postwar economic boom rendered the communist movement less popular in Canada. Both factors brought a rapid decline in AUUC membership,[105] causing Ukrainian communists to rethink their agendas, focussing on mass campaigns for world peace and a ban on the atomic bomb.

As for Japanese, the fall of Imperial Japan, their long-term source of ethnic pride and Japan's negative postwar reputation, led to growing indifference toward the homeland. Domestically, since they had been officially marginalized for a long time, the creation of citizenship and acquisition of the federal franchise provided a great sense of satisfaction. These developments, plus the gradual removal of other restrictions, the provincial enfranchisement in British Columbia in 1949, and an initial settlement over compensation, made Japanese less inclined toward organized activities. In 1953, the CCJC, which had worked for removal of the wartime discriminatory measures against Japanese, was officially disbanded. The NJCCA, whose budget depended on membership, faced financial problems. At the same time, the weakening of a sense of ethnic community beyond the local sphere and the necessity to maintain organized ethnic activities at the national level especially were often discussed. For example, despite the contention that the NJCCA was "necessary to safeguard Japanese Canadian interests,"[106] its lack of an agenda and the decentralization of power around local groups were obvious. In the late 1950s, the NJCCA frequently looked at its past achievements, such as the acquisition of compensation and citizenship, while expressing a certain pessimism for the future: "[N]JCCA has meant many things to many people. It has been a symbol of our ideals; it has been a means through which we were able to maintain our self-respect; it has taught us the ethics and machinery of organization; it has been our tool to handle with the best of our skill; it has been our unifying force for good intent; it has been a taskmaster and our teacher. Yet it is now reaching the point where it may easily become a thing of historical moment."[107]

Such comments suggest how important were common goals and agendas to the maintenance of ethnic groups, especially as organized and focussed communities. In this sense, Ukrainian nationalists were rare in that they possessed a long-term agenda because of their statelessness and as such maintained their ethnic boundaries collectively more than did some other groups.

The post-World War II period can be characterized by the rise of pan-Canadian identity around democracy and citizenship. Both mainstream and ethnic elites anticipated and supported the great impact that Canada, as a democratic country, could have on the world. Domestically, the Citizenship Act in particular promoted people's sense of belonging to Canada. Mainstream Canadians saw the construction of a strong sense of national community as an important task. The war made them long for peace and changed how they perceived ethnic minorities in Canada. Ukrainians and Japanese regarded the Citizenship Act as long-overdue recognition as full-fledged citizens and had great expectations of dramatic changes. At one level, mainstream and ethnic boundaries merged in the name of freedom, democracy, and citizenship. Yet, at another level, the interests of mainstream leaders remained remote from those of ethnic elites. Mainstream policy makers' Canadianism placed issues directly related to Canada as their top priority, taking into account specific ethnic agendas only when they affected Canada's image or national strength. Japanese issues—such as wartime property losses, lack of the franchise, and deportation—were thus discussed widely as symbols of racism since they were unjustifiable in democratic nations. Issues outside Canada's jurisdiction, such as Ukrainian nationalists' lobby for an independent Ukrainian state free of Soviet control, were neglected. In pursuit of their respective goals, both ethnic elites challenged the federal government, thereby redefining and expanding Canadian democracy and citizenship on their terms, tying them to ethnic pluralism. Yet certain factors made Ukrainian nationalists best equipped to promote the ideas of multiculturalism and group rights. Ukrainian statelessness in Europe and fear of cultural assimilation in Canadian society convinced them to strive for cultural and linguistic survival. Ukrainian nationalists thus actively maintained ethnic consciousness and activism, while both communist Ukrainians and Japanese increasingly lost momentum for organized action.

CHAPTER 5

The Canadianization and Ethnicization of Myths, Collective Memories, and Symbols

After World War II, not only Ukrainian and Japanese elites but also Scots enthusiastically incorporated new political discourses around democracy and citizenship into their collective memories and group myths, thereby modifying them to be relevant in the contemporary Canadian context. At the same time, they ethnicized past events in Canada and consolidated their ethnic boundaries. Through both processes, these leaders contributed to the construction of a more encompassing Canadian identity defined by ethnicity and characterized by the merger of Canadian and ethnic identities. First, Canadian citizenship had a great impact on the acceleration of such a merger. During this period, the myths and collective memories that Scots, Ukrainians, and Japanese produced were positive, reflecting appreciation for their new status as Canadian citizens and the optimism that they had for a postwar reborn Canada. Second, the continuity of myths and collective memories from the interwar period, as a factor in helping to maintain ethnic identity, varied among the three groups. Ukrainians kept their homeland symbols, such as Taras Shevchenko and the Cossacks, and their Canadian pioneer myths on the Prairies, around which they built a sense of community. Japanese, in contrast, saw their homeland symbols, such as the emperor, and their Canadian myths in British Columbia interrupted by the war, and they had to reconstruct new symbols and myths. Scots' interest in their myths, symbols, and collective memories was more sporadic, based on movements such as the promotion of Gaelic and Scottish traditions in Nova Scotia. Third, the regional boundaries of the interwar period, both physical and imagined, constituted a crucial factor in shaping communities. Here again Ukrainian nationalists provided the best example of intertwined ethnic and regional identities, which focussed on and identified with the Prairies. For both Japanese and Scots, neither British Columbia nor Nova Scotia necessarily reflected their demographic concentrations and were rather more imagined. In this chapter, I examine the above points through three types of myths and symbols—homeland, Canadian, and regional.

Homeland Myths and Symbols

Myths and symbolic figures imported from the homeland remained effective in the maintenance of ethnic identity in postwar Canada. Yet, as pride in being Canadian was boosted by the implementation of Canadian citizenship, these myths and memories were Canadianized, reflecting postwar optimism and victory in the war. Despite common tendencies, how the three ethnic elites preserved and used these myths and symbols after the war varied significantly, having different implications for and impacts on their respective ethnic communities and identities. Ukrainian nationalist elites were the most effective in using homeland myths and symbols to retain a strong ethnic consciousness among their people. Unlike Scots, who promoted their myths, symbols, and collective memories for Canadian or provincial purposes, Ukrainians kept their myths and symbols ethnically distinctive for their unchanging cause of Ukrainian independence.

The first difference among the three groups concerned the consistency of myths and symbolic figures. The maintenance of ethnicity, as a dynamic political phenomenon defined by identity, not common blood, required ethnic elites' efforts to keep homeland myths and symbols alive and to stimulate their ethnic pride constantly, even though obstacles often hindered such efforts. Among the three groups, and in comparison with their rival communists, Ukrainian nationalists preserved heroes such as Taras Shevchenko and Bohdan Khmelnytsky most continuously, both because these figures did not meet with any obvious objections from mainstream Canadians, who did not always see or ignored them as symbols of loyalty to Ukraine, and because they were intertwined with Ukrainian independence. Although Ukrainian communists also saw historical homeland heroes as useful, their emphasis was more on the promotion of the class consciousness of the international proletariat than on ethnicity, at least until the late 1940s, when they began focussing on the ethnic significance of such heroes. While Japanese had always valued their homeland heroes and myths, World War II did not allow them to promote interwar ones, particularly the emperor, resulting in a period of discontinuity. Japan's defeat in the war neither ended Emperor Hirohito's throne nor reduced his significance to Japan, but it did terminate the myths that tied Emperor Hirohito with imperialism and ultranationalism. Scots were another peculiar case; their homeland collective memories and symbolic figures were always present, but they frequently became more broadly "Canadian" rather than distinctively "Scottish." For example, the birthday of Robert Burns on 25 January was celebrated and often featured in a mainstream newspaper such as the *Globe and Mail*.[1] Also, the "Scottish movement" that had thrived in Nova Scotia lost momentum after the death of the greatest promoter of Scottish culture and premier of the province, Angus L. Macdonald, in 1954.[2]

The second difference among the three groups was seen in the political agendas attached to these myths and symbols. While at a fundamental level the "myth of common descent" was always closely tied to ethnic groups' respective pasts, roots, and collective memories in their homelands,[3] the political messages attached to them depended on ethnic leaders' contemporary political interests. Such interests did not necessarily involve nationalist aspirations for or independence of the homeland, but when they did they provided the ethnic group with a strong motivation for unity and a sense of community.

In this vein, Ukrainian nationalists kept making the most effective use of national heroes and the myths of Ukraine's "golden age" to strengthen ethnic consciousness,[4] tying them to the renewed lobby for Ukraine's independence. That Ukrainians remained an "oppressed" nation after World War II, despite their desire to become independent, increased the significance of these homeland myths and symbols, which, they believed, would justify the claim of Ukraine as a separate state historically. To raise support for the independence movement, Ukrainian nationalists cited Ukraine's history, emphasizing the fact that Ukrainians had once been an autonomous nation and therefore had to continue fighting for "freedom" to recover their state. For example, they highlighted the golden age of Ukraine in the "great and powerful Ukrainian state" under Volodymyr the Great,[5] and they celebrated Khmelnytsky as a fighter who physically led the Cossacks in pursuit of Ukrainian nationhood.[6] Above all, Shevchenko continued to be enshrined as a leader in every aspect of Ukrainian national life and democracy, as is clear from the following:

> They [Ukrainians] have great kings, hetmen, religious leaders, cultural and educational leaders, novelists, poets, and composers. But among all the heroes in its history, the figure of Shevchenko appears above the horizon of people's life. Beyond God's gift, he showed the depth of his intellect and the heart and soul of language by his

> alluring poems and became a nationalist prophet, leader, historian, teacher, and people's defender against the authoritarianism and slavery of tsarist Russia. He was the voice of the nation, who could not put his words into practice in his defence in the political and economic situation. Yet Shevchenko was not only in his defence, but he also set a clear goal for liberation, realizing that only in one's home were rights, strength, and freedom.[7]

Shevchenko thus was elevated to a sacred figure who could lead God's "chosen people"[8] to their freedom, and he was celebrated as a figure "that God sent to us [Ukrainians] in order that he could guide the Ukrainian nation to live."[9] This sort of fusion between Shevchenko and God's will made the Ukrainian nation eternal, at least in the minds of Ukrainian nationalists. Even at critical times when "the Poles and Muscovy tried to destroy Ukrainian life," *Ukrainskyi holos* argued, "they could not destroy the Ukrainian soul."[10] Such comments, implicitly tying the Ukrainian situation in the past to the contemporary one, sent the Ukrainian masses a clear message that the failure to make Ukrainians independent after World War II should never undermine Ukrainian national consciousness.

Scots, too, stressed their glorious past, but they differed from Ukrainian nationalists in that their interests lay in Scottish superiority in Canada rather than in Scotland's politics. At the same time, Scottish Canadians' celebration of anything Scottish was by no means politics free, for Scots manipulated their myths, symbols, and collective memories to claim to be a "chosen people" who had come to Canada with the democratic mission to build a new British colony.[11] As the Citizenship Act promoted the notion of "all Canadians" and memories of the old world and the British Empire began to fade, Scots stressed their distinctiveness as founders of the free West and a democratic and free Canada as opposed to growing communist powers. In this context, Burns became a symbol of the worldwide Commonwealth and democratic West, as Macdonald reminded his audience on Burns night in 1951: "On this very night, in a thousand cities and towns in every part of the English-speaking world, in old Scotland herself, in England, in Ireland, in Wales, in the United States and in Canada, in far off Australia and New Zealand, in many a ship on distant seas, and in many a camp under strange skies, the thoughts of thousands of men and women will turn to Burns for inspiration and courage, for pleasure and for hope."[12] After quoting a couple of poems by Burns, Macdonald stressed the poet's relevance to the postwar international scene: "Burns dignified the common man and the common pursuits of life, and in a time when democracy and the rights of the common man are threatened by ruthless and tyrannous foes, it is well that we should recall this aspect of Burns's poetry—message of Burns to our time."[13]

Canada's new fight for equality, democracy, and freedom in the Cold War was also encouraged in the context of the Scottish past. Justice J. Keiller Mackay of the Supreme Court of Ontario, for example, stressed the benefits of freedom and human rights, tying them to how Scots had survived as a strong and influential nation, when he responded to the toast to Scotland at the North British Society meeting in Halifax on the feast of St. Andrew in 1950: "Empires rise and fall, kings, tyrants and conquerors come and go, but Scotland has contrived throughout the centuries to preserve her ancient love of freedom and her passionate avowal of the dignity and nobility of our common humanity."[14] More specifically, the event was often dramatized as a rebellion for Scottish independence and freedom. Angus L. Macdonald, for example, called it the "final stand for an independent Scotland."[15] As Ian McKay points out, Flora Macdonald, a Scottish heroine who helped Charles Edward Stuart to lead the Highland clans in the uprising, was enshrined in Canada as well.[16] That she helped Stuart to escape from British forces after his defeat at the Battle of Culloden in 1746 demonstrated her "loyalty" and "self-sacrifice"[17]—qualities admired and needed by Canadians, who had just experienced World War II and faced a new challenge in the Cold War. Scots thus were defined as a special people possessing democratic principles and loyalty, but the racism that had accompanied the Scottish sense of superiority for much of the first half of the twentieth century, particularly during World War II, was largely forgotten.[18]

Postwar Japanese leaders reinstated the emperor and his family as symbols of their loyalty to Japan, yet naturally they no longer identified with Japan's nationalism or imperialism. This decline of nationalist discourse around the emperor made the Japanese homeland symbol different from that of Ukrainian nationalists. The royal family was now viewed as a central national symbol that would lead Japan's postwar reconstruction and its relationship with other countries, particularly Canada. Memories of the war and Imperial Japan, which postwar Japanese Canadians always identified with property losses and internment, had to be separated from the royal family. The new role assigned to Japan's throne became apparent when Prince Akihito visited Canada in 1953 on behalf of his politically controversial father, often seen as having been responsible for the Pacific War. Japanese throughout Canada, both *issei* and *nisei*, widely celebrated the occasion, though the *New Canadian* insisted that the celebration be done in a very "modest" and "democratic way,"[19] as opposed to a nationalist way, reflecting concern about the reaction of mainstream society. The visit signified a resumed relationship between Japan and Canada and the end of lingering suspicion of Japan. The purpose of the royal visit, as the speech that the prince gave in Victoria noted, was "to contribute to the further development of friendship between Canada and Japan."[20] The *New Canadian* endorsed this goal: "Prince Akihito could have been regarded merely as another visitor from a foreign land but our role as Canadian citizens does not mean that we should be completely invisible citizens detached from a land which has given us cultural heritage of its customs, aesthetics, philosophy, art, and moral code that we can help impart to Canadian life. The visit of Prince Akihito, we hope, will bolster friendly relations between Canada and Japan, and if we, as Canadian citizens, have helped in making his visit a successful one, then the effort will have been worthwhile."[21] *Tairiku nippô*'s successor, *Tairiku jihô,* expanded on the significance of the visit, maintaining that the improved relationship should not only complete the normalization of the diplomatic relationship but also end the continued ban on Japanese immigration to Canada.[22] Prince Akihito's visit was indeed received with exhilaration and "tears in the eyes."[23] If Emperor Hirohito represented the bitter memory of the war, Prince Akihito brought great expectations for a new Japan and the future. As the *New Canadian* stated, "Japan's moderns hope that he will return with ideas of becoming an important force in the country and a modern monarch, less tied up with religious ritual and more concerned with current trends of Japanese history."[24] Such a comment manifested resistance to conventional practices and rituals that *issei* Japanese had maintained. *Tairiku jihô* no longer identified Akihito with the "golden age" of Japanese nationalism and reported on his tour with enthusiasm as an "honourable" and a "memorable" event that would lead "Japan's postwar policies in the right direction" and guide "Japan to join democratic Western nations."[25] For Japanese, Akihito's visit removed the contradictions in Japanese Canadians' dual loyalty.

The third difference among the three groups concerned the impact of homeland myths and symbols on internal divisions. When competing elites share the same myths and symbols, rivalry often intensifies over representation of the ethnic group and mobilization of its members. This phenomenon, which Paul R. Brass describes as "the process by which elites and counter-elites within ethnic groups select aspects of the group's culture, attach new value and meaning to them, and use them as symbols to mobilize the group, to defend its interests and to compete with other groups,"[26] was most obvious among Ukrainians. Fuelled by the Cold War, competition between Ukrainian nationalists and communists over Ukrainian historic figures such as Shevchenko intensified. They competed over symbols and myths more vigorously than did Scottish and Japanese elites, who were rarely divided ideologically during this period by the use of ethnic symbols. Obviously for Scots, who did not need to rely on ethnicity to gain greater power in Canadian society or politics, homeland myths and symbols were highlighted only by a circle of interested politicians, scholars, and others and were rarely sources of conflict. The difference between Ukrainians and Japanese is therefore the focus here.

Ukrainian nationalists and communists both adroitly manipulated the myths around Kievan Rus' and Shevchenko for their own purposes so that they could win the political competition to represent the Ukrainian ethnic community. For nationalist Ukrainians, Shevchenko, in addition to his traditional role as a national prophet, played a part as a symbol of resistance against neighbouring foreign powers in Europe. A spirit of struggle against communism, which gained significance as the Cold War escalated, was derived from his poetry and acquired contemporary political connotations, as the following quotation shows:

> Not only Ukrainians but also foreigners know who Shevchenko was, for what he fought and perished. Shevchenko fought not only for the social and economic liberation of Ukrainian people. He fought not only for the political liberation of Ukraine about which he often wrote in his poems. Most precisely, the ingenious work of Shevchenko turned against the Russian tsar who subjugated the Ukrainian people and their state. He rebelled against this hostile authority, which was in Ukraine in his time. Clearly, he was not able to stand against communists, such as Lenin and Stalin and all contemporary soldiers in Ukraine, because he was no longer alive. But nobody doubted that, if Shevchenko were to live today, and had the freedom to write as he had from the tsar, he, without any contradiction, would have cursed the contemporary communist red Muscovite tsars and called on the Ukrainian people to rise and break their chains.[27]

Clearly, such comments, which equated Russian tsars with communists, portrayed Shevchenko as a fighter against their authoritarian power. Among communist Ukrainians, Russian tsars were depicted as "Russian militarist-feudal-capitalist oppressors."[28] In this context, Shevchenko was a hero who represented the exploited class of "serfs" and worked "for the overthrow of feudalism and the democratic unification of the Slavic peoples."[29] Both factions also competed over the interpretation of historical memory and myth. Their ideal of Slavic unity and insistence on the legitimacy of the Soviet Union made communists refute the nationalist notion of Kievan Rus' as a distinctively "Ukrainian" state and argue that it was a Slavic empire that "embraced all the Rus' people."[30] This communist interpretation of Kievan Rus' was a message to Ukrainians in Canada that they should not lobby for Ukrainian independence. According to communists, Khmelnytsky did not fight for Ukrainian independence, as nationalists argued, but "brought to fruition the age-old dream of the Ukrainian people—their unification with the Russians, the people of the same blood and religion," to return to "the ancient glory of the Rus.'"[31]

Such competition over symbols surfaced most clearly when communists erected a monument of Shevchenko on 1 July 1951 in North Oakville, Ontario, on the occasion of the sixtieth anniversary of Ukrainian settlement in Canada.[32] Communists, naturally, celebrated the success of the project and the appeal that the monument had to the public, calling it "a great triumph" and stating that, "while there were a couple of thousand visitors from other parts of Canada and even from the United States, and while there were undoubtedly several thousand non-Ukrainians present, there could not have been 45,000 people at the celebration if the great majority of the Ukrainian people in this district had not turned out. Despite the false and insidious propaganda of the 'nationalist' leaders, the Ukrainian Canadian people joined hands to mark the 60th anniversary and together greeted the Shevchenko monument."[33]

Obviously, this was an opportunity to showcase the work of communists and its innocuous nature and to defeat negative views of the Soviet Union. It was also a public gesture to show their possession of the Ukrainian hero. Nationalist elites, never pleased with the attention that communists received from the public, criticized their patriotism as superficial:

> Having realized that Ukrainians feel very sentimental toward Shevchenko and have profound love for him and his achievements, the communists attached to a monument of Shevchenko brutally and carelessly, manipulating this honest sentiment of Ukrainians for their evil goal, spreading hostile propaganda, collecting donations from Ukrainians, and using them for their weak cause.... Moscow in the era of Shevchenko and at present has only one goal: to conquer all Slavic and other nations with their despotic power and government. Shevchenko vigorously rebelled against Moscow, the worst prison house of people, and led his people in the correct direction: the liberation of the Ukrainian people from Moscow. On this road, Ukrainian leaders and the entire people stand today.[34]

For nationalists, then, the statue was an evil manipulation of the Ukrainian spiritual symbol and thus not legitimate. Their statue was erected in 1961 in Manitoba on the occasion of the seventieth anniversary of Ukrainian settlement in Canada and the centennial of the poet's death. Nationalists demonstrated the legitimacy of their statue, inviting the prime minister and other government officials to the ceremony; John G. Diefenbaker unveiled the statue, while Dufferin Roblin, premier of Manitoba, gave an address. Inviting mainstream politicians was a statement that nationalists were Ukrainians' representatives in Canada and shared interests with other Canadians. Yuzyk, for example, stressed the "universal" nature of Shevchenko, describing the day of the ceremony: "This man of lowly birth, who used his rare talents of poetry and painting to fight Russian tsarist tyranny for the rights and dignity of the common man and for freedom of his and other subjugated nations and who suffered a martyr's fate in exile, is to-day the most revered man among Ukrainians throughout the world."[35]

Japanese differed considerably from Ukrainians in terms of competition over myths and symbols within their community since they lacked an intense rivalry between *issei* and *nisei* over interpretation of the Japanese past and role of the emperor. Both groups agreed, if not completely, on the role that the emperor could play. Such agreement was due to changes in *issei*'s attitudes toward Japan and the royal family caused by the demise of Imperial Japan. While *issei* had always seen the emperor as a symbol of imperialism and the head of the superior Yamato race, they now accepted the new role of the emperor as the representative of a normalized relationship between Canada and Japan. Rather than imposing their loyalty to Japan on *nisei*, they only hoped that Akihito's visit would promote pride in being Japanese among *nisei*, who had grown up believing that maintaining distance from Japan was politically appropriate in Canada. "The biggest product" of Akihito's visit to Canada, *Tairiku jihô* reported, was "to impress the *nisei* who tended to underestimate Japan." Since Canada had "invited him as an official guest," it continued, "the *nisei* must have realized the special status that Canada assigned to Japan."[36] Now that their adopted homeland recognized Japan, *issei* thought, the visit of Akihito could also help *nisei* to appreciate Japan as a democratic country and take pride in their ethnic background. In addition, the royal tour was officially laid out by the Canadian and Japanese governments and thus, unlike the construction of monuments, not a demonstration of possession of the Japanese symbolic figure by any group.

Crystallization of Canadian Ethnic Myths, Symbols, and Histories

Postwar Canada saw two opposite tendencies in the development of myths and collective memories. On the one hand, the fusion between ethnic and Canadian myths and collective memories advanced; on the other hand, ethnic groups tried to establish their own histories that could be detached from Canada's past. In many ways, coexistence of the two tendencies suggests that ethnic groups always tried to be both ethnic and Canadian. The postwar expansion of specifically Canadian myths and symbols, already found in the interwar period, reflected a sense of roots in and attachment to Canada and Canadian citizenship by both ethnic groups and their elites. The emphasis on Canadian experiences by ethnic leaders made ethnicity integral to Canadian identity and Canada to ethnic identity. For late-nineteenth-century and early-twentieth-century Ukrainian and Japanese immigrants, who had resided in Canada for many years, and for their Canadian-born descendants, Canada became a more familiar land. For Ukrainian and Japanese elites, one of the most notable and common ways of demonstrating Canadian ethnic myths and symbols was celebration of their anniversaries in Canada and enshrinement of the first immigrants to Canada. The 1951 diamond jubilee of the settlement of Ukrainians in Canada was the most organized manifestation of the maturity of community life in comparison with other groups. Japanese had not yet established a precise date for their first settlement, but they still commemorated fifty years of their experiences in Canada during this period. The case of Scots, as builders of the British Empire and Canada, showed a different tendency in creating Canadian myths and requires a separate category of analysis because the boundary between Scottish and mainstream myths and anniversaries was less clear-cut. Yet, at the same time, all groups tried to establish their own histories, which celebrated their own ethnic heroes and events, thereby redefining their boundaries.

"Canadian" stories and collective memories, which stressed ethnic groups' contributions to Canada's nation building and cultural, economic, and political achievements in Canada, had their origins in the interwar period. Yet this movement had some postwar dimensions. The first was integration of the notion of Canadian citizenship that could be seen in the public discourses of rival factions—Ukrainian nationalists and communists, *issei* and *nisei* Japanese.[37] Ukrainian and Japanese leaders wished to show that their groups had deep roots in the country and therefore deserved equal status and rights as citizens. Yet Ukrainian elites had a better opportunity than did Japanese to make an explicit connection between their pioneer symbols and citizenship since their hero, Wasyl Eleniak, was among the first people to gain Canadian citizenship, together with the prime minister and the mother of a Polish soldier. The ceremony in Ottawa was a sign that the Ukrainian pioneer had gained an equal status with these individuals, and *Ukrainskyi holos* reported on it with great enthusiasm: "Respectfully and firmly for his age, he [Eleniak] walked into the court. And when he received the certificate, the applause never stopped. The next person after him was Mrs. Mynarska from Winnipeg. Her son, a pilot, perished heroically in the war and achieved a great distinction: the Victoria Cross. And Mrs. Mynarska equally received a lot of sincere applause. Then another person followed, and in total there were twelve people."[38] That Eleniak became one of the first Canadian citizens was valued by Ukrainians, not simply because his contribution as a Ukrainian pioneer was recognized by mainstream leaders but also because he was selected to participate in the citizenship ceremony, representing Ukrainians who had roots in Canada. This sense of uniqueness was well illustrated by Vera Lysenko: "Eleniak symbolizes today, as perhaps does no other man of any ethnic groups in Canada, the entire period of their settlement for the Ukrainian Canadians."[39]

Japanese, in contrast, had no such perfect symbol. The alleged first Japanese immigrant to Canada, Manzô Nagano, who landed in British Columbia in 1877, was not always based in the province, moving back and forth among Canada, Japan, and the United States. Neither did he live long enough to receive Canadian citizenship since he died at his home in Nagasaki in 1923. Yet Japanese elites also considered contributions to citizenship and the franchise when they selected their heroes. In 1950, the *New Canadian* "officially" elevated thirty-six people as "the Japanese Canadians of the Half-Century,"[40] based on nominations and votes by subscribers. Besides Manzô Nagano, they included individuals such as Etsu Suzuki, a newspaper editor and leader of the Japanese-Canadian labourers' rights movement; Tomekichi Honma, who led the Japanese campaign for the vote and equal rights as citizens; and Yasutarô Yamaga, who built a foundation for better Japanese-(white)-Canadian relations in the interwar years so that the future generation could become full-fledged citizens of Canada.[41] Suzuki gained the largest number of votes in the competition, reflecting the fact that the labourers' movement was one of the few concrete ways at that time to unite Japanese and other Canadians in local communities and combat racism. The *New Canadian* noted the impact that his work had on the field of citizenship: "We are indeed putting into practice what he had advocated twenty some years ago. It was to build our lives in Canada permanently and establish our lives in Eastern Canada. In short, it was a plea that we become Canadians."[42] While Suzuki did not represent the entire span of Japanese settlement, he symbolized much of the Japanese fight for equal rights in Canada.

The postwar features of Canadian ethnic myths also included an emphasis on ethnic groups' accomplishments and the reflection of expectations rather than the negative sides of their pasts. Since the introduction of Canadian citizenship and the end of World War II were critical steps for ethnic groups toward full recognition in Canada, both Ukrainian and Japanese elites developed myths and collective memories that made a transition from the "difficult" past to the "better" present in terms of both material conditions and social acceptance. In this way, they could conceptualize their histories as linear progressions that overlapped with the experiences of Canada. As part of the initial batch of stories, pioneers were honoured for the hardships that they encountered in the new land and celebrated for building the foundations of ethnic communities. On the sixtieth anniversary of Ukrainian settlement, tributes to pioneers were the main focus. At a concert held by nationalists in Winnipeg on 8 September 1951, the organizers stressed the contrast between past and present in congratulatory tones:

> The foreign land and language, the foreign customs and habits, the wild forest and the prairies—all laid down difficulties in your mind at the very doorstep of the promised land. Quite often immigration officers left you with spouses and children on the foreign, unfriendly prairies, in the bleak isolated forest, far away from cities and people, without a roof over your head, without any money and livelihood, without anything. Though without anything, you had your precious treasures, talismans which at times transformed endless forests and grassy prairies into a sea of golden grain.... With your courage, endurance, and hard work, you enriched not only yourself but also your children and grandchildren.[43]

This sort of collective memory reflected the ideas that evolution of Ukrainian Canadians and the Canadian community occurred side by side and that distinctively Ukrainian qualities were great assets to Canada. Communist Ukrainians, while placing more emphasis on labourers' struggles in the pioneer era, also exhibited a bright picture of their present and future and a sense of contribution to Canada. The *Ukrainian Canadian* celebrated Ukrainians and Canada on Dominion Day in 1956, stating that "the Ukrainian Canadians have already contributed greatly in labour, in helping to build up the country, in bringing the traditions of their people into the common store house of Canadian culture."[44]

Japanese, settled mainly on the West Coast before World War II, did not possess a sense of being a major force in Canada's nation building but nonetheless saw their participation as a great achievement: "Fifty years ago our pioneers came to Canada without anything. All they had was a spirit of endurance, persistence, and unlimited ability of development. Despite the fact that they faced discrimination and intolerance, they built strong roots on the Canadian land—created a seed of real Canadianism. This seed has now grown, and the dreams and hopes of the pioneers came true in Canada. Canada is now one of the international powers. Today the Japanese Canadians are no longer politically and socially marginalized or isolated."[45] Such a depiction of the difficult past was written in retrospect to contrast with the better postwar period and thus showed how much Japanese felt that they were part of Canada by this time. The striking similarity between Ukrainian and Japanese emphases on the hardships that immigrants had confronted in terms of both racism and economic conditions in the pioneer era reflected their perceptions that their situations had improved greatly in the postwar era.

The final postwar feature of Canadian myths and collective memories was the fact that they began taking shape as more sophisticated ethnic histories, predecessors of the scholarly works that started appearing in the 1960s and became common in the 1970s. This tendency reflected ethnic elites' determination to preserve "their" pasts, distinguishable from Canadian experiences, and thus to produce their own histories, making all ethnic groups' experiences independent of each other and mainstream history. In other words, the production of ethnic groups' own histories was a claim that they were participants in Canada's growth as a nation-state but as distinctive groups of people who made positive contributions to Canada. Their monographs thus differed considerably from the interwar studies produced by mainstream assimilationist scholars in terms of ethnic groups' self-assertion.

Examples of such ethnic histories for Ukrainians are Vera Lysenko's *Men in Sheepskin Coats: A Study in Assimilation,* published in 1947, and Paul Yuzyk's *Ukrainians in Manitoba: A Social History,* published in 1953. Although the authors had different ideological orientations—the former was funded by the AUUC, and the latter was a nationalist—and interpreted Ukrainian-Canadian history from their own political perspectives, they were similar in their belief that their history could be written independently of mainstream landmark events and great individuals. Their works, in fact, were some of the earliest studies to use the format that later became the norm in writing ethnic history, dividing their chapters into themes such as settlement, organizational life, the press, culture, and assimilation. Written in a journalistic style, Lysenko's book outlined Ukrainian life in Canada from the arrival of Ivan Pylypiw and Wasyl Eleniak to the development of a community—particularly around the Ukrainian Labour-Farmer Temple Association (ULFTA)—and assimilation. Yet her history also went back to the old world, particularly to the time of the Cossacks under Bohdan Khmelnytsky, thereby providing Ukrainian-Canadian history with primordial roots as a nation.[46] Reflecting the priorities and censorship of the communist sponsor of *Men in Sheepskin Coats,* the AUUC, Lysenko focussed on Ukrainian songs, poems, and other cultural works, which the AUUC used to attract people to communism and increase its membership.[47] Yuzyk's monograph was based on much more thorough research yet followed a similar line of events, from the Cossack era in Europe to immigration to Canada, and the economic and cultural activities of the Ukrainian community. It was provincial, not national, in scope, understanding Manitoba as the focal point of Ukrainian-Canadian identity and in that context enumerating, for example, events, names, cultural activities, presses, and secular organizations in the province.[48] Both monographs thus perceived the ethnic group from a similar primordial perspective, as a community of people bonded by common roots and cultural traits, which became the major way of conceptualizing Ukrainian history in Canada.

For Japanese elites, the establishment of Japanese-Canadian history became particularly imperative in the 1950s because they were searching for a new cause. Since most wartime restrictions on Japanese had been lifted by then and the franchise achieved, they needed a project to replace such political campaigns. In a way, their institutionalization of ethnic history was more obvious and intentional than that of Ukrainians. The newly formed Japanese Canadian Citizens Association (NJCCA) officially called for the production of Japanese-Canadian history in the late 1950s. A sense of possession of Japanese Canadians' past and the will to make their ethnic boundary something permanent were well illustrated when the *New Canadian* wrote in 1957 that "a History of the Japanese in Canada will be Our Story.... This history is a necessity of the annals of Canada and to future generations of Japanese Canadians, showing the record of progress of one minority group which under unique circumstances rose from the pall of racial discrimination to make contributions to almost every field of Canadian life."[49]

This project should not be regarded merely as an effort to record the past; it was also the claim that the NJCCA had the authority to carry out the plan, determining who would be the author and what should be written. The emphasis on political correctness and control was evident when the association justified its choice of Ken Adachi, then a journalist, as project leader on the ground that it had found "no major faults with Adachi's work, which we assigned to him" in previous years.[50] The history committee added that "the history" should be "written by a Japanese Canadian able to feel and extract the true meaning and picture experienced by our pioneers."[51] Although the committee acknowledged that mainstream studies of Japanese Canadians—including Charles Young and Helen Reid's *The Japanese Canadians* (1938) and F.E. LaViolette's *The Canadian Japanese and World War II* (1948)—shed light on the Japanese-Canadian community, it rejected them as official historical interpretations of Japanese-Canadian life. These studies, according to the committee, focussed more on statistics and failed to incorporate a "clear-sighted view into the hearts and minds of the people they are about."[52] LaViolette's study, in particular, was censored because of the federal government's wartime policy.[53] Implicitly, the NJCCA was denying mainstream practices and power to define the Japanese community since the interwar period. It was also criticizing the lack of celebration of Japanese-Canadian history in those books, indicating that this history had entered a new phase, which claimed self-definition of the past and uniqueness of the community. More specifically, the NJCCA's project rejected a "straightforward, chronological marshalling of events" and focussed more on "an interpretative study of the struggle, upheaval, and achievement of the Japanese Canadians."[54] Adachi, in his article "History of Japanese Canadians in B.C., 1877–1958," a prelude to the history project, argued that "the story of the Japanese in British Columbia, of all the groups in the province, is easily the most dramatic, and disturbing in its ramifications."[55] More precisely, he emphasized various types of long-term discrimination and internment during World War II, thereby determining the future foci of Japanese-Canadian history.

As part of the mainstream British group, Scots fit into a different category from Ukrainians and Japanese in terms of writing ethnic history. Notably, they did not try to construct a dichotomy between their past and Canada's past as clearly as Ukrainians and Japanese did, yet they highlighted the Scottish experience and contribution to nation building.[56] Such a tendency was well illustrated by Angus L. Macdonald, who, in referring to Scottish contributions to Canadian education, maintained that "these [educational institutions, including universities] owe their beginnings to men of Scottish birth or Scottish descent. So that the Scot in Canada, as elsewhere, has established a goodly record in the educational world."[57] The Scottish system of education was celebrated not only as a Scottish achievement but also as the foundation of mainstream Canada. A similar tendency of ethnicizing Canadian achievements can be seen in Charles W. Dunn's *Highland Settler: A Portrait of the Scottish Gael in Nova Scotia* (1953). Following a linear development from emigration to the cultural and economic developments of Highland Scots in the province, the study used the same format as Ukrainian- and Japanese-Canadian histories. Yet it differed slightly from Ukrainian and Japanese efforts to create their histories in terms of who wrote them. Dunn was a Harvard-trained Scottish scholar of literature who was born and raised in Scotland and thus rather an "outsider" to Nova Scotia. His book was more a celebration of Gaelic cultural heritages, which were well preserved in Nova Scotia, than a politically motivated representation of the Scottish voice. Undoubtedly, he gave Highland Scots a special "ethnic" status, not as imperial colonists but as people brought to Canada after their clan system was destroyed in 1746.[58] Yet his main interest was the retention of a rare language away from Highland Scotland. Devoting a large part of his book to Gaelic literature, poems, and presses, he stressed their survival: "The quantity of Gaelic pamphlets, papers, and books published in North America is considerable and somewhat astonishing."[59] In this case, then, Gaelic identity was promoted also by homeland scholars whose works helped to identify Nova Scotia with Highland characteristics.

Yet public interest in Scottish roots seemed to have declined to a certain degree in the 1960s. An example is the failed attempt of a Scottish popular writer and native of Pictou, Henry R. Beer, to commemorate the 200th anniversary of the arrival of the *Hector* in 1973.[60] He was very enthusiastic about writing a history of Scottish immigrants on this occasion. In search of both financial and referential assistance, he made various contacts, including the Gaelic College on Cape Breton, the Nova Scotia Museum, and the National Library of Scotland.[61] Yet he rarely seemed to receive positive responses. For example, W.A. MacCulloch, executive manager of the Hector Bicentennial Commission, in his response to Beer's proposal for financial aid, pointed out "the lack of local interest." The commission, he continued, "decided not to support, in a capital way, any projects for summer."[62] His application for a research grant funded under the Canadian Horizons Program of the Canada Council was also rejected. Norman Mackenzie, Scottish scholar and former president of the University of British Columbia, wrote to him that he was "very disappointed" with the decision.[63]

Region and Identity

Ethnic myths and collective memories were often closely tied to an imagined region. Anthony D. Smith provides the useful concept of "ethnoscape" to describe "the idea of an historic and poetic landscape" that becomes imbued with "the culture and history of a group."[64] Regional identity helps to consolidate ethnic identity rather than overwhelm it. In other words, specific regions in Canada gained significance in the consolidation of ethnic identity, though regional boundaries carried different meanings for and had different impacts on different groups. I argue in this section that region, both physical and imagined, as a component of ethnic identity, was another factor that made Ukrainian ethnic consciousness distinctive, especially compared with that of Japanese, focussing on the following issues: how region was related to the ethnic group's concept of time and progress, how region was tied to an imagined homeland, and how the ethnic group was incorporated into the region by both ethnic and mainstream elites.[65]

Region was strongly intertwined with ethnic leaders' perception of time and progress in various ways. More precisely, it symbolized a certain era in the history of each ethnic group. Ukrainians exhibited the deepest sense of attachment to a particular region among the three groups. As Frances Swyripa has shown, the progress of the Prairies and Ukrainian communities were often seen side by side, and region thus symbolized their long continuous history in Canada.[66] The concentration of Ukrainians in the three prairie provinces for more than half a century without any major interruption and their contribution to the Canadian economy through cultivation of the land stimulated a profound sense of roots. Japanese, in contrast, perceived the geographical boundary between the West Coast and the rest of the country as the dividing line between the difficult "past" and the prosperous "future." The mass evacuation from the West Coast to the interior camps in 1942, and the subsequent resettlement east of the Rockies after World War II, broke Japanese-Canadian ties with British Columbia. For Scots, region was also strongly intertwined with their sense of time, and Nova Scotia, as Ian McKay has pointed out, symbolized the romantic past of Highland Scotland. The Scottish elite's efforts to ethnicize Nova Scotia around Scottishness comprised a project to go back to the past, reflecting resistance to "the products of twentieth-century modernity" such as urbanization, professionalization, and rise of the positive state.[67]

For Ukrainians, the Prairies symbolized their entire period in Canada, since Ukrainian farmers entered western Canada in the late nineteenth and early twentieth centuries. A sense of "struggle" during the settlement period and of "achievement," especially in agriculture, over many years on the prairie, where immigrant farmers had been in great demand, produced the conviction that the region belonged particularly to Ukrainians. Their attachment to it was often highlighted, particularly in comparison with other groups. P.I. Lazarovich, a Ukrainian lawyer and teacher, for example, emphasized the exceptional role that Ukrainians played in pioneering the west at the second congress of the Ukrainian Canadian Committee in 1946: "I took the Alberta statistics as an example.... Our farmers cultivated more land than Anglo-Saxons where there was mixed population. I know such regions very well, where in ten to fifteen years the British had mixed with us. Today there are no British in general in Ukrainian areas or will be no British very soon. Our people cultivated their lands without exception. Therefore, our possession grows every year, covering a large amount of land."[68]

Obviously, for Ukrainians, the claim that they were involved in province building more than other ethnic groups was the key factor that Ukrainianized the prairie provinces. This belief was further illustrated on the occasion of the golden jubilees of Saskatchewan and Alberta in 1955, when such landmark events served as great chances for Ukrainians to demonstrate their cultural and economic contributions.[69] *Ukrainskyi holos,* for example, stressed Ukrainians' commitment to these two provinces: "With the possible exception of Manitoba, there are no other provinces in Canada where Ukrainians have made a greater contribution to development." Economic foundations were the major focus: "Ukrainians have [a] full right to feel that they were productive participants in these fifty years of progress," and "the present condition of growth and prosperity of both provinces" was a "product of their effort." The article added that, "when Saskatchewan and Alberta became provinces in 1905, Eleniak and Pylypiw had already been farming in Alberta for many years."[70] For Ukrainians, then, western Canada embodied a claim to both influence and rights that they deserved as builders of Canada and was a symbol of economic progress for both Ukrainians and Canada.

For Japanese, moving from the West Coast to east of the Rockies identified British Columbia with the unappealing "past" and lingering racial discrimination. In the late 1940s, the memories of racial and political marginalization in the province before the war remained vivid, and some wartime measures and restrictive prewar policies, including the denial of fishing licences and the franchise to Japanese, were still in practice. Japanese elites thus excluded British Columbia from democratic Canada as well as from citizenship, which symbolized the bright future. More precisely, the zone within 100 miles of the Pacific coast, where the interwar Japanese population had been concentrated, became the darkest symbol of the Japanese past. Equation of the West Coast with the past reflected the determination of Japanese that they would not return to the region and was well illustrated by the following statement in the *New Canadian:* "The *New Canadian* believes that the great majority of those who have moved east of the Rockies will not return. They are relatively well established or becoming so with the assistance of placement officers and friends.... The coast offers the advantage of a milder climate and certain familiar fields of employment as in gardening, fishing, berry-farming, etc. But the coast also retains its deep-rooted discrimination in the broad field of economic activity, which older Niseis and Isseis [sic] will remember."[71] The new lands on which Japanese had resettled or were resettling, in contrast, were seen as representing democracy, justice, and economic prosperity. Immediately after the war, the *New Canadian* expressed the optimism associated with the region east of the Rockies: "Now, however, they [the evacuees] are made to realize that there is little discrimination in eastern Canada, and that the termination of the war has resulted in no heightened ill-feeling against the people of Japanese race. Nor does serious depression threaten in Canada in the foreseeable future—on the contrary Canada stands at the threshold of a period of great economic expansion.... It is worth noting that a number of Niseis, and Isseis [sic] too, have tackled the problem of re-establishing themselves in the east with remarkable success."[72]

A sense of hope was expressed not only in political and economic terms but also in terms of productivity of the land and potential for permanent settlement. The *New Canadian* maintained that farming in Alberta looked very promising: "For anyone who decided to establish roots on the soil of Canada, Alberta would offer great opportunities, with its rich natural resources such as sugar, grass, livestock, lumber, fish, crops, oil and coal."[73] Such a portrayal of the area east of British Columbia, even with some exaggeration, symbolized a bright future, which might erase bitter experiences of the past completely. Furthermore, the Japanese elite argued that arrival of Japanese en masse in the camps in the BC interior, created a great economic impact on somewhat deserted places and thus benefited those small towns. Celebrating the golden jubilee of Greenwood in the interior in 1947, the *New Canadian* pointed out that, before the influx of Japanese in 1942, Greenwood was a "ghost town," but Japanese evacuees "revitalized the town, renovating houses and cleaning up the streets."[74] The article was filled with success stories showing how the town resumed local activities such as the exploration of gold mining and the production of insulation. Japanese participation in anniversary events in Greenwood illustrated both their determination to plant roots and their aspirations for a better life, as the titles of two Japanese floats showed: "The Arrival of Japanese Evacuees" and "Toward a Goal."[75] Intriguingly, such commemoration indicated that Japanese did not treat the evacuation as taboo; rather, they took a positive approach to the worst event in their history, exhibiting these floats as public statements of moving on from the painful memories of the past.[76]

For Scots, identification with Nova Scotia represented a bygone and romanticized past, focussed on the Gaelic language and entirely symbolic elements such as Highland Gaelic music, dance, and poetry, which had been threatened by modernization.[77] Gaelic was most relevant for its exoticism, rareness, and antiquity. Scottish folklorist J.L. Campbell, for example, stressed how Gaelic spurred the memory of the remote past: "This [Gaelic] literature was of enormous extent, including heroic folktales dating back to pagan times, so-called Ossianic ballads about the wars of the Gaels with the Vikings in the 9th century."[78] By celebrating and promoting in Nova Scotia the preservation of Gaelic culture and language, Scottish leaders tended to imagine that the province, or at least Cape Breton Island, maintained the good qualities—namely, folk traditions—of the premodern era. Such a romanticized and fictionalized vision of Cape Breton was strengthened, for example, by Dunn's account of Scots in Nova Scotia; describing the late eighteenth and early nineteenth centuries, Dunn wrote that "Gaelic folk-culture played an important part in the everyday activities of the Highlanders" in Cape Breton despite the spread of "modern scepticism."[79] He further associated such preservation of folk culture with pioneering when he maintained that Highlanders in Cape Breton overcame hardships in the settlement era by singing their songs, which "were centuries old." Yet, for Dunn, such culture was not only imported from Scotland but also created in Cape Breton, thereby making Nova Scotia unique and "the last strong-hold of the old Gael." A number of Gaelic poets and musicians, according to him, emerged as "the stress of pioneering life" prompted such creativity.[80]

This sort of identification of one place with the past was also reflected in ethnic groups' reminiscences about and idealism toward their homelands—particularly for Scots and Japanese. Scots' romanticism always went back to the old world and Highland Scotland, where they themselves, for the most part, had not lived, while Japanese collective memory returned to the West Coast, where virtually all postwar Japanese had once actually lived. Thus, both places evolved as lost homelands to which neither group could go back in reality. Ukrainians exhibited a somewhat different tendency in this regard. While Ukrainian nationalists often saw themselves as refugees who had been "persecuted" in their homeland, they kept fighting for the independence of Ukraine, and it therefore was real. A lost homeland was thus a phenomenon unique to Scots and Japanese.

For Nova Scotian Scots, romanticized Highland Scotland was a creation of individuals reflecting the postwar idealization of and desire for an ancient landscape unaffected by industrial development.[81] The Highlands were depicted as a poetic and idyllic land and incorporated into Scottish identity in the province. This merger between homeland and Nova Scotian landscapes was unique given that both Ukrainians and Japanese did not identify their particular regions with their homelands. The fact that Highland Scotland and Cape Breton Island especially had common natural features of island, ocean, and hills, which were seen favourably, helped Scots to fantasize both places together. If Scotland was "a country of wondrous natural beauty, a land of rugged mountains and shadowed glens, of brooding lochs and leaping streams, of dark forests and of stormy seas,"[82] Nova Scotia obviously matched the scenery, for the province was a "land of entrancing beauty, this glory of mountain and glen, of lake and river, of forest and sea."[83]

Japanese exhibited a unique case in which they created a "lost homeland" in Canada because of the mass evacuation from the West Coast.[84]Although

Japanese identified the West Coast with the memory of injustice and discrimination, they also developed a somewhat favourable vision of a "home" in which they had settled for a long time. Clearly, that the West Coast could evoke both negative and positive images appears paradoxical, yet it only reflected the complexity of evacuees' collective memory. No matter how problematic life in the past, the homeland, which had once been a core of Japanese-Canadian cultural activities and businesses, was viewed with nostalgia and fantasized. The Japanese elite often depicted Powell Street as a symbol of success, emphasizing the good aspects of Japanese life and detaching them from the province's discriminatory politics. Thus, in their memory, the street existed on its own as Japanese space. A college student in English, for example, called Powell Street "their main street, dream street, wall street, park avenue [sic]" and the "nucleus of a grander scheme, of a better world to come."[85] Such comments reflected the sorrow and longing not just for the street itself, which had been ruined, but also for a sense of neighbourhood and ethnic community. Another Japanese said, "gone was the heart, the heart of Little Tokyo."[86] The street, then, was a symbol of Japanese ethnic bonds, which had to be maintained in people's minds. The sentiment was reflected in an essay by a regular anonymous columnist in the *New Canadian:* "I shall never revisit Powell Street. I want to leave it intact as I knew it—a gay, courageous and colorful thoroughfare which was part of me."[87]

How region was identified officially with a particular ethnic group differed and reflected Canada's ethnic hierarchy. Only Scottishness could be promoted to define official space and regional identity. For Scots, the regional boundary had been drawn as a provincial project of Nova Scotia since the interwar period, even though Nova Scotia was ethnically diverse—a type of project that neither Ukrainians nor Japanese had.[88] For the former, region strengthened the bond of ethnic community by setting the space to which the majority of Ukrainians felt attached. Unlike Scots, their regional boundary was not official, yet it was recognized by mainstream leaders. The Japanese case was the opposite of the Scottish case; postwar Canadian policies, which prohibited Japanese from going back to the West Coast and dispersed them east of the Rockies, were part of an official and deliberate plan to prevent Japanese from concentrating in a specific region and thus wiped out British Columbia's racialized image. Yet this scheme was not just a geographical or political measure but also had a great psychological impact on both the mainstream and the Japanese population. It hindered the Japanese elite from identifying with any specific region, depriving them of a sense of roots, particularly in British Columbia. For mainstream Canadians, it removed a sense of burden and promoted assimilation of Japanese. For Japanese, then, region was used to undermine their identity. For this reason, Scots and Ukrainians are the focus here.

They make an interesting comparison since both were incorporated into their respective regions positively. Yet the prairie region historically was more relevant to Ukrainians than Nova Scotia was to Scots. As Ian McKay has pointed out, the Scottish elite led by Angus L. Macdonald publicized their ethnicity in part for the sake of tourism, and thus the targets of his scheme were both Scots and the general population outside the province.[89] While Macdonald's frequent addresses helped to attach to Scottish identity concrete purpose and meaning, including advertising the province, they were full of rhetoric, emphasizing more visible cultural symbols such as folk songs, music and tales, and place names than direct contributions to the province's history or development.[90] In this context, McKay argued that the enshrinement of Flora Macdonald, whose plaque was unveiled by the premier in Windsor in 1951, commemorating her short stay in the province, was irrelevant to its history.[91] In contrast, Ukrainianness was promoted neither as an official identity of any province nor as an artificial project, but a link between the two evolved more naturally. Ukrainianness in the cultural sphere, particularly in folk art, music, and dance, was celebrated in various places and recognized as an element of the region, yet the focus was more on economic contributions. The lieutenant governor of Manitoba, R.F. McWilliams, for example, told the fourth congress of the UCC that Ukrainians "are contributing greatly and will in the days to come contribute much more greatly to the up-building of this province."[92] However, though such comments recognized Ukrainian contributions as significant, they were directed toward the Ukrainian community rather than the general public.

~

The postwar period was characterized by idealism and optimistic attitudes toward the future, reflecting the end of World War II, the introduction of Canadian citizenship, and renewed ties with ethnic groups' homelands. Scots, Ukrainians, and Japanese all produced or redefined myths and collective memories, reflecting the consolidation of pan-Canadianism. In this context, a merger between Canadian and Ukrainian and Japanese myths and collective memories occurred, for both Ukrainian and Japanese elites tied their homeland symbols and myths to Canada and incorporated Canadian or regional elements into their collective memories. For Scots, such an overlap had always been the case, but they often tried to ethnicize Canadian identity, thereby making ethnicity an important means of self-expression in Canada. At the same time, both Ukrainian and Japanese elites sought to consolidate their ethnic communities, thus keeping ethnic diversity as an integral part of Canadian identity. A major result was the production of formal Ukrainian- and Japanese-Canadian histories that placed the particular ethnic experiences at the centre of Canadian history. Despite these similarities, homeland, Canada, and region had different impacts on the three ethnic groups. Above all, Ukrainians were the most equipped to develop their ethnic myths and collective memories to enhance their ethnic identity effectively, mainly for the continuity of homeland and Canadian myths and symbols, and to stress the relevance of the prairie provinces as the core of their imagined community. Japanese, in contrast, needed to invent a new way of associating with homeland and region, which never carried the same meanings as they did in the interwar period. Scots also highlighted their ethnicity, producing Scottish-Canadian history, promoting Scottishness as Nova Scotian identity, and fantasizing their Highland roots, thereby resisting being just Canadians.

CHAPTER 6

Ethnic Movements and the Road to Multiculturalism

The 1960s witnessed a dramatic transformation in the situation of ethnic groups in Canada. Influenced by increasing international awareness of the need to protect fundamental human rights, Prime Minister John Diefenbaker adopted the Canadian Bill of Rights in 1960, which, for the first time, officially banned discrimination based on ethnicity, religion, race, or sex. By then, ethnic elites had already had an impact on Canadian ethnic pluralism and democracy, trying to insert their agendas into mainstream politics. Yet major changes occurred in ethnic politics during the first half of the 1960s connected to the rise of French nationalism in Quebec, which coincided with modernization of the province in fields such as education, politics, and economy. French Canadians began challenging the federal government for removal of unequal treatment as well as protection of their cultural and linguistic rights as equal partners of British Canadians. Results included appointment of the Royal Commission on Bilingualism and Biculturalism (B&B Commission) in 1963 and introduction of the Official Languages Act in 1969.

These new developments gave Ukrainian and Japanese elites another opportunity to gain more influence within their communities and Canadian society. Recognizing that the mainstream Canadian elite, then still dominated by those of British origin, could no longer ignore the voices of ethnic minorities and their impacts both within and outside Canada, Ukrainians in particular intensified ethnic activism in pursuit of equal partnership. They launched a vigorous campaign against the B&B Commission's initial reports, which defined Canada as a bilingual and bicultural rather than multicultural nation. The B&B Commission's understanding that the British and French only were co-builders of Canada fuelled such resistance. Their lobby led the B&B Commission to publish its fourth report, *The Cultural Contribution of the Other Ethnic Groups,* in 1969 and to recognize their participation in Canadian cultural and economic life.[1]

My goal in this chapter is to construct the evolution of multiculturalism from ethnic elites' eyes, highlighting the differences among their views. I argue that ethnic input was fundamental to the birth of the federal policy of multiculturalism, yet the Ukrainian definition dominated the period. The first part of the chapter focuses on the different political goals that Scottish, Ukrainian, and Japanese elites attached to multiculturalism. It examines why Ukrainian nationalists led the multiculturalism movement, as opposed to the lack of enthusiasm among Japanese, and argues that multiculturalism designed to guarantee collective rights was more relevant to Ukrainian nationalists than to Japanese. Although it became an accepted fact that "the multicultural movement was spearheaded largely by Ukrainian Canadians,"[2] the reasons why they and not other groups led the lobby have not been fully explored. Political scientist Bohdan Bociurkiw, one of the founding members of the Ukrainian Canadian University Students' Union (UCUSU) and a lobbyist for multiculturalism, outlined some of the possible reasons. They included Ukrainians' "historical aversion to assimilation," a "strong sense of collective responsibility for the preservation of the group's ethnocultural values in Canada," "the lasting commitment of Ukrainian churches to the preservation of the national cultural-linguistic heritage," "the group's highly developed capacity for grass-roots organization," and "the nature of Ukrainian settlement in the Prairie provinces."[3] While all of these points seem convincing, some preconditions, which created these features, deserve closer examination. Ukrainians' constructed distinctiveness as an influential ethnic minority can best be highlighted through comparison with a more marginalized racial group, just as looking only at Ukrainians would hide other groups' input into the policy of multiculturalism.[4] In the second part of this chapter, I thus argue that, despite differences between Ukrainians and Japanese and between mainstream Canadians and both ethnic elites in terms of how they viewed multiculturalism, all parties promoted the concept as Canada's new identity. "Unity in diversity" was widely celebrated, for example, during the Canadian Centennial in 1967. For both Ukrainians and Japanese, the federal implementation of multiculturalism in 1971 was the culmination of a long quest. I thus focus in this chapter mainly on Ukrainians and Japanese. Although Scots produced many individuals who advocated the mosaic, such as Watson Kirkconnell and Lord Tweedsmuir, they were not active in the multicultural movement and rather supported bilingualism and biculturalism. This was mainly because the multiculturalism movement initially focussed on a linguistic question.

Defining Canadian Multiculturalism: Ukrainian Leadership and Priorities

The divergence between Ukrainian nationalists and both Japanese and their fellow communist Ukrainians resulted from a number of things. First, the rise of Ukrainianism was due to a few Ukrainian nationalists appointed or elected to high-level offices in the federal government. Japanese, in contrast, did not possess such leaders, and thus their voice was limited if not silent, and communist Ukrainians were associated mainly with the marginalized Communist Party of Canada. Second, the demand of French Canadians for rights equal to those of the British, based on the conviction that they were a founding people of Canada, prompted Ukrainian nationalists to claim that they were also participants in western Canada's nation building. In addition to their numbers in the west, cultivation of the prairie soil, in which Ukrainians took part, made them feel fundamental to Canada's economic development. This view was also advocated by communist Ukrainians, though for democratic equality rather than multiculturalism. Japanese, in contrast, neither had a large population nor established the same sense of roots in Canada after resettlement, and thus they tended to acquiesce to British and French leadership. Third, French-Canadian nationalism, which stressed linguistic and cultural rights, provided the impetus for Ukrainian nationalists to insist on preservation of their own language and culture because of both their whiteness and their lack of a homeland.[5] However, in the Japanese case, marginalization based on race hindered any campaign for collective linguistic and cultural rights, convincing Japanese that their ethnocultural boundary was permanent. Rather, as in the years immediately after the war, they were more interested in individual rights, hoping to be liberated from their often negative image. Fourth, Ukrainian nationalists continued to have their homeland cause—the independence of Ukraine—into the 1960s, while Japanese no longer possessed any clear homeland political agenda tied to nationalism. Ukrainians' fight for liberty naturally was tied to the principle of human rights and called for scrutiny of the protection of rights in Soviet Ukraine. For these reasons, I inevitably focus in this section on Ukrainian nationalists, with some comparisons with Japanese and communist Ukrainians.

By the 1960s, a number of Ukrainian nationalists had been appointed and elected to high-level federal and provincial offices[6] where they could influence mainstream policies and try to insert their own interests. Scholars have often attributed success of the multicultural movement to Ukrainian individuals such as Paul Yuzyk and Jaroslav B. Rudnyckyj, linguist and professor of Slavic studies at the University of Manitoba. Rudnyckyj was appointed to the B&B Commission, and Yuzyk to the Senate, in 1963. That they appeared on the mainstream political scene at this time was not a coincidence. Given mounting pressure from the French and ethnic groups such as Ukrainians, the Canadian government needed to show the ethnic diversity of policy makers. That Rudnyckyj was among ten commissioners who were mainly French and British in origin, yet included a Ukrainian and Pole,[7] indicated the government's scheme to include, at least in the public eye, the voices of other ethnic groups. These prominent individuals, both strongly identified with the nationalist camp, were supported by influential organizations such as the Ukrainian Canadian Committee (UCC) and UCUSU.

Mainstream politicians were also concerned about attracting ethnic votes, which constituted another factor that distinguished Ukrainians from Japanese. The former were still concentrated in particular constituencies in the Prairies, which made their vote desirable to count,[8] while Japanese, despite their enfranchisement in 1948, never had ethnic blocs that could produce or appear to produce a collective vote. The relocation policy after World War II only made the situation worse. Whether or not Ukrainians, particularly after the war, voted automatically or in large numbers for their "own" candidates was another issue, but the fact that mainstream leaders believed that voting behaviour was affected by ethnicity is more important here.[9] Such a belief was promoted, to some degree, by the Ukrainian elite, who claimed to represent their people. Yuzyk, in a letter to Prime Minister Diefenbaker just one month before the federal election in 1963, stressed how successful he had been in the campaign to woo Ukrainians on behalf of the Progressive Conservative Party.[10] He wrote that he had enticed Ukrainians to a meeting by speaking to "14 priests and many leaders of organizations, who made enthusiastic announcements in the churches and halls." "The response of the Ukrainians was good," he continued, "as about 3,000 were in the Auditorium or in the large crowds outside."[11] While Yuzyk utilized his ethnic origin to sell himself to Diefenbaker, he was well aware that his strong commitment to Ukrainian affairs, particularly those beyond Canada's jurisdiction, would not benefit him among mainstream politicians. He thus presented himself as primarily an enthusiastic Progressive Conservative member: "I have actively worked for our Party in every federal and Manitoba provincial election since 1957, and have received acknowledgements."[12] His stance of putting the party before his ethnicity, at least in communications to his leader, was clear when he stated that "you may hear the criticism that I am involved too much in 'Ukrainian' affairs. I do keep in close touch with the leading Ukrainian organizations, both secular and church, for I believe that this kind of involvement helps to produce sympathy and support for the Conservative party. It is a good way to promote a broad and dynamic Canadianism. But as you are aware, I am constantly active in general Canadian affairs."[13] Such a comment suggests that a dichotomy between Canadian and ethnic issues persisted. His own political campaigning thus required an adroit negotiation between the party and ethnicity, showing ethnicity as a means of mobilizing Ukrainian voters but otherwise downplaying it.

The Ukrainian nationalist elite, however, had to be perceived more as Ukrainian representatives than as party officials by their fellow Ukrainians to win the competition within their own circles. It was a necessary step toward gaining influence in Canadian politics to collect as much support as they could inside the ethnic community. The interdependency between people such as Yuzyk and the Ukrainian community was obvious. When the senatorship in Manitoba became available, Basil Kushnir, president of the UCC, wrote to Diefenbaker to clarify the UCC's official request "to reserve this position for a Ukrainian candidate." The UCC supported Yuzyk, stating that he "would treat their positions with seriousness" and "be associated with their organized life." Kushnir also argued that his opinion and support represented "the Ukrainian community in Canada," suggesting that the masses were behind him.[14] Obviously, for Kushnir and the UCC, having an ethnic Ukrainian in the Senate was important or even necessary to have Ukrainian voices heard. Kushnir thus made it clear that, once Yuzyk was appointed, both he and Progressive Conservative leaders must listen to Ukrainians and their demands: "If any party would wish to exploit the UCC exclusively for its own advantage or use its platform to gain political influence that would result only in a loss both to the party and to the UCC."[15] Such comments indicated that Kushnir was also using ethnicity as a negotiating tool to build his influence, making the most of his leadership at the UCC. Yuzyk, on the other hand, regarded the support from Kushnir and other leaders of the UCC as the key to his success since it gave him collective power. "Mr. W. Kochan, Executive Director of the Ukrainian Canadian Committee which unites the activities of some 28 dominion-wide organizations," he wrote, "was kind enough to notify me that a letter was sent to you last week in the matter of the Manitoba senatorship." "I am very happy," he added, "that the President of the UCC, Monsignor Dr. W. Kushnir, is giving me his full support."[16]

Once appointed to prominent positions, Ukrainians such as Yuzyk always placed priority on agendas that appealed to many Ukrainians, speaking on behalf of the UCC and its member organizations. This points to the extent that ethnicity provided elites with strength when they competed with other politicians for further influence and power. Yuzyk advocated the notion of a multicultural Canada, while Rudnyckyj on the B&B Commission pushed the principle of regional bilingualism and linguistic rights for major ethnic groups. Both men were concerned with collective rights, which Ukrainians should get as a group and which should be equal to those of the British and French. Yuzyk's maiden speech in the Senate in 1964, entitled "Canada: A Multicultural Nation," stressed the contributions of "Third Element ethnic groups" as "co-builders of the West and other parts of Canada."[17] It acquired a symbolic status as an address that established the foundations on which Canada and Ukrainians should stand. In a similar vein, Rudnyckyj became a key figure in claiming cultural and linguistic rights for "other groups" in the British- and French-led B&B Commission. Although these two men only confirmed the view that Ukrainian nationalists had nurtured since the interwar period, the significance of their roles lay in the fact that their claims were officially made and perceived in the context of rising ethnonationalism in Canada.

That the Japanese elite, during the same time, had to devote much space in the *New Canadian* stressing the need for the National Japanese Canadian Citizens Association (NJCCA) and its branches, in response to the general decline in membership and lack of interest, is suggestive. The promotion of Canada as a bilingual and bicultural country seemed, to a greater or lesser degree, acceptable to Japanese or at least not something that stirred up a collective demand among them as nation builders. While the *New Canadian* supported Yuzyk and his activities, it tended to just cover what was happening and look at it favourably but not express its stance.[18] That the Japanese represented the only non-white racial group that presented a brief indicated lack of interest among other racial groups. The sheer number of Ukrainian conferences, seminars, meetings, and printed materials that examined the status of Ukrainians and multiculturalism, and of Ukrainian proposals submitted to the B&B Commission, suggested that the issue was basically a Ukrainian one.[19] For example, in response to the first volume of the B&B Commission's report, the UCC issued a white paper in 1968 calling for inclusion of other ethnic groups' rights in the Constitution.[20] Besides many UCC meetings, one of the most notable events was the Thinkers' Conference on Cultural Rights held in Toronto in 1968. Organized by Yuzyk, the conference was a public demonstration of resistance against bilingualism and biculturalism.[21]

Ukrainians were more apt than Japanese to react to the idea that Canada was an "equal partnership" between the British and French since their past experiences were less marginalized. Resenting the B&B Commission's mandate to investigate "what steps should be taken to develop the Canadian

Confederation on the basis of an equal partnership between the two founding races," while "taking into account the contribution made by the other ethnic groups to the cultural enrichment of Canada,"[22] Ukrainians stressed their accomplishments, emphasizing the celebratory side of their past from immigration to community building. Japanese, in contrast, because of long-term marginalization, had not developed positive myths. Also, since they had established a new life after relocation, the immediate postwar tendency to look to the future with hope rather than at the past gradually faded away. Instead, the 1960s witnessed a growing emphasis on injustice and racism in the past. It was particularly difficult, under such circumstances, for Japanese to claim a part in Canada's "national" experience. There were many differences in how the two groups remembered their pasts in Canada during this period. My focus here will be on myths of immigration and settlement as well as the two world wars, which represented "integration" into Canada for Ukrainians but "exclusion" for Japanese.

That the Canadian government needed Ukrainian immigrants but not Japanese in the late nineteenth century created a gap in terms of how they produced myths and collective memories. Although recognizing that their people had been categorized as ethnically "undesirable" immigrants, Ukrainian leaders often stressed the fact that Canada had been in need of farmers who could settle and cultivate the prairie land in the late nineteenth and early twentieth centuries. For example, the brief to the B&B Commission from the UCC national headquarters emphasized how "the Canadian Government discovered the great potential value of Ukrainian settlers and in many ways directed their movement to Canada."[23] Another brief stated that the influx of Ukrainian immigrants was a result of "the insistent call from the Government of Canada who badly needed hard-working people to open up the West and develop the land."[24] That Canadians had also had doubts about Ukrainians was ignored for the moment, for the history of "inclusion" was more relevant in the pursuit of full partnership with the British and French. The Japanese collective memory of immigration, in contrast, did not have a celebratory side since Japanese were considered racially "undesirable" and economically unnecessary. The Gentlemen's Agreement of 1908 between Canada and Japan, which limited Japanese male immigrants to Canada to 400 annually, indicated that they were never wanted. The "prejudice and discrimination inflicted upon the people of Japanese ancestry from the time they arrived," and the fact that British Columbians hoped to keep their province a "British society" now, became a common start to their immigration story.[25] The Japanese elite thus tended to believe that they were fortunate just to enter Canada and never could or would be equal to the British and French.

The scale of settlement in the west and its impact on Canada's economic growth were other factors that made it easier for Ukrainians than Japanese to promote themselves as equal partners. Undoubtedly, that the Ukrainian population was up to seven times larger than its Japanese counterpart in the first half of the twentieth century rendered Ukrainians greater contributors to Canada's economy. Yet the gap was the result of the Ukrainian elite's tactics and myth making as well as sheer numbers. Ukrainian leaders adroitly overestimated the scale of their settlements and cultivation of the prairie land, while Japanese rarely developed such a psychology of mass contribution, both because their participation in Canadian society had just begun and because the relocation severed Japanese roots in British Columbia. Eloquent and exaggerated statements of the Ukrainian role in developing the national economy could be found in Yuzyk's speeches and book, which compared the acres that Ukrainians had cultivated with those of the French and listed their subsequent involvement in the economy, such as owning small stores.[26] These accomplishments were due to Ukrainians' physical and mental attributes. According to Yuzyk, Ukrainians' "centuries-old background of farming in their native land and their devotion to hard work and their families" made them achieve "the most spectacular progress in agriculture," and "the size of the average farm" was still increasing. Ukrainians thus were uncontroversial "builders of Western Canada"[27] and "unquestionably 'founders' in their own right just as much as British or French settlers of earlier vintage."[28] Communist Ukrainians also adopted the position that "Ukrainians were the spearhead of the great human army that was to conquer the Prairies and open the West," which earlier groups had failed to do.[29]

In contrast to the firm determination of Ukrainians to claim equal partnership with the British and French, though Japanese leaders did emphasize their part in Canada's economy, such comments were rare. A brief that the NJCCA submitted in 1960 to Ellen L. Fairclough, minister of citizenship and immigration, for the removal of restrictions on Japanese immigration provides a good example of how the Japanese elite positioned their people in Canada: "In times of peace, too, Japanese Canadians can claim to have helped in strengthening the structure of Canada as a nation. Japanese immigration began about the time that Western Canada entered into a period of rapid expansion and development. New rail lines pushed through the mountains to the Pacific, and the rich resources of the coastal area ... were being tapped. Manual labor was in high demand and the immigrants from the Orient met this demand.... The contribution of these immigrants towards the early economic development of the West cannot be regarded as small."[30] Obviously, such a comment indicated the Japanese elite's attempt to incorporate the contributions of Japanese to the nation's collective memory. Yet Japanese differed from Ukrainians in that their point of such comments was to demand the end of discrimination rather than equal partnership.

Although the idea that Ukrainians could be a "third nation" in Canada had already been launched in the interwar period, Yuzyk in particular tried to incorporate other ethnic groups into one collective entity in pursuit of equal status with the British and French. He often acted as a coordinator of non-British and non-French peoples, whom he referred to as the "Third Element" even though ethnic groups had rarely cooperated or communicated with each other. According to his theory, there were "three elements" in Canada: the British, the French, and the rest, "consisting of all the other ethnic groups, including the Indians and Eskimos."[31] While categorizing Natives and others as one group, the special reference to Natives was significant. They were not in the B&B Commission's frame of reference, but Yuzyk recognized that they had been in Canada before the British and French and were thus considered to be entitled to rights. In the same speech, he pointed out the decline of the British population in Canada between 1901 and 1961, to less than 50 percent since 1951, before arguing that "the Third Element ethnic groups, now numbering approximately five million persons, are co-builders of the West and other parts of Canada, along with the British and the French Canadians, and are just as permanent a part of the Canadian scene."[32] Ukrainian organizations tended to adopt his viewpoint and repeated it especially in their briefs to the B&B Commission pushing for multiculturalism. All the same, the "Third Element" was a concept that targeted the mainstream elite more than the ethnic groups. The lack of reference to it in the *New Canadian*, for example, indicated that the "third force" did not catch the Japanese imagination.[33] Although Yuzyk did try to promote some communication among ethnic groups, organizing a number of meetings, he was more engaged in dialogue with the British and French. The Thinkers' Conference, attended predominantly by mainstream leaders and Ukrainians, for example, stated in a rather tentative tone that "the Conference should in no way be considered a formation of a third political force, but rather the expression of a serious concern by those citizens making up the third element of Canada's population in the cultural development of our country."[34]

Participation in the world wars was regarded by both Ukrainian and Japanese elites as proof of their contributions to Canada, yet it created the greatest gap between the two ethnic groups, stressing inclusion among the former and exclusion among the latter. In both wars, Ukrainians were not without problems, facing suspicion from mainstream Canadians. The fact that in World War I many of them, as Austro-Hungarian subjects, became enemy aliens and were interned showed that Ukrainians were also marginalized.[35] World War II also imposed on them a test of loyalty, yet it provided them with the first decisive moment in which they were expected to join other Canadians for a common cause.[36] Despite this discrimination, the Ukrainian elite once again tended to emphasize the better side of the story—Ukrainians' participation in the war as historical evidence of their equal partnership. For Japanese, in contrast, except for special cases, that they were not only banned from enlisting in the Canadian military forces in the latest war but also interned delayed the emergence of a heroic and glorious story of wartime achievements.[37]

Although their loyalty had often been divided during the wars, nationalist Ukrainians promoted heroes and stories from the wars that stressed patriotism to Canada. A typical statement, such as the one that appeared in the brief of the Ukrainian branch of the UCC presented to the B&B Commission, commented on equal partnership and a sense of unity in the struggle: "Many of the comrades of these Ukrainian Canadian veterans gave their lives on the fields of battle. They believed that their sacrifice was for the full democratic equality of all Canadians. No distinction was made in battles between a Ukrainian-Canadian soldier, a French-Canadian soldier, or a soldier of British racial origin. It would be manifestly unjust to make that distinction now among these same veterans or their children or their languages and cultures."[38] Obviously, the history of World War II was being rewritten as an event of cooperation and full participation among all Canadians—especially the British, French, and Ukrainians. The fact that it intensified suspicions of certain ethnic groups was completely erased. In this context, Philip Konowal, awarded the Victoria Cross for his accomplishment during World War I, became a symbol of "bravery" and "the extreme sacrifices" of Ukrainian soldiers who fought for "Canadian freedom and democracy."[39] In contrast, Japanese turned more toward stories of segregation and persecution to revitalize ethnic consciousness during the 1960s, which had declined to a large degree after the postwar removal of restrictions and acquisition of the franchise.[40] The *New Canadian* illustrated the tendency to focus on the tensions among Canadians rather than their cooperation: "World War II then overshadowed this tense local confrontation—but set events in motion which involved the whole of white Canada in the destruction of our community. The conquerors of the Indian now declared war on their Asian cousins.... The perceived threat was eliminated by destroying the Japanese community through internment."[41] Such a memory became a drive for Japanese to continue fighting against racism; *Tairiku jihô* encouraged them not to "forget the inhumane treatment" and to work against "discrimination" and for "racial equality."[42]

Integration versus marginalization also created a gap between Ukrainian nationalists and Japanese in terms of how they defined and envisioned multiculturalism. The first difference appeared in how the two elites perceived the roles that the federal and provincial governments could play in the promotion of ethnic identity. Ukrainian nationalists tried to define the mainstream by incorporating themselves into the leading groups, while Japanese still sensed their separateness from mainstream Canadians, always waiting for recognition. For Ukrainian nationalists, multiculturalism involved "official" intervention in the preservation of their ethnicity, while Japanese chose to express their ethnic distinctiveness and contribution by their own means. Consequently, Ukrainian nationalists were more active in terms of negotiating with governments.

The policy of multiculturalism as Ukrainian nationalists envisioned it expanded on bilingualism and biculturalism to include the institutionalization of ethnic languages and cultures as an official Canadian identity. For them, it was the legitimization of the ethnic pluralism that they had nurtured since the interwar period. Formal support for Ukrainian language and culture had to be encouraged through public infrastructure such as schools and media on the ground that it was their natural right as equal partners of the British and French. The UCC, together with other groups such as Poles and Germans, submitted a brief to Ottawa in 1962 criticizing "the fact that the CBC ignores the interest of a quarter—and sometimes even a half—of the Canadian population." Yet these Canadians, according to the brief, fulfilled "all the duties flowing from their citizenship," which once again included clearing the land, founding industries, and serving in wars. The brief then stressed the government's responsibility, arguing that "much more could be done in music, literature, the arts, theatre and variety shows to give a wider view of the contributions and activities of the ethnic groups."[43] A similar claim was made with regard to language education in public schools. Ukrainian nationalist organizations saw both secondary and postsecondary education as the main vehicles in this field. Although Ukrainian instruction in Manitoba's schools continued to be on the agenda,[44] recommendations sent to the B&B Commission by the USRL included the teaching of Ukrainian "as a credited, second language subject on an optional basis" in schools and universities,[45] instruction in Ukrainian "wherever a sufficient number of students"[46] could be expected, and standardization of the level "according to accepted academic requirements for French and English."[47] The fourth volume of the B&B Commission's report never satisfied Ukrainians, for it did not provide any concrete plan for the promotion of ethnic culture and language. For example, Bohdan Krawchenko, president of UCUSU, criticized the report, arguing that recognition of ethnic groups' cultural contributions to Canada was not sufficient and that more public money should be available for Ukrainian programs at school, the National Film Board, and the CBC.[48]

Japanese, in contrast, had not yet reached the stage of claiming their linguistic and cultural rights within the public infrastructure given that the government had always discouraged them from remaining distinctive. They chose to showcase the virtues of Japanese culture and language in the first place by their own means and resources, relying on their own ethnic organizations and trying to attract participation from mainstream Canadians. As always, they tried to eliminate racial discrimination, exhibit the best parts of Japanese cultural heritage, and bolster mutual understanding with other Canadians, as an article in the *New Canadian* argued: "The ideal form for an ethnic group is one that allows free access to Canadian citizens of different ethnic origins."[49] The NJCCA's role in this area was emphasized frequently in the *New Canadian,* which contended that the organization had been "most active in presenting to the public … the culture and beauty of the Japanese people."[50] The NJCCA brief, submitted to the B&B Commission, encouraged promotion of non-English and non-French languages, saying that "the study of other ethnic languages be encouraged whenever and wherever possible."[51] But it wanted such encouragement as a means of furthering communication among ethnic groups rather than a right or through public funding. The priority on unity and cooperation was clear when the brief maintained that "we further believe that the emphasis should be placed, not on multi-national or racial origin, not on the hyphenated Canadian, but on 'Canadianism'—one and indivisible."[52]

Such an ambition did not exist only at the theoretical level and was reflected in the construction of the Japanese Canadian Centre in Toronto in 1964. Although built as a meeting place for Japanese, it was more than a recreational facility. As the first large-scale Japanese project since the end of World War II, the centre symbolized how Japanese were now incorporated into mainstream Canada and reflected how they conceptualized their role in the context of multiculturalism. For them, according to an article on the new centre, multiculturalism was more a matter of harmonious coexistence and understanding between mainstream society and the Japanese community than a guarantee of collective rights. As a manifestation of "Canadianism" that was not confined to cooperation between the British and French, it also recognized "the composition of the Canadian population" and challenged the B&B Commission's notion that "two languages and cultures only, or two solitudes," made Canada.[53] A second article on the centre made its view of multiculturalism and its own role clear. "A prime position" among the centre's activities, it said, "is given to the cultural aspects of exchange and contribution to Canadian society, which can only be achieved by opening the door wide to the Canadian public."[54] In addition to opening Japanese to other Canadians, the centre was a means to join with them for the creation of Canadian identity since it was called a "belonging through participation" project.[55] The centre thus was highly politicized as a statement of improved relations between Japanese and mainstream society. Prime Minister Lester B. Pearson, in turn, admitted at the opening ceremony that the Japanese evacuation was "a black mark against Canada's traditional fairness and devotion to the principles of human rights." However, he continued, there was "one compensation" in that "relocation brought to the attention of other parts of Canada the strong character and the fine qualities of our Japanese citizens and settlers."[56] Although Pearson's speech was appreciated by Japanese as the first official statement that admitted Canada's fault, it met with criticism from mainstream Canadians, who thought that Canada's wartime action was justifiable.[57] Such a conflict showed that the Japanese goal to build a better relationship with mainstream society had just begun.

The second difference in how Ukrainians and Japanese defined multiculturalism was seen in the kinds of rights that each group attached to it. Ukrainian nationalists, as "white ethnics," saw multiculturalism as a means to protect their collective cultural and linguistic rights, stressing their participation in Canadian society on the one hand and safeguarding their distinctiveness as an ethnic group on the other.[58] In contrast, Japanese, whose racial visibility would always hinder their integration into Canadian society, avoided highlighting their ethnic boundaries.[59] For them, multiculturalism was another form of democracy that guaranteed individual rights and freedoms regardless of cultural, linguistic, or racial background. The legacy of the federal government's postwar resettlement scheme, which rejected the creation of any identifiable Japanese communities, dominated Japanese mass psychology, making the establishment of ethnic compartments something negative.[60]

Provoked by the federal government's launch of bilingualism and biculturalism, Ukrainian nationalists developed their own theory of a cultural and linguistic territory belonging to Ukrainians. Their argument was twofold. First, French Canadians' cultural and linguistic privileges should be kept within Quebec; second, other ethnic languages and cultures should be promoted alongside English in the rest of Canada.[61] By drawing the line between French-speaking and English-speaking territories and referring to the basic French rights that the British North America Act guaranteed, Ukrainian nationalists recognized "the fact that Canada's official languages" were

"English and French, in the restricted sense."[62] The UCC vigorously denied the constitutionality of the Official Languages Act, arguing that "the attempts by the federal government to pass the Official Languages Act Bill C-120 and to amend the entrenched language provisions of the British North America Act are not only unconstitutional but also without historical foundation."[63] Ukrainians' biggest concern was the fact that the special status of English and French would once again make those who spoke other languages second-class citizens. Thus, the UCC argued, "it is submitted that the term 'official' in itself suggests a superior status. It is further submitted that to brand two of our Canadian languages as being 'official' places other Canadian languages in an inferior secondary connotation and one which, we feel, will eventually lead to varying degrees of discrimination. All languages used in Canada are Canadian."[64]

Outside Quebec, the UCC argued, bilingualism should mean "the use of the mother language plus the dominant language of the respective province."[65] Such attempts to draw territorial boundaries for ethnic linguistic and cultural privileges were expanded by Jaroslav Rudnyckyj. His position, which divided ethnic groups into language families—Germanic, Latin, Slavic, and Eskimo-Indian—refuted the idea of a "Third Force" that categorized non-British and non-French groups into one group.[66] For him, such a categorization overestimated the superiority of English and French and ignored the hierarchy among the other languages. He argued instead that Ukrainian, "as representative of the Slavic group,"[67] not only deserved an official status with English and French but also should be recognized on the Prairies as a "regional language" since it was "used by 10% or more of the population of a province or territory," according to the 1961 census.[68] The status of "regional language" should include privileges in "education," "media," and "usage in the internal organizational life of the given group."[69] Rudnyckyj's view gained popularity among other Ukrainian leaders as a new interpretation of bilingualism.[70]

The Japanese elite avoided any attempt to territorialize their ethnic community or to create a closed Japanese society in Canada. Facing a dilemma between the race and ethnicity often regarded as inseparable by mainstream Canadians, they saw multiculturalism as a solution to racism and a key for promoting an individual's fundamental human rights. The *New Canadian* clearly suggested that the human rights issue began preoccupying the Japanese elite.[71] For them, the promotion of ethnic identity through the NJCCA was still valuable for the upward mobility of Japanese in Canadian society, but community leaders were well aware that overemphasis on ethnoracial distinctiveness would only accelerate the alienation of their own grassroots from the organized Japanese community. The masses' general indifference to the NJCCA and multiculturalism and the tendency of not wanting "to be reminded of their Japanese-ness" were apparent by the 1960s.[72] The NJCCA thought that it had to justify and explain its activities and raison d'être, advertising the roles that it had played or could play in the field of fundamental human rights. The *New Canadian* published one appeal, which pointed out lingering discrimination against Japanese in employment and argued that the NJCCA was still needed "to meet the challenge of prejudice."[73] The NJCCA, according to its advocates, was "a single link in a strong chain of minority organizations, which find their legal outlet in the Human Rights Commission [of Ontario]" in their pursuit of civil liberty and freedom.[74] Influenced, to some extent, by the Japanese American Citizens League (JACL), the NJCCA assigned itself the role to work "so that all Canadians may enjoy the full measure of citizenship and opportunity that should be the birthright of every Canadian."[75] While it was not as vigorous as its American counterpart in this regard, it kept in close contact with mainstream groups such as the Ontario Human Rights Commission and the Ontario Royal Commission on Civil Rights.[76] Its activities were moderate, focussing on issues such as banning the term "Jap" and eliminating discrimination in employment and housing.[77] It also emphasized the necessity of cooperation and organized activities for human rights by pointing out "the problem of 'just being human,'" without any ethnoracial affiliation.[78] Lucien C. Kurata, reeve of Swansea, Ontario, for example, criticized the lack of interest in the NJCCA's general meeting in 1964. "The greatest problem within racial minorities," he said, was "the basic selfishness of human beings, being exemplified by their ignorance, intellectual dishonesty, and sometimes the problem of an inferiority complex."[79]

Communist Ukrainians took a slightly different approach to multiculturalism than did both nationalist Ukrainians and Japanese. Although their arguments had less impact on policy making than those of their nationalist rivals, they were unique in that they represented the voice of Canadians still facing prejudice for their political ideology. Rather than defining multiculturalism, communist Ukrainians tended to refute others' definitions and activities. While they obviously advocated preservation of Ukrainian language and culture as a means of promoting communism, their stance differed from that of nationalists, for they supported neither cultural and linguistic collective rights nor the notion of the "third force" and took a moderate approach to Quebec sovereignty.[80] In their view, following the communist position, ethnicity was transient, and, in a brief submitted to the B&B Commission together with communist organizations from eleven other ethnic groups, they criticized the notion of the mosaic as making ethnicity "static" and creating "permanent little islands of immutable cultural values."[81] In addition, they argued that the "third force" implied "identity of a homogeneous power," which had never existed.[82] Communists envisioned a Soviet type of federalism in Canada and criticized Anglo-Saxon chauvinism.[83] Implicitly, they were sending a message to nationalist Ukrainians that the idea of Ukrainian independence in Europe was equally dangerous. Their multiculturalism had some similarities with Japanese demands, in terms of placing civil rights and an end to discrimination over collective rights, but communist Ukrainians were more concerned about discrimination on an ideological basis.[84] They stressed the promotion of fundamental human rights and argued that the only way to solve Canada's ethnic conflicts would be found in the policies of the Canadian left, which represented "the labour and democratic base in our society."[85]

Although mainstream elites and organizations could not ignore the political pressure and activism of Ukrainian nationalists, their understanding of ethnic pluralism leaned more toward equal rights for all Canadians and national unity. Facing the French-Canadian separatist movement in Quebec, they had to avoid divisions within the rest of Canada. The B&B Commission's fourth report, which demonstrated the historical contributions of other groups to Canadian economy and culture, was intended to recognize non-British and non-French peoples—particularly Ukrainians—without promoting further ethnic divisions. As such, the report did not propose any future plans, especially for protecting collective rights.[86] For example, Rudnyckyj's proposal for the "constitutional recognition" of "regional languages" was rejected by the B&B Commission and widely criticized as something that might "Balkanize" Canada.[87] The Canadian Citizenship Council also provided a good example of how the mainstream elite saw collective rights when it pointed out that they were "not the rights listed in the Declaration which have preoccupied the United Nations in recent years." "The revolutionary doctrine of collective rights," it continued, "is the one which is threatening our unity."[88] The council's work, as it declared, was limited to fields such as "the maintenance of human rights" that "should be the basic objectives of the citizens of Canada."[89]

Mainstream policy makers faced another dilemma in multiculturalism: namely, the extent to which they should take into account ethnic groups' homeland politics. For the mainstream elite, "culture" did not include much of the politics that defined ethnic groups' identities. For ethnic elites, in contrast, multiculturalism was a principle that recognized not only their cultural traditions but also their roots and identities that stretched beyond Canada.

Obviously, then, their homeland politics were inseparable from the "culture" that determined who they were, and multiculturalism should include official recognition of their dual loyalty to Canada and their respective homelands.

Yet only Ukrainian nationalists, because of Ukraine's lingering statelessness, were actively involved in homeland politics and their expanded definition of multiculturalism. While Japanese and communist Ukrainians both kept their loyalty to Japan and the Soviet Union respectively, international politics, to a large extent, were left to their formal homeland delegations in Canada and elsewhere. Ukrainian nationalist leaders, in contrast, tried to increase their scope of activity both as self-appointed diplomats on behalf of their homeland and as Canadian representatives, believing that Ukrainian independence would benefit Canada by destroying communism.[90] Their activities took on a new outlook in response to international developments in the cooperation of nations in postwar organizations such as the United Nations and North Atlantic Treaty Organization (NATO).[91] Yuzyk and Kushnir, for example, frequently discussed problems in the Soviet Union in government and international circles. Yuzyk, having served as part of the Canadian delegation to the eighteenth General Assembly of the United Nations in 1963 and as chairman of the Human Rights Commission for the World Congress of Free Ukrainians since 1961, was a devoted activist for Ukrainian independence. The UCC was also active in trying to influence the United Nations on behalf of Ukraine's right to sovereignty, submitting several memoranda to this effect to the assemblies in the 1960s.[92]

The representation of Ukraine by Ukrainian-Canadian leaders often conflicted with the interests of Canadian politicians. Although Canada, as part of the West in the ideologically polarized world, stood against communism, it tried to maintain peaceful relations with the Soviet Union to prevent a nuclear war. Prime Minister Pierre Trudeau, who endeavoured to strengthen the Soviet-Canadian relationship in particular, often needed to reconcile the two contradictory priorities. One of the most significant encounters between Ukrainian nationalists and the federal government occurred in 1971 when Trudeau signed the USSR-Canada Protocol, which approved scientific, technical, educational, cultural, and other exchanges between the two countries. In the same year, Trudeau visited Moscow, and Soviet premier Aleksei N. Kosygin spent several days in Ottawa. Such actions clearly demonstrated Trudeau's indifference to the sensitivity of the issue to Ukrainian nationalists and provoked the Ukrainian-Canadian community. Yuzyk criticized Trudeau strongly for failing to "bring up problems regarding particular nationalities within the Soviet Union, which have been deprived of certain freedoms," in his conversations with Kosygin.[93] Nationalist Ukrainian anger peaked when Trudeau, on his return to Canada from Moscow, made a comparison on the CBC between the Front de libération du Québec (FLQ), a left-wing terrorist organization that demanded the independence of Quebec from Canada, and imprisoned Ukrainian dissidents in the Soviet Union. For nationalist Ukrainians, Trudeau's comment not only supported the Soviet Union but also ignored the fact that the FLQ possessed an opposite ideology from that of Ukrainian nationalists. Yuzyk introduced in the Senate a memorandum submitted by the UCC to Trudeau saying that the community "was deeply hurt by his failure to acknowledge the legitimate aspirations of the Ukrainian people."[94] At the same time, the UCC and Yuzyk used the opportunity to bring up the Ukrainian question, asking the government to work on behalf of Ukrainians' rights in the Soviet Union.[95]

In this context, Ukrainian nationalists paid much attention to civic rights and freedoms in Soviet territory, for the immediate postwar optimism for Ukraine's independence faded with the increasing power of the Soviet Union. Such a humanitarian approach, they believed, would be more effective in the current context because they could suggest that the Ukrainian national question was no longer simply "their" problem but more a Canadian and even universal issue. In doing so, they became leading activists for the promotion of fundamental human rights. They actively petitioned the federal government about and reminded their masses of the "injustices" experienced by Ukrainians under the Soviet regime. Yuzyk, for example, frequently brought the question of fundamental human rights before the Senate, emphasizing the role that Canada could play in this field "as a signatory of the Universal Declaration of Human Rights."[96] In 1968, Kushnir submitted a memorandum on behalf of the UCC to Prime Minister Pearson:

> The observance of the International Year for Human Rights is followed by all Canadians of Ukrainian origin with special attention, as we are all greatly concerned with the new wave of violations of the fundamental human freedoms in Ukraine under the Soviet Regime. Thousands of letters received from relatives and first hand reports brought over by Canadian tourists confirm beyond any doubt the revival of secret police rule in today's Ukraine, which consequently results in an open breach of basic human rights such as the freedom of opinion, freedom of religion, the right to personal security and to public trial, the right to equal education and employment as well as the right to use the Ukrainian language and to participate in developing Ukrainian culture—not to mention the freedom of speech, of assembly and association and the sacred right to self determination and national independence.[97]

Another of Yuzyk's speeches, entitled "Canadian Freedom and Ukrainian Freedom," highlighted and even exaggerated the difficulties that Ukraine faced in comparison with the paradise-like image of Canada. Although Canada inherited "civilization and the democratic forms of government" from Britain, Ukraine's experience was full of hardship, injustice, and humiliation. Ukraine, Yuzyk explained, "fell victim in the seventeenth century to a backward, tyrannical and ruthless Muscovite Russia" and then to "the communist regime" that "continued the policy of an indivisible monolithic Russia."[98] Such a view of the struggling homeland reflected, in part, current positive developments toward the recognition of Ukrainian culture and language in Canada.

The multiculturalism movement, as a form of resistance to bilingualism and biculturalism, thus began under the initiative of Ukrainian nationalists. Having representatives in the Senate and on the B&B Commission who were motivated by cultural and linguistic survival as well as pride as nation builders equipped them for this leadership. While both communist Ukrainians and Japanese also joined the movement, they understood it in terms of ending discrimination and prejudice.

Making Multiculturalism Pan-Canadian: The Canadian Centennial

Multiculturalism, though interpreted variously by Ukrainian and Japanese elites to meet their own political agendas, was also a uniting force at another level. Internationally, multiculturalism enhanced a sense of distinctiveness and pride among Canadians since the introduction of such a policy was one of the first in the world. Domestically, when incorporated into Canada's 100-year history, the policy was believed to promote a sense among its peoples of being rooted in the country. "Unity in diversity" entered the popular vocabulary as the phrase that could bridge the two contradictory forces in Canadian identity. Although the federal government did not necessarily have a definite vision of how the policy could be developed as distinctively Canadian, it tried to elevate it to something more dynamic and inclusive than the earlier cultural mosaic so that it appealed to all Canadians. Such Canadianism was expected to overcome ethnic elites' hidden or unhidden political agendas. Undoubtedly, landmark occasions such as the Centennial in 1967 and its supplement, Expo 67, helped to define pan-Canadian identity based on multiculturalism but were also politically manipulated by both ethnic and mainstream elites.[99]

Incorporation of multiculturalism into Canada's origins had international implications, such as that Canada was different from the United States, where ethnic identity was expected to blend in the melting pot. This

Canadian self-image was not new, but it was particularly significant in the 1960s, when Canada's national unity was in question. The *Globe and Mail*, for example, quoted Lester B. Pearson from when he was leader of the opposition, claiming that Canadian Confederation "meant the rejection not only of political and economic annexation by the United States, but also of the American melting-pot concept of national unity," and "a settlement between the two founding races of Canada."[100] Similarly, the newspaper cited E.C. Manning, premier of Alberta, speaking at Alberta Day at Expo 67: "I am against special status for any province. I am also against the melting-pot concept. Each area has its differences and these should be fostered and preserved."[101] Obviously, his comment was directed at Quebec, yet it indicated his belief that the ethnic rights movement did not always have to take a form of regional separatism.

Ukrainian nationalists also rejected the American melting pot theory as a source of racial conflict in the United States and stressed Canada's uniqueness in pursuit of multiculturalism. Walter Tarnopolsky, a professor of law at the University of Saskatchewan and a human rights activist, argued that the melting pot theory, which claimed "the superiority of 'the American way of life,'" created both "intolerance internally" and "many of the difficulties in foreign policy as well."[102] Since Canada differed from both the "assimilationist" United States and the "totalitarian" Soviet Union, Ukrainian nationalists thought that it could become a world leader in terms of the peaceful coexistence of multiple ethnic or national groups. This perspective was best illustrated by Yuzyk when he exaggerated Canada's ethnic pluralist stance: "If we succeed, and we are well on the road to succeeding, to evolve the pattern of unity in continuing diversity through the application of the principle of Confederation and compromise, this will serve as precedent for other states in the world having similar population and cultural problems.... In Canada we have the world in miniature. World peace and order could be achieved if the principles of unity in continuing diversity, brotherhood, compromise and the recognition of the freedom and dignity of individuals and nations are honestly applied."[103]

As Canada reached its centennial year, the idealism of and aspirations for unity in diversity were projected back into Canadian history since Confederation, thereby giving multiculturalism historical roots. This interpretation of history asserted that Canada was a multicultural nation from the beginning and had maintained such traits for 100 years, a vision that it was hoped would help to promote a pan-Canadian spirit for the centennial celebrations and reduce the conflict of identities. The Canadian Citizenship

Council wrote as if multiculturalism had evolved in Canadian history without any major problems when it described Canada as "a country in which its people of diverse traditions, racial origins, religious beliefs and stations of life have learned to live with one another on the basis of equality and mutual respect."[104] Interwar and wartime racism and British dominance were erased from the past. Such idealization could also be seen in some Ukrainian writing during this period. *Ukrainskyi holos,* for example, stressed unity in diversity, calling it a "fundamental philosophy of our nation building, [which] should not be a propagandistic phrase of cheap politics."[105] Tarnopolsky went further:

> Our pluralistic society became a necessity for Canada more than a century before Sir Wilfrid Laurier. It became inevitable in 1763, when, following the defeat of the French by the British on the Plains of Abraham in 1759, New France was ceded to Great Britain. From that time on, when the British conquerors realized that they could neither liquidate nor assimilate the French-speaking population on the banks of the St. Lawrence, it became clear that this land would not be unilingual and homogeneous. Once ... the Quebec Act of 1774 recognized that a person did not have to be [an] English-speaking Protestant to participate in public life, these same rights had to be granted to others as well. Once these "others" started to enter Canada later in the nineteenth century, it became clear that there was not going to be just one way to be Canadian.[106]

Obviously, history was rewritten so that Canada might appear uniquely successful in the coexistence of ethnically diverse populations even though early in the twentieth century "Anglo-conformity" had hoped to create a homogeneous nation. In this context, distinguished politicians from the past and interwar advocates of the mosaic such as Watson Kirkconnell and Governor General Tweedsmuir became multiculturalists.[107] Yuzyk also elevated one of the Fathers of Confederation, Hector L. Langevin, to "a prophet of multicultural Canada," quoting his statement from 1865 that, "under Confederation, there will no longer be domination of one race over another, and if one section should be desirous of committing an act of injustice against another section, all the others would unite together to prevent it."[108] The fact that late-nineteenth- and early-twentieth-century immigrants were not in Langevin's vision at that time was ignored. Yuzyk also made Laurier an advocate of multiculturalism, calling him "a great Canadian leader who could foresee the shape of things to come" and "had the vision of a multicultural Canadian nation."[109]

Ukrainians' own version of Canada's 100 years, which situated their efforts at the centre of the story, exhibited a contrast with the official vision by emphasizing that the political activism of ethnic groups had created ethnic pluralism. *Ukrainskyi holos*, for example, talked about the peoples who were neither British nor French in origin: "In an effort to preserve them [ethnic traditions and values], these groups of citizens hoped to lobby and help two levels of governments, federal and provincial."[110] This statement suggests that Canada was not born multicultural and that it was ethnic groups' activities that provided the catalyst. Furthermore, nationalist Ukrainians implied, Ukrainian consciousness, which became the basis of multiculturalism, would not have been maintained without their efforts. *Ukrainskyi holos* argued that "the fundamental idea of the Ukrainian Self-Reliance League was to keep Ukrainians in Canada conscious Ukrainians, and to create the healthy foundation of Canadian citizenship among them."[111] Although communist Ukrainians had just recently converted to multiculturalist views, they joined this self-applause and emphasized the ULFTA's and later the AUUC's contributions in the promotion of Ukrainian heritage and identity in Canada for a century.[112]

Japanese, also looking back on Canada's past and their own past in the centennial year, stressed that their campaigns against discriminatory policies had built a foundation of ethnic pluralism. Japanese-Canadian history was interpreted as a history of struggling for civil rights, reflecting both the discrimination that they had faced in the past and a feeling that they were finally included in Canada's mainstream event. The Japanese franchise movement was highlighted as having helped to produce contemporary civic rights and multiculturalism, and thus the fight for full citizenship would continue to be their focus.[113] The *New Canadian* also related the Centennial to the developments in Canadian immigration policy, which had recently removed all racial restrictions on selection criteria, and argued that the policy was "won by the continuous fight of the Japanese and the JCCA."[114] Clearly, such comments suggest that Japanese, too, saw the growing consensus toward multiculturalism as the product of their work and not as mainstream society's design for Canada.

The Centennial thus incorporated the multiethnic nature of Canada into its programs, but at the same time national unity was a top priority. The Centennial served as a meeting place for all ethnic groups, and the obligation to participate was emphasized in the Centennial Commission's declaration of 1964, which stated that the purpose of the Centennial was "to stimulate and promote a pride in Canada by Canadians, a greater sense of unity between all Canadians and a personal involvement in the celebrations by every citizen."[115] Use of the term "Canadian" without distinguishing ethnically one from another in the declaration well illustrated that mainstream leaders hoped that there would be no tensions among Canadians of different ethnic origins on this occasion. Ethnic groups were strongly encouraged to participate to exhibit their ethnic heritages as components of the Canadian mosaic. At the conference that established the Folk Arts Council in 1964, Pearson, now prime minister, expressed his hope that the council would "ensure … full and vibrant participation of all our ethnic groups in our Centennial celebrations" to make it "an active force for national unity."[116] On another occasion, Judy LaMarsh, secretary of state, for example, stressed that the primary goal of the Centennial was to bring Canadian nationhood to another level, resisting any forces that might divide Canada politically or ethnically.[117]

The largest ethnic contribution to the Centennial was made by the Canadian Folk Arts Council, which included ethnic groups' cultural performances in music, art, dance, and food in the celebrations.[118] The occasion was designed to showcase Canada's multicultural nature and was welcomed with enthusiasm by Ukrainian nationalists and Japanese as an opportunity to develop all-inclusive Canadian identity. The Folk Arts Council was established as an organization for ethnic, religious, and cultural associations throughout Canada to encourage their participation in the Centennial. Leon Kossar, Ukrainian in origin and founder of the council, stressed the significance of ethnic folk arts and their incorporation into Canada's birthday: "The vigorous growth of the folk arts throughout the country in the past three years has been a source of pride and pleasurable surprise to the many community church and ethnic organizations that have done so much throughout Canada's history to preserve the valued cultural traditions of the past." Quoting the Folk Arts Council's brief to the Centennial Commission, he continued that "we have seen recently how much interest there is across our land in the multicultural composition of the nation. We also feel that this would be directly translated into Centennial programming that will make Canada's birthday one of close personal identification with every citizen of our country."[119] His comments indicated how members of the ethnic elite also adopted a somewhat rhetorical unity in diversity, recognizing that folk arts would be the best route to reflect their peoples' dual loyalty in the Centennial. The Japanese elite also valued the invitation to the Canadian Folk Arts Festival and the Canadian Pavilion at Expo 67 on the ground that ethnic groups would make a "kaleidoscope of color, music and fun."[120] Yet such celebration of the mosaic was also translated into their mission as an important component of Canadian identity, and active participation was encouraged. Edward Ide, president of the NJCCA, acknowledged the work of Kossar and called for the active involvement of all Japanese organizations in the Folk Arts Festival, regarding such an opportunity as a "privilege."[121] For Japanese, who had been focussing on their own means to promote culture, the council provided a great chance to show their cultural traditions to others.

For ethnic groups, the Centennial was an opportunity to display the harmony between their ethnic and their Canadian identities and served as a test case of how multiculturalism could or would be depicted on special public occasions. Ukrainian nationalists saw it as another great opportunity for group performances that would show the federal government how ethnic elements could prevent the Centennial from being monotonous and thus that these cultures should be preserved through state funding. Nationalist Ukrainians held various concerts, exhibitions, and dances and participated in the Folk Arts Festivals in many cities. In Saskatchewan, for example, a special committee of the UCC organized a children's concert to commemorate Canada's birthday at which 250 children appeared in traditional Ukrainian costumes and sang in both Ukrainian and English.[122] On another occasion in 1967, also under the leadership of the UCC, Ukrainian youth groups got together for an assembly on Parliament Hill in Ottawa and met with Pearson on Ukrainian Youth Day, in conjunction with the government's tribute to the Ukrainian contribution to Canada.[123] The focus on children and youth had a political purpose in that the UCC tried to demonstrate that Ukrainian culture and language were not only retained among the pioneers and older generations but also vital for younger people. In this sense, while the Centennial tended to stress the past and historical contributions of Ukrainians as nation builders of Canada, it also carried messages for the future in terms of the preservation of languages and traditions.

Participation in the Centennial provided a special mission and responsibility for Japanese and communist Ukrainians, who had not yet overcome marginalization. It was the first time since the end of World War II that Japanese were asked to take part in a mainstream landmark event, while communist Ukrainians felt politically stigmatized during the Cold War. Both groups tried to show their enthusiasm for participation and a sense of being part of Canada. For Japanese, it was a "special year" when they renewed their "pride" and "awareness" as a "model element, which constituted Canadian society."[124] A sense of cooperation was publicly demonstrated through various projects, such as floats on Dominion Day, Japanese gardens in Alberta and Ontario, and Canada's Expo Pavilion. The Nikka Yuko Centennial Garden built in Lethbridge in 1967 was unique in the sense that it commemorated both the Centennial and the roots of Japanese—both pre–World War II settlers and evacuees—in the area. A project of local Japanese and the

City of Lethbridge, it symbolized the fact that Japaneseness had already been part of local identity in southern Alberta before the focal point of ethnic identity shifted from British Columbia. Explaining why Lethbridge had chosen the Japanese project for the Centennial, a local Japanese stated that the garden was "evidence of how much economic contribution Japanese made in the area."[125] Communist Ukrainians also pointed out how important their participation was in the Centennial, regarding the occasion as the biggest chance to merge both Canada's and Ukrainians' experiences. The AUUC, which regarded its celebration of the seventy-fifth anniversary of Ukrainian settlement in Canada as "an integral part of the Canadian centenary," organized a number of concerts by over 350 performers at Expo 67 as well as ceremonies at the Shevchenko Memorial Park in Ontario.[126] The *Ukrainian Canadian* also stated that "the Ukrainian Canadian contribution to the events of this historic year can be summed up as worthy of our Canadian heritage and a further stepping stone to future successes."[127]

Both communist Ukrainian and Japanese elites saw the Centennial and Expo 67 as opportunities to show their ties to Japan and the Soviet Union respectively. The fact that homeland pavilions and delegates were incorporated into the Canadian event symbolized the compatibility of their dual identities. The Soviet exhibition at Expo 67 showcased both the real representative of Ukraine and "Soviet technology, science, culture, education and other achievements, both economic and spiritual."[128] Together with the performances by the AUUC, the National Day of the Ukrainian Soviet Socialist Republic at Expo 67 was a celebration of Ukraine as "one of the top ten industrially developed nations in the World" as well as a country with a rich cultural heritage, as opposed to the totalitarian image that it had.[129] Likewise, Japan's pavilion was designed to present Japan's merits, contrasting its developing industries with its traditional high culture, such as *ikebana* ("flower arrangements"), *kabuki* ("drama"), and *nihon teien* ("gardens"). Yoshiharu Takeno, director of the Japan External Trade Organization, made this goal clear, stating that visitors to the pavilion would get "a greater understanding of Japan's love of things beautiful, her way of life, and her foremost place in world technology and science."[130] For Japanese Canadians, it was particularly useful to detach themselves from undemocratic and backward images that had always been associated with their community and to promote the traditional culture and spirit that they really represented. Such an effort was well illustrated by the Nikka Yuko Centennial Garden's focus on authenticity when the organizers invited Tadashi Kubo, an architect from Osaka Prefecture University in Japan, imported construction materials from Japan, and adopted traditional Japanese landscaping.[131]

Promotion of the positive images of their homelands, both communist Ukrainians and Japanese believed, would also strengthen ties between Canada and their respective countries. Such political messages were further reinforced by the participation of official homeland delegations. Communist celebrations at the Shevchenko Memorial Park at Palermo were attended by the Soviet ambassador to Canada, Ivan F. Shpedko, while the Japanese pavilion was visited by Prince and Princess Takamatsu, who also attended the official opening of the Nikka Yuko Centennial Garden. Shpedko, together with AUUC members, laid a wreath at the Shevchenko monument and made an address, hoping that "the peoples of Canada and the Soviet Union" would "strengthen their bonds of friendship and act together in the interests of world peace."[132] Communist Ukrainians could emphasize in public that, even if the Cold War had seen the relationship between communist and Western countries deteriorate, Canada had nonetheless recognized the Soviet Union officially. For Japanese, the royal visit was not the first since the end of World War II, yet incorporation of the delegates from Japan into the Centennial symbolized that the two countries had finally normalized their relationship.

Yet unity in diversity had its limits, especially when homeland politics were involved. Ideological conflict reared its head on some occasions and divided ethnic communities. Illuminating Ukrainian examples included the exclusion of communists from the Folk Arts Council and its program for the Centennial and the Soviet representation of Ukraine at Expo 67. Neither the council nor expo organizers wanted to attach conflict to the Folk Arts Festival and Expo 67, yet homeland politics affected the situation. That the council was established under the leadership of Kossar, a nationalist Ukrainian, who regarded the UCC as the representative organization of Ukrainians in Canada, explains the exclusion of communists. Communist Ukrainians expanded the issue beyond the Ukrainian community, criticizing the government appointment of the committee members as "shameful" and claiming their "right" to have their representatives on it.[133] For them, such resentment was based on solid grounds, for the council was funded by the federal government to promote ethnic cultures in the Centennial. Kossar's deliberate exclusion of communists, AUUC members argued, both violated the "spirit of co-operation" that should characterize the landmark Canadian event and discriminated against "progressive, democratic-minded Ukrainians" who "played a tremendous role in winning civil rights and recognition for Ukrainians on an equal basis with other fellow Canadians in the social, economic, and cultural life of the country."[134] Obviously, this comment suggested that folk arts had become politicized and the main vehicle for ethnic groups to show their contributions to and participation in Canada beyond the cultural realm. After the first national conference in 1964, which gave birth to the Folk Arts Council, the AUUC formally appealed to the federal government in writing, stressing the AUUC as nation builders of Canada, its members' country of citizenship.[135] Nationalist Ukrainians, in turn, were not pleased with the Soviet Union's representation of Ukraine at Expo 67. They believed that Ukraine should be included in Expo 67 independently. The UCC criticized the Soviet pavilion, arguing that it demonstrated the "complete domination of Soviet Russia" over Ukraine yet pointing out that the exhibition of Ukrainian arts and dance performances also indicated that Ukrainian identity survived under the Soviet Union.[136]

Although ideology was not as obvious as in the Ukrainian case, the Japanese celebration was not completely free from politics. Conflict sometimes appeared between Japan-led Expo 67 and Japanese-Canadian events in terms of how they presented Japan. Japanese Canadians focussed on Japanese cultural traditions, for example, featuring an *ikebana* headmaster from Japan at the Cultural Centre in Toronto and organizing an *obon odori* ("folk dance") festival. Recognizing the Centennial as a celebration of the mosaic, they were well aware that such presentations were most relevant to the occasion. Japan, however, understood Expo 67 more as a scientific show and emphasized the economic development of Japan, demonstrating how the country had rebuilt itself as an economic power. An article in the *New Canadian* criticized how "poor" the Japanese pavilion was, exhibiting cars and motorcycles at the entrance and not showing any traditional sense of pride.[137] Attacking a Tokyo reporter's point of view that the Japanese-Canadian exhibitions belonged to "amateurs," a Japanese Canadian wrote that "it was a Canadian Japanese voice speaking for the Centennial Celebrations for Canada's birthday. It was not a Japanese voice." The Centennial, she continued, was meant "to show our feelings as Canadians of Japanese extraction and as Canadian citizens, expressing our joy and gratitude for Canada's hundredth birthday."[138]

~

In the 1960s, Canada experienced a dramatic transformation in terms of its identity, facing two contradictory realities. First, the rise of nationalism in Quebec and subsequent lobbying by other ethnic groups led by Ukrainian nationalists divided the nation, thereby making formal policies addressing ethnic cultures and languages a pressing task for the federal government. Canadian leaders were threatened by both Quebec separatism and other ethnic groups' protests as they tried to define Canadian identity in their own ways. In this process, Ukrainian nationalists were by far the most active group in pursuit of multiculturalism and collective ethnic rights for many reasons: integration of high-ranking individuals, enthusiasm for linguistic and cultural survival, and statelessness of Ukraine. Groups such as Japanese and communist Ukrainians, in contrast, tended to stress basic human rights regardless of race, ethnicity, and ideology, while they also valued their cultural traditions as the means to express their identity and negotiate with mainstream society. Second, though Canada witnessed mounting ethnic tensions within its boundaries during this period, the Centennial, which promoted a pan-Canadian identity, made both Ukrainians and Japanese, to greater and lesser degrees, feel part of the Canadian mainstream.

CONCLUSION

In this study, I examined the role of ethnic elites in the transformation of Canadian identity from Anglo-conformity to multiculturalism through five decades, from the 1920s to 1971. Such a change involved a complex interplay between ethnic leaders and mainstream Canadians as well as a complex interaction among various group boundaries, including mainstream, ethnic, ideological, and regional. I analyzed how ethnic elites envisaged Canada and their own ethnic communities, using mainly Japanese and Ukrainian examples but also incorporating examples from the mainstream Scottish group. Each group had a particular relationship with mainstream Canadians. I regarded Scots for the most part as an integral part of mainstream Canadian society and introduced Scottish ethnicity to clarify the nature of Ukrainian and Japanese ethnic identity. Because Scots alone, among the three groups, participated in the mainstream, ironically they produced fewer records relating specifically to their sense of ethnicity and thus received the least analysis.

My main goal was to set forth the idea that ethnic leaders were instrumental in the construction of a pan-Canadian identity based on ethnic pluralism. Their role was to bridge the gap between their own and mainstream British Canadian notions of democracy, freedom, and pluralism. In this process, they sought to adjust their own visions to those of mainstream Canadians. In addition to traditional political activism, they developed a way to claim their rights and places in Canada intellectually. They tried to convey messages to their communities through ethnic presses and speeches and by employing ethnic myths and symbols. Some successful ones, such as the Scottish elite and some Ukrainians, gained power as ethnic leaders, eventually joining the Canadian mainstream elite.

I sought in this study to understand ethnicity as a dynamic political phenomenon defined not by common culture, language, and origin alone but by ethnic elites' interactions with Canadian society. My analytical framework had two central aspects. First, I focussed on negotiations in which ethnic elites used ethnicity instrumentally: that is, to gain more political power, influence Canada's official identity, and change the legal position of ethnic minorities. In this process, ethnic elites made ethnicity both a significant negotiating tool in Canadian politics and a component of Canadian political decision making. Ukrainian and Japanese leaders in particular engaged in these negotiations. Second, I examined both Canadian and ethnic identities. Building on Anthony D. Smith's ethnosymbolist theory, I emphasized the role that historical myths, memories, and symbols played in maintaining strong ethnic consciousness and identity. In the process of negotiating full participation in Canadian life, both Ukrainian and Japanese elites relied on a number of homeland-made and Canadian-made collective memories, symbols, and myths, both to inspire their masses' emotional attachment to their ethnic communities and to make ethnicity an integral part of Canadian identity. Some influential Scots, even though Scottishness was usually indistinguishable from Canadian identity, emphasized Scottish superiority, seeing Scots as a people who came to Canada with a lofty mission to establish a world-wide empire defined by high ideals. In this sense, even for Scots, ethnicity was a means to gain power and obtain influence. I can now make some conclusions about the roles of elites in changing attitudes toward ethnic groups, shifting Canadian identity, and transforming ethnic boundaries.

Generally speaking, mainstream/ethnic boundaries declined over this period as the thinking of ethnic and mainstream elites coalesced and multiculturalism became a more integral part of Canadian identity. At official levels, significant changes occurred in how mainstream society saw the roles that ethnic groups had played or could play in Canadian society. The ethnoracial hierarchy and deep-rooted discrimination, dating from the early twentieth century, that favoured Scots while making Ukrainians and Japanese second-class citizens peaked during World War II. The end of the war was a turning point since all ethnic groups began to be tolerated and recognized in Canada. The question of loyalty among both Ukrainian and Japanese elites, the evacuation and internment of Japanese in British Columbia, and the horrors of the racism of Nazi Germany made mainstream Canadians more aware of human rights issues. At the same time, most ethnic Canadians were expected to participate in Canada's war effort. Both the marginalization and the integration of ethnic groups impacted people's views of Canada, replacing a British-dominated nation with a multicultural one. As a result, the postwar era witnessed a number of changes, including passage of the 1947 Citizenship Act and gradual abolition of discriminatory policies against previously marginalized groups such as Japanese. The Cold War served to increase awareness of freedom and democracy among Canadians who felt threatened by the expression of communism led by the Soviet Union. In the 1960s, the rise of French-Canadian nationalism, which aggravated other ethnic groups, was another turning point. Once again mainstream Canadian leaders faced a crisis in national unity, forcing them to think that a new perspective was necessary to govern an ethnically diverse Canada. The Royal Commission on Bilingualism and Biculturalism appointed in 1963, the Official Languages Act of 1969, and federal multiculturalism introduced in 1971 reflected this change and, for the first time, recognized ethnicity as an official component of Canadian identity.

Such a transformation would never have occurred had it not been for the activism and campaign for pluralism of ethnic elites. Both Ukrainian and Japanese leaders—in particular nationalist Ukrainians and *issei* Japanese—had seen Canada as a multicultural nation since the interwar period. Such a view simultaneously allowed them to cultivate loyalty to their respective homelands and gain full recognition in Canadian society. This notion of ethnic pluralism became an expression of resistance to prewar and interwar Anglo-conformity, which had assumed British-Canadian superiority and a long-standing special dual loyalty to Canada and Britain. Both Ukrainian and Japanese elites pressured the Canadian government to introduce multiculturalism, guaranteeing the equal rights of people of all ethnic origins and recognizing their roles in articulating official Canadian identity. For Ukrainian nationalists, upward mobility, cultural and linguistic survival in Canada, and independence of their homeland were all factors in their lobby for multiculturalism. For both *issei* and *nisei* Japanese, acquisition of the federal franchise was the major cause attached to multiculturalism before 1948. Both Ukrainian nationalist and Japanese activism gained momentum as the end of World War II and the Cold War made democracy and human rights central political principles in Canada. Ukrainian nationalists worked on opening Canada's doors to Ukrainian refugees, while Japanese sought compensation for the wartime evacuation and internment, on the grounds of both democratic ideals and protection of fundamental human rights. Communist Ukrainians, while increasingly marginalized with the start of the Cold War, also joined the lobby for multiculturalism after World War II, in pursuit of their own notion of democracy based on equality among all classes of people. For Ukrainians and Japanese, the federal multiculturalism policy announced in 1971 was a goal that they had long envisioned and finally reached.

Japanese, disenfranchised until 1948 federally and numerically small, did not have such a foundation from which to work with mainstream leaders, particularly before and during World War II. Then, too, Ukrainians since the 1920s were divided between communists and nationalists and thus more actively competed among themselves to mobilize their people than Japanese did among theirs. Japanese elites were also divided between *issei* and *nisei* since the 1930s, but the fact that such categories were determined by birth and often interdependent made them less competitive and less active in terms of influencing their masses. New developments in the postwar period, especially the influx of Ukrainian nationalist refugees into Canada and the start of the Cold War, intensified the ideological competition between Ukrainian nationalists and communists. In contrast, the rivalry between *issei* and *nisei* among Japanese lost intensity after the war as the *issei* population declined. Finally, Ukrainian nationalists remained strongly tied to their homeland, perceiving Ukrainian independence as their most important cause, while Japanese, who tried to unite themselves behind Imperial Japan in the interwar period, were increasingly detached from homeland politics after the war.

Comparing Scots with Ukrainian and Japanese elites illustrates internal competition among ethnic leaders in the promotion of ethnic identity. Scots, for example, did not have to first become the official or unofficial representatives of their ethnic communities to become mainstream leaders. As a result, they neither mobilized Scots as part of a nation-wide ethnic community nor competed strongly among themselves to control representation of their people. That they did not have to turn ethnicity into political strength contributed to the loss of ethnic identity. In other words, for Scots, ethnicity was useful to claim Canadian democratic values as their invention.

These differences were well reflected in the ways that elites maintained ethnic myths, symbols, and collective memories. Ukrainian leaders maintained homeland myths and Canadian collective memories more consistently than Japanese elites. Ukrainian nationalists in particular always tied their fight for the independence of Ukraine to homeland heroes throughout the five decades and continuously cultivated the myth of common descent that promoted ethnic consciousness. Shevchenko, for example, as a poet who could enrich the Canadian mosaic just like Burns, was a great choice for their symbolic figure in Canada. The intense conflict between nationalists and communists over what Shevchenko represented—whether the struggle for Ukrainian independence or the proletarian fight against imperialist oppressors—also contributed to the consolidation of Ukrainian ethnic consciousness. Japanese elites, in contrast, did not maintain homeland symbols such as the emperor. He was always regarded as politically irrelevant in Canada, and after the fall of Imperial Japan the impact of the emperor as a core of ethnic identity obviously declined. Furthermore, Ukrainians benefited from the fact that they had been concentrated and built roots in the Prairies. Their collective memories associated with the Prairies were nurtured positively, focussing on their contributions to nation building. Yet Japanese regional myths were often painted with stories of discrimination and marginalization and thus became negative over the years. Scottish elites highlighted their myths and symbols when they distinguished themselves from other Canadians, showing that Scots were racially, culturally, and intellectually superior to them.

Multiculturalism, which stressed ethnic groups' collective rights to preserve their languages and cultural traditions through public funding and programs, was particularly significant for Ukrainian nationalists, who thought that their linguistic and cultural survival was threatened both in Canada because of accelerating assimilation of the younger generation and in Ukraine because of the Soviet policies. Unlike Ukrainians, who tried to protect their ethnic distinctiveness by all means, however, Japanese, having faced long-term marginalization because of their race and concentration in British Columbia, did not always emphasize their cultural and linguistic uniqueness. They regarded multiculturalism as a principle that ought to secure individual rights to maintain ethnic identity without any legal barriers and discrimination because of racial background. In the 1960s, Ukrainian multiculturalism won over other definitions and became more common than the Japanese one, making the promotion of different languages and cultural traditions a top priority of the policy.

Ethnic elites contributed to the evolution of Canadian multicultural identity by creating transnational spaces between their respective homelands and Canada. The comparison here among Japanese, Ukrainian, and Scottish elites highlighted both the common and the different roles that they played in this process. They differed significantly in their goals attached to ethnic pluralism. Scottish elites regarded multiculturalism as a means to define Canada with their "superior" political and cultural traditions as builders of a world-wide empire. For Japanese elites, ethnic pluralism represented both homeland growth from Imperial Japan to a democratic state and antiracism legislation in Canada. For Ukrainian elites—particularly nationalists—ethnic pluralism was a way to ensure their cultural and linguistic survival. Yet they all played a similar role, bridging their homelands and Canada both politically and symbolically.

NOTES

Introduction

1 The term is taken from Howard Palmer, who first used it in the context of ethnic history. See his "Reluctant Hosts: Anglo-Canadian Views of Multiculturalism in the Twentieth Century," in *Reading in Canadian History: Post-Confederation,* edited by R. Douglas Francis and Donald B. Smith (Toronto: Harcourt Brace and Company Canada, 1976), 143–61.

2 Will Kymlicka, *Multicultural Citizenship: A Liberal Theory of Minority Rights* (Oxford: Clarendon Press, 1995), 10, 78. A similar process by which immigrants became more conscious of their "ethnic" identity after immigration to Canada was pointed out by some historians. See, for example, Marlene Epp, "Pioneers, Refugees, Exiles, and Transnationals: Gendering Diaspora in an Ethno-Religious Context," *Journal of the Canadian Historical Association* 12 (2001): 151.

3 Royden Loewen and Gerald Friesen, *Immigrants in Prairie Cities: Ethnic Diversity in Twentieth-Century Canada* (Toronto: University of Toronto Press, 2009), 4–5.

4 This theory of the relationship between upward mobility and mobilization of the masses is well articulated by Paul R. Brass, for whom ethnicity is nothing but a by-product of political competition among elites. Using the controversy of cow protection and slaughter between Hindu and Muslim elites in South Asia as an example, he demonstrates how they manipulated cultural or religious symbols to win political and economic clout, consequently defining ethnic boundaries. See his "Elite Groups, Symbol Manipulation, and Ethnic Identity among the Muslims of South Asia," in *Political Identity in South Asia,* edited by David Taylor and Malcolm Yapp (London: Curzon Press, 1979), 35–77. See also Orlando Patterson, "Context and Choice in Ethnic Allegiance: A Theoretical Framework and Caribbean Case Study," in *Ethnicity: Theory and Experience,* edited by Nathan Glazer and Daniel P. Moynihan (Cambridge, MA: Harvard University Press, 1975), 305–49; Michael Hechter, "A Rational Choice Approach to Race and Ethnic Relations," in *Theories of Race and Ethnic Relations,* edited by D. Mason and J. Rex (Cambridge, UK: Cambridge University Press, 1986), 268–77.

5 Patterson, "Context and Choice in Ethnic Allegiance," 312.

6 Wsevolod W. Isajiw, "Multiculturalism and the Integration of the Canadian Community," *Canadian Ethnic Studies* 15, 2 (1983): 110. See also Bohdan

S. Kordan, "The Intelligentsia and the Development of Ukrainian Ethnic Consciousness in Canada: A Prolegomenon to Research," *Canadian Ethnic Studies* 17, 1 (1985): 22–33.

7 Franca Iacovetta, "Manly Militants, Cohesive Communities, and Defiant Domestics: Writing about Immigrants in Canadian Historical Scholarship," *Labour/Le travail* 36 (1995): 239.

8 Benedict Anderson, *Imagined Communities: Reflections on the Origin and Spread of Nationalism* (London: Verso, 1983), 21, 37–46.

9 Anthony D. Smith, *The Ethnic Origins of Nations* (Oxford: Blackwell, 1986).

10 Anthony D. Smith, *Myths and Memories of the Nation* (Oxford: Oxford University Press, 1999), 68.

11 Anthony D. Smith, *Chosen Peoples: Sacred Sources of National Identity* (Oxford: Oxford University Press, 2003).

12 Herbert J. Gans, "Symbolic Ethnicity: The Future of Ethnic Groups and Cultures in America," in *On the Making of Americans: Essays in Honor of David Riesman,* edited by Herbert J. Gans (Philadelphia: University of Pennsylvania Press, 1979), 193–220. See also his "Symbolic Ethnicity and Symbolic Religiosity: Towards a Comparison of Ethnic and Religious Acculturation," *Ethnic and Racial Studies* 17, 4 (1994): 577–92.

13 See Lubomyr Luciuk and Stella Hryniuk, eds., *Canada's Ukrainians: Negotiating an Identity* (Toronto: University of Toronto Press, 1991); Lubomyr Luciuk, *Searching for Place: Ukrainian Displaced Persons, Canada, and the Migration of Memory* (Toronto: University of Toronto Press, 2000); and Bohdan S. Kordan, *Canada and the Ukrainian Question, 1939–1945* (Montreal: McGill-Queen's University Press, 2001).

14 Orest Martynowych, *Ukrainians in Canada: The Formative Years, 1891–1924* (Edmonton: Canadian Institute of Ukrainian Studies Press, 1991).

15 Frances Swyripa, *Wedded to the Cause: Ukrainian-Canadian Women and Ethnic Identity, 1891–1991* (Toronto: University of Toronto Press, 1993).

16 D. Campbell and R.A. MacLean, *Beyond the Atlantic Roar: A Study of the Nova Scotian Scots* (Toronto: McClelland and Stewart, 1974), 281.

17 See, for example, Wilfred Campbell, *The Scotsman in Canada* (London: S. Low Marston, 1911); John M. Gibbon, *Scots in Canada: A History of the Settlement of the Dominion from the Earliest Days to the Present Time* (Toronto: Musson, 1911); James H. Walker, *A Scotsman in Canada* (London: Cape, 1935); Neil MacNeil, *Highland Heart of Nova Scotia* (New York: Scribner, 1948); and Charles W. Dunn, *Highland Settler: A Portrait of the Scottish Gael in Nova Scotia* (Toronto: University of Toronto Press, 1953).

18 Allen Andrews, *The Scottish Canadians* (Toronto: Van Nostrand Reinhold, 1981), 64.

19 Jenni Calder, *Scots in Canada* (Edinburgh: Luath Press, 2003), 137.

20 Matthew Shaw, *Great Scots! How the Scots Created Canada* (Winnipeg: Heartland Associates, 2003); Paul Cowan, *How the Scots Created Canada* (Edmonton: Dragon Hill, 2006).

21 Ken McGoogan, *How the Scots Invented Canada* (Toronto: HarperCollins, 2010), xi.

22 Ian McKay, "Tartanism Triumphant: The Construction of Scottishness in Nova Scotia, 1933–1954," *Acadiensis* 21, 2 (1992): 16.

23 Gilbert Foster, *Language and Poverty: The Persistence of Scottish Gaelic in Eastern Canada* (St. John's: Institute of Social and Economic Research, Memorial University of Newfoundland, 1988), 80.

24 Celeste Ray, "Transatlantic Scots and Ethnicity," in *Transatlantic Scots,* edited by Celeste Ray (Tuscaloosa: University of Alabama Press, 2005), 31.

25 Ray, *Transatlantic Scots*; Peter E. Rider and Heather McNabb, eds., *A Kingdom of the Mind: How the Scots Helped Make Canada* (Montreal: McGill-Queen's University Press, 2006). For the strong influence that Scottish writers had on Canadian literature, see Elizabeth Waterston, *Rapt in Plaid: Canadian Literature and Scottish Tradition* (Toronto: University of Toronto Press, 2001).

26 Barry Broadfoot, *Years of Sorrow, Years of Shame: The Stories of Japanese Canadians in World War II* (Don Mills: Paperjacks, 1977); Keibo Oiwa, ed., *Stone Voices: Wartime Writings of Japanese Canadian Isseis* (Montreal: Véhicule Press, 1991); and Takeo Ujo Nakano and Leatrice Nakano, *Within the Barbed Wire Fence: A Japanese Man's Account of His Internment in Canada* (Halifax: Goodread Biographies, 1980).

27 Maryka Omatsu, *Bittersweet Passage: Redress and the Japanese Canadian Experience* (Toronto: Between the Lines, 1992).

28 Ann Sunahara, *The Politics of Racism: The Uprooting of the Japanese Canadians during the Second World War* (Toronto: James Lorimer and Company, 1981); and Ken Adachi, *The Enemy that Never Was: An Account of the Deplorable Treatment Inflicted on Japanese Canadians during World War Two* (Toronto: McClelland and Stewart, 1976).

29 Roy Miki, *Redress: Inside the Japanese Canadian Call for Justice* (Vancouver: Raincoast Books, 2004).

30 Patricia Roy, *The Oriental Question: Consolidating a White Man's Province, 1914–41* (Vancouver: UBC Press, 2003); and *The Triumph of Citizenship: The Japanese and Chinese in Canada, 1941–1967* (Vancouver: UBC Press, 2007).

31 Stephanie Bangarth, *Voices Raised in Protest: Defending North American Citizens of Japanese Ancestry, 1942–49* (Vancouver: UBC Press, 2008).

32 Loewen and Friesen, *Immigrants in Prairie Cities,* 5–6. A similar approach was adopted for rural areas in the Prairies by Frances Swyripa in *Storied Landscapes: Ethno-Religious Identity and the Canadian Prairies* (Winnipeg: University of Manitoba Press, 2010).

33 Fredrik Barth, "Introduction," in *Ethnic Groups and Boundaries: The Social Organization of Cultural Difference,* edited by Fredrik Barth (Boston: Little, Brown and Company, 1969), 10.

34 One of the most prominent primordialist theorists of ethnicity is Clifford Geertz. See his *The Interpretation of Cultures: Selected Essays by Clifford Geertz* (New York: Basic Books, 1973). Max Weber's classic 1921 article defines race and ethnicity as "self-ascribed" since members perceive "common traits." See his "Ethnic Groups," in *Theories of Ethnicity: A Classical Reader,* edited by Werner Sollors (New York: New York University Press, 1996), 52–66.

35 Barth, "Introduction," 22–24.

36 Roberto Perin, "Writing about Ethnicity," in *Writing about Canada: A Handbook for Modern Canadian History*, edited by John Schultz (Scarborough: Prentice-Hall Canada, 1990), 207.

37 See W. Stanford Reid, *The Scottish Tradition in Canada* (Toronto: McClelland and Stewart, 1976).

38 José E. Igartua, *The Other Quiet Revolution: National Identities in English Canada, 1945–71* (Vancouver: UBC Press, 2006), 226.

39 Ibid., 227.

40 C.P. Champion, *The Strange Demise of British Canada: The Liberals and Canadian Nationalism, 1964–1968* (Montreal: McGill-Queen's University Press, 2010), 13.

41 Ibid., 12.

42 Ibid., 11.

43 Ibid., 138–64.

44 Ross Lambertson, *Repression and Resistance: Canadian Human Rights Activists, 1930–1960* (Toronto: University of Toronto Press, 2005). For the human rights movement after World War II, see also Carmela Patrias and Ruth A. Frager, "'This Is Our Country, These Are Our Rights': Minorities and the Origins of Ontario's Human Rights Campaign," *Canadian Historical Review* 82, 1 (2001): 1–35; and James W. Walker, "Human Rights in a Multicultural Framework: Defining Canadian Citizenship, 1945–1970," *Canadian Issues* (2002): 32–34.

45 Franca Iacovetta, *Gatekeepers: Reshaping Immigrant Lives in Cold War Canada* (Toronto: Between the Lines, 2006), 51–63.

46 Smith, *Myths and Memories of the Nation;* and Eric J. Hobsbawm, *Nations and Nationalism since 1780: Programme, Myth, Reality* (Cambridge, UK: Cambridge University Press, 1990).

Chapter 1: Changing Ethnic Profiles

1 Leo Driedger, *Race and Ethnicity: Finding Identities and Equalities* (Oxford: Oxford University Press, 2003), 216.

2 Ibid.

3 J.S. Woodsworth, *Strangers within Our Gates or Coming Canadians* (1909; reprint, with an introduction by Marilyn Barber, Toronto: University of Toronto Press, 1972), 112.

4 Ibid., 154–55.

5 Arthur Herman, *How the Scots Invented the Modern World* (New York: Three Rivers Press, 2001), 345–85.

6 Andrew Wilson, *Ukrainian Nationalism in the 1990s: A Minority Faith* (Cambridge, UK: Cambridge University Press, 1997), 2.

7 J.M. Bumsted, *The Scots in Canada* (Ottawa: Canadian Historical Association, 1982), 10.

8 On the first immigration, see David J. Hall, "Clifford Sifton: Immigration and Settlement Policy, 1896–1905," in *The Settlement of the West*, edited by Howard Palmer (Calgary: University of Calgary Press, 1977), 60–85;

Martynowych, *Ukrainians in Canada*, 3–70; and John C. Lehr, "Peopling the Prairies with Ukrainians," in *Canada's Ukrainians*, 30–51. On the second immigration, see, for example, Myron Gulka-Tiechko, "Ukrainian Immigration to Canada under the Railways Agreement, 1925–30," *Journal of Ukrainian Studies* 16, 1–2 (1991): 29–60; and Brian Osborne, "'Non-Preferred' People: Interwar Ukrainian Immigration to Canada," in Luciuk and Hryniuk, *Canada's Ukrainians*, 81–102.

9 Dominion Bureau of Statistics, *Census of Canada* (Ottawa: Dominion Bureau of Statistics, 1931).

10 Masako Iino, *Nikkei Kanadajin No Rekishi* (Tokyo: University of Tokyo Press, 1997), 6–7. The numbers of immigrants included those who did not stay in Canada.

11 Dominion Bureau of Statistics, *Census of Canada* (Ottawa: Dominion Bureau of Statistics , 1921).

12 Swyripa, *Storied Landscapes*, 29.

13 Lehr, "Peopling the Prairies with Ukrainians," 30–51.

14 William Darcovich and Paul Yuzyk, eds., *A Statistical Compendium on the Ukrainians in Canada, 1891–1976* (Ottawa: University of Ottawa Press, 1980), Series 20.60.

15 J.M. Bumsted, "Scots," in *Encyclopedia of Canada's Peoples*, edited by Robert R. Magocsi (Toronto: University of Toronto Press), 1139.

16 See, for example, Andrij Makuch, "Narodni Domy in East Central Alberta," in *Continuity and Change: The Cultural Life of Alberta's First Ukrainians*, edited by Manoly R. Lupul (Edmonton: Canadian Institute of Ukrainian Studies Press, 1988), 202–10.

17 Iino, *Nikkei Kanadajin No Rekishi*, 15.

18 Bumsted, *The Scots in Canada*, 12.

19 Presbyterian Church in Canada Archives, 2001-5002-9-2, Reverend Alexander MacMillan and Family Collection, "Looking Back: Reminiscences of the Rev. Alexander MacMillan, D.D., Mus.D, 1864–1961: Written between 1940–1945," edited by Keith MacMillan and Pat MacMillan, 1987–88.

20 Martynowych, *Ukrainians in Canada*, 155. See also Andrii Krawchuk, "Between a Rock and a Hard Place: Francophone Missionaries among Ukrainian Catholics," in Luciuk and Hryniuk, *Canada's Ukrainians*, 206–17. On Anglican missions in western Canada, see, for example, Barry Ferguson, ed., *The Anglican Church and the World of Western Canada, 1820–1970* (Regina: Canadian Plains Research Center Press, 1991). On United Church activities, see Dennis L. Butcher, ed., *Prairie Spirit: Perspectives on the Heritage of the United Church of Canada in the West* (Winnipeg: University of Manitoba Press, 1985).

21 For Methodist activities among Japanese, see, for example, Adachi, *The Enemy that Never Was*, 111–13; and Bob Stewart, "The United Church of Canada in British Columbia," in *Circle of Voices: A History of the Religious Communities of British Columbia*, edited by Charles P. Anderson, Tirthankar Bose, and Joseph I. Richardson (Lantzville: Oolichan Books, 1983), 201.

22 Martynowych, *Ukrainians in Canada*, 186, 197.

23 Paul Yuzyk, "Religious Life," in *A Heritage in Transition: Essays in the History of Ukrainians in Canada,* edited by Manoly R. Lupul (Toronto: McClelland and Stewart, 1982), 166. For Ukrainian religion in Canada, see also David J. Goa, ed., *The Ukrainian Religious Experience: Tradition and the Canadian Cultural Context* (Edmonton: Canadian Institute of Ukrainian Studies Press, 1989).

24 Jinjiro Nakayama, *Nikkeiimin Shiryôshû* vol. 10 (1922; reprint, Tokyo: Nihon Tosho Senta, 1994), 1285–88. For Japanese Buddhism in Canada, see also Yasuo Izumi, "Buddhists in British Columbia," in Anderson, Bose, and Richardson, *Circle of Voices,* 27–33; Terry Watada, *Bukkyo Tozen: A History of Jodo Shinshu Buddhism in Canada* (Toronto: HPF Press and Toronto Buddhist Church, 1996); James Placzek and Larry Devries, "Buddhism in British Columbia," in *Buddhism in Canada,* edited by Bruce Matthew (New York: Routledge, 2005), 1–29; Masako Iino, "Bukkyôkai and the Japanese Canadian Community in British Columbia," in *Issei Buddhism in the Americas,* edited by Duncan Ryûken Williams and Tomoe Moriya (Champaign: University of Illinois Press, 2010), 27–40; and John S. Harding, Victor Sōgen Hori, and Alexander Soucy, eds., *Wild Geese: Buddhism in Canada* (Montreal: McGill-Queen's University Press, 2010). For Buddhism during World War II, see Akira Ichikawa, "A Test of Religious Tolerance: Canadian Government and Jodo Shinshu Buddhism during the Pacific War, 1941–1945," *Canadian Ethnic Studies* 26, 2 (1994): 46–69.

25 For a detailed discussion of mobilizing the Ukrainian grassroots, see Martynowych, *Ukrainians in Canada,* 155–308; and Swyripa, *Wedded to the Cause,* 143–82.

26 The socialist movement started around 1907, and local associations emerged in urban centres in Manitoba and British Columbia, all of which were united in 1909 under the nation-wide Federation of Ukrainian Social Democrats in affiliation with the Socialist Party of Canada. Nationalist activities in the early twentieth century focussed on some organized local associations, which included the government-funded Ruthenian Training School for bilingual teachers and the Ukrainian National Home in Winnipeg. For more details, see Martynowych, *Ukrainians in Canada,* 252–53.

27 For visible minorities and World War I, see James W. Walker, "Race and Recruitment in World War I: Enlistment of Visible Minorities in the Canadian Expeditionary Force," *Canadian Historical Review* 70, 1 (1989): 1–26.

28 The number of veterans was claimed by the National Association of Japanese Canadians. See http://www.najc.ca/thenandnow/history6.php (accessed 16 April 2012).

29 Peter Melnycky, "The Internment of Ukrainians in Canada," in *Loyalties in Conflict: Ukrainians in Canada during the Great War,* edited by Frances Swyripa and John Herd Thompson (Edmonton: Canadian Institute of Ukrainian Studies Press, 1983), 1.

30 See ibid., 1; and Martynowych, *Ukrainians in Canada,* 323–24.

31 Martynowych, *Ukrainians in Canada,* 237–44.

32 The BC government disenfranchised Japanese, both naturalized and Canadian born, in 1895. In 1902, Japanese were denied the vote in every election in British Columbia: federal, provincial, municipal, school board.

See Yoko Urata Nakahara, "Ethnic Identity among Japanese Canadians in Edmonton: The Case of Pre-World War II Immigrants and Their Descendants" (PhD diss., University of Alberta, 1991), 11.

33 Isajiw, "Multiculturalism and the Integration of the Canadian Community," 110.

34 See Oleh W. Gerus and Denis Hlynka, eds., *The Honourable Member for Vegreville: The Memoirs and Diary of Anthony Hlynka, MP* (Calgary: University of Calgary Press, 2005).

35 "Kurata Becomes 1st JC Appointed Magistrate," *New Canadian*, 16 March 1966, 1. See also "Jo Ann Miyagawa Believed First JC Woman Called to the Bar," *New Canadian*, 1 April 1969, 1; and "Nisei Potato 'King' Becomes First JC Mayor in Alberta," *New Canadian*, 8 December 1970, 1.

36 Dominion Bureau of Statistics, *Census of Canada* (Ottawa: Dominion Bureau of Statistics , 1951, 1961).

37 Orest T. Martynowych, "Introduction," in *Prophets and Proletarians: History of the Rise and Decline of Ukrainian Communism in Canada*, edited by John Kolosky (Edmonton: Canadian Institute of Ukrainian Studies Press, 1990), xxvi.

38 Dominion Bureau of Statistics, *Census of Canada* (Ottawa: Dominion Bureau of Statistics, 1951, 1971).

39 Ibid., 1941, 1951, 1961.

Chapter 2: The Consolidation of Ethnic Boundaries and the Rise of the Mosaic

1 See Kate A. Foster, *Our Canadian Mosaic* (Toronto: Dominion Council, YWCA, 1926); and John Murray Gibbon, *Canadian Mosaic: The Making of a Northern Nation* (Toronto: McClelland and Stewart, 1938).

2 For the Canadian mosaic and its emphasis on cultural aspects of Ukrainians, see Frances Swyripa, *Ukrainian Canadians: A Survey of Their Portrayal in English-Language Works* (Edmonton: University of Alberta Press), 42–45.

3 Many of the issues regarding the promotion of Scottish identity as a provincial identity of Nova Scotia by Angus L. Macdonald are discussed in McKay, "Tartanism Triumphant," 5–47.

4 Canada officially recognized the Soviet Union in 1924. The first Soviet ambassador to Canada, Georgi Nikolayevitch Zarubin, was appointed in 1944. In 1941, the proposal that Canada should establish full diplomatic relations with the Soviet Union was vigorously opposed by nationalist Ukrainians. See Kordan, *Canada and the Ukrainian Question, 1939–1945*, 65–74.

5 Martynowych, *Ukrainians in Canada*, 224.

6 "My dlia partii—chy partiia dlia nas?," *Zakhidni visty*, 20 June 1930, 4. See also "Korin pomylok," *Zakhidni visty*, 15 August 1930, 4; and "Vorohy i pryiateli," *Ukrainskyi holos*, 21 October 1925, 4.

7 See, for example, "Pravo holosovnia i listy holosuiuchykh," *Ukrainskyi holos*, 5 October 1921, 4; "Dominiialni vybory i my," *Zakhidni visty*, 18 April 1930, 4; and "Ukrainski kandydaty v Manitobi," *Ukrainskyi holos*, 8 June 1927, 4.

8 There were some exceptions, including World War I veterans who gained the franchise in 1931, and Japanese who lived in Alberta who had the provincial and municipal franchise, but they constituted less than 2 percent of all Japanese in Canada. See Yoko Urata Nakahara, "Ethnic Identity among Japanese Canadians in Edmonton: The Case of Pre-World War II Immigrants and Their Descendants" (PhD diss., University of Alberta, 1991). For the interwar franchise movement for Japanese veterans, see Hiroko Takamura, "The Tangled Identity of Issei Japanese in Their Fight for Franchise, 1900–1931," in *Changing Japanese Identities in Multicultural Canada,* edited by Joseph F. Kess et al. (Victoria: University of Victoria Press, 2003), 233–40.

9 On the role of the Legation, see Klaus H. Pringsheim, *Neighbours across the Pacific: Canadian-Japanese Relations, 1870–1982* (Oakville: Mosaic Press, 1983), 31–65.

10 "Zaika dôhô no ankoku jidai, 10," *Tairiku nippô,* 24 December 1926, 1.

11 Japanese-language schools were often organized by interested groups of parents and local secular or Buddhist organizations. The first one opened in Vancouver in 1906, and by 1935 there were approximately forty schools in British Columbia. See Adachi, *The Enemy that Never Was*, 127.

12 A number of criticisms of the consul were expressed in *Tairiku nippô* in 1926; see, for example, "Zaika dôhô no ankoku jidai, 6," *Tairiku nippô,* 20 December 1926, 1.

13 "Dôhô shakai wa kiki ni aru to nikkai o satta hito ga shinchônaru kôryo o kibô," *Tairiku nippô,* 20 March 1926, 5.

14 For his general biography, see the Inventory of Yasutarô Yamaga Collection created by Greg Yavorsky. The collection can be found in Special Collections, University of British Columbia Library. Yasutarô Yamaga regularly contributed to *Tairiku nippô.* See, for example, his series of articles, "Dôhô nôsha no haiseki mondai," *Tairiku nippô,* 1 June 1926, 1, and 3 June 1926, 1. Some of his earlier works appeared as *History of Haney Nokai*, translated by T.W. Hashizume (Toronto: Nikkei Books, 2006).

15 See, for example, "Zaika dôhô seikatsu ni shidôseishin no teishô," *Tairiku nippô,* 11 October 1934, 3. The JCCL's activities focussed on the franchise, and it was always on the agenda. See University of British Columbia Archives, Japanese Canadian Research Collection (hereafter JCRC), box 7, file 4, Vancouver Chapter of the Japanese Canadian Citizens League (hereafter JCCL), minutes, 1936–41.

16 Bumsted, "Scots," 1139.

17 Library and Archives Canada (hereafter LAC), MG 28 V 2, vol. 6, St. Andrew's Society of Ottawa, minutes, 1868–1929; Beaton Institute, University College of Cape Breton (hereafter Beaton Institute), MG 6-26, C 8, Scottish Catholic Society Collection, 1920–46, Scottish Catholic Society, minutes.

18 For ideological divisions and mobilization of the masses, see Martynowych, *Ukrainians in Canada,* 486–510.

19 Mitsuru Shinpo, Norio Tamura, and Shigehiko Shiramizu, *Kanada no nihongo shinbun: Minzokuidô no shakaishi* (Tokyo: PMC shuppan, 1991), 41.

20 While *issei,* with a few exceptions, did not speak out for the franchise as actively as did *nisei,* they always confronted attempts by white British Columbians to strip all rights from Japanese, which included restrictions on land ownership and fishing licences in the early twentieth century.

21 "Naibilshe lykho v hromadskim zhyttiu," *Ukrainskyi holos,* 30 December 1925, 4.

22 "Shoho ne treba zabivaty!," *Ukrainskyi holos,* 11 February 1920, 4. See also "Ukrainska kultura i chervoni ianychary," *Ukrainskyi holos,* 7 March 1923, 4; "Praktychna propozytsiia," *Ukrainskyi holos,* 22 April 1925, 4;and "Ugrupuvannia kanadiiskykh ukraintsiv," *Ukrainskyi holos,* 9 May 1928, 4.

23 D.M. Elcheshen, "Bolshevik Imperialism," *Ukrainian Review,* 4 January 1937, 8.

24 "Nikkei shiminkyôkai no hôshin ni tsuite," *Tairiku nippô,* 28 March 1932, 8.

25 Kenzô Ikago sent his articles on the education of *nisei* to *Tairiku nippô* throughout the 1930s. Numerous public seminars were also held to discuss how to educate *nisei.* See, for example, a series of articles on the educational workshop in Vancouver, starting on 8 June 1935 in *Tairiku nippô.*

26 Christopher Harvie, *Scotland and Nationalism: Scottish Society and Politics, 1707 to the Present,* 3rd ed. (London: Routledge, 1998), 13.

27 Murray G.H. Pittock, *Scottish Nationality* (Houndmills: Palgrave, 2001), 82.

28 Carl Berger, *Sense of Power: Studies in the Idea of Canadian Imperialism, 1867–1914* (Toronto: University of Toronto Press, 1970), 259.

29 "An Embassy to Canada," *The Scotsman,* 3 August 1927, 8.

30 A number of Ukrainian-Canadian scholars examined Ukrainian nationalism and search for freedom in postwar Canada. Representative works include Swyripa, *Wedded to the Cause,* 105–42; and Martynowych, *Ukrainians in Canada,* 453–85.

31 See, for example, "Poslidovnist," *Ukrainskyi holos,* 1 April 1921, 4; "Pozychka dlia Halychyny," *Ukrainskyi holos,* 13 July 1921, 4; "Na pomich ridnyi zemli!," *Ukrainskyi holos,* 21 December 1921, 4; "Na shcho e halytska pozychka svobody," *Ukrainskyi holos,* 10 August 1921, 4; and "Velykyi zymovyi oboviazok," *Ukrainskyi holos,* 19 January 1921, 4.

32 "Do ukrainskoho hromadianstva v Amerytsi y Kanadi!," *Ukrainskyi holos,* 4 October 1922, 5; "Narodna sprava," *Ukrainskyi holos,* 13 December 1922, 4; and "Robota dlia ukrainskoi spravy," *Ukrainskyi holos,* 8 July 1925, 4.

33 Construction of the modern Japanese nation-state started in 1868 when the Meiji government took over Tokugawa *bakufu* ("polity") and introduced policies of modernization in education, the military, and government systems. Yet scholars identified the emergence of national consciousness or nationhood before the Meiji restoration, especially among local samurai who tried to restore the emperor's power, which had been under the shogun's control. See, for example, Anderson, *Imagined Communities,* 94–98.

34 "Dôhô shakai ha kiki ni aruto nikkai o satta hitobito ga shinchônaru koryo o kibô," *Tairiku nippô,* 20 March 1926, 5.

35 See, for example, "Dôhôshoshi ni kangaete itadakitai koto," *Tairiku nippô,* 31 August 1939, 2; and Noboru Inamoto, "Dainisei no watashi ga hunki no tokikuru," *Tairiku nippô,* 16 February 1939, 2.

36 "Zairyû dôhô no seishin sôdôin," *Tairiku nippô,* 23 January 1939, 4.

37 "Kaigai zairyûmin ha dôhôshakai o wasureruna," *Tairiku nippô,* 9 August 1938, 5.

38 "Zairyûhôjin no seishinsôdôin," *Tairiku nippô,* 23 January 1939, 4.

39 Ibid.

40 Ibid.

41 "Telegrama v ukrainskii spravi," *Ukrainskyi holos,* 28 January 1920, 5.

42 "Memoriial do premiera Kinga," *Ukrainskyi holos,* 12 July 1922, 3.

43 "Ukrainets liubyt voliu," *Ukrainskyi holos,* 5 May 1937, 4.

44 "Ukraina domahaesia povnoi svobody," *Ukrainskyi holos,* 1 January 1919, 1. For discussion on democracy, see also "Voroh demokratii," *Ukrainskyi holos,* 12 July 1933, 4; "Syla i slabict demokratii," *Ukrainskyi holos,* 19 July 1933, 4; and "Poshana zakoniv," *Ukrainskyi holos,* 25 July 1937, 4.

45 "Pislannytstvo kanadiiskykh ukraintsiv," *Ukrainskyi holos,* 29 June 1938, 4.

46 "Zairyû dôhô no seishinsôdôin," *Tairiku nippô,* 23 January 1939, 4. See also "Nentô ni Atari dôhôshoshi ni tsugu," *Tairiku nippô,* 1 January 1939, 1; "Dainisei no watashi ga huntô no toki itaru," *Tairiku nippô,* 16 February 1939, 2; Eikichi Kagetsu, "Jiko no seishin o saikentôseyo," *Tairiku nippô,* 7 July 1939, 3; and "Dôhôshoshi ni kangaete itadakitai koto," *Tairiku nippô,* 31 August 1939, 2.

47 "Zaibei dôhô ni tsugu!," *Tairiku nippô,* 5 November 1938, 4.

48 Yasuharu Kadoguchi, "Jihen to dai nisei," *Tairiku nippô,* 10 November 1937, 2.

49 See also Edward C. Banno, "The Sino-Japanese Affair and the Second Generation Japanese," *Tairiku nippô,* 1 January 1938, 2.

50 "Immigrants Who Are Not an Asset," *Saturday Night,* 14 March 1925, 1.

51 Ninety-five percent of CPC members came from Finns, Jews, and Ukrainians. Martynowych, "Introduction," in *Prophets and Proletarians,* xxiii.

52 Charles Lugrin Shaw, "Japan's Finger in Canada," *Maclean's,* 15 October 1937, 11, 53.

53 W. Peter Ward, *White Canada Forever: Popular Attitudes and Public Policy toward Orientals in British Columbia* (Montreal: McGill-Queen's University Press, 1978), 100.

54 Hilda Glynn-Ward, *The Writing on the Wall* (1921; reprint, with an introduction by Patricia E. Roy, Toronto: University of Toronto Press, 1974), 143.

55 F.W. Baumgartner, "Central European Immigration," *Queen's Quarterly* 37, 4 (1930): 190.

56 See Kay Anderson, *Vancouver's Chinatown: Racial Discourse in Canada, 1875–1980* (Montreal: McGill-Queen's University Press, 1991).

57 A.L. Horton, "A Protest from Vegreville," *Maclean's,* 15 August 1930, 48.

58 This sort of belief is well expressed by Griffin Frederick, "Catching Up with Canada," *Star Weekly,* 1 December 1928, 3.

59 *Canada Year Book* (Ottawa: Dominion Bureau of Statistics, 1927–28), 191.

60 W.A. Carrothers, "The Immigration Problem in Canada," *Queen's Quarterly* 34, 2 (1929): 521.

61 Charles Lugrin Shaw, "The Oriental Wants to Vote," *Maclean's,* 1 April 1937, 24.

62 For a discussion on the liberal tendencies of Canadian scholars who moved away from narrow racism to ethnic pluralism, see Susan Bellay, "Pluralism and Race/Ethnic Relations in Canadian Social Science, 1880–1939" (PhD diss., University of Manitoba, 2001).

63 For studies of assimilation of ethnic groups published during this period, see also James T.M. Anderson, *The Education of the New Canadian: A Treatise on Canada's Greatest Education Problem* (London: J.M. Dent and Sons, 1918); and C.A. Dawson, *Group Settlement: Ethnic Communities in Western Canada* (Toronto: Macmillan Company of Canada, 1936).

64 W.G. Smith, *Building the Nation: A Study of Some Problems Concerning the Churches' Relation to the Immigrants* (Toronto: Canadian Council of the Missionary Education Movement, 1922), xiv.

65 Ibid., 170.

66 George M. Weir, "Introduction," in *The Central European Immigrant in Canada,* by Robert England (Toronto: Macmillan Company of Canada, 1929), x.

67 Ibid., 99.

68 Robert England, *The Colonization of Western Canada: A Study of Contemporary Land Settlement* (London: P.S. King, 1936), 167.

69 Helen R.Y. Reid, "Foreword," in *The Ukrainian Canadians: A Study in Assimilation,* by Charles H. Young and Helen R.Y. Reid (Toronto: Thomas Nelson and Sons, 1931), v.

70 Young and Reid, *The Ukrainian Canadians,* 76–77.

71 Ibid., 77.

72 Charles H. Young, Helen R.Y. Reid, and W.A. Carrothers, *The Japanese Canadians,* edited by H.A. Innis (Toronto: University of Toronto Press, 1938), 171–74.

73 Smith, *Building the Nation,* 129.

74 England, *The Central European Immigrant in Canada,* 85.

75 Ibid., 73, 83, 88, 96–97.

76 See also Denzel G. Ridout, "European Sources of Non-Anglo-Saxons in Canada," *Canadian Geographical Journal* 2 (1931): 204.

77 Young, Reid, and Carrothers, *The Japanese Canadians,* 78–81, 85–118.

78 Acadia University Archives and Special Collections, Watson Kirkconnell Collection, vol. 26, file 56, Watson Kirkconnell, "Scotland and Things Scottish."

79 Focussing on the images of Ukrainian women, Swyripa, *Wedded to the Cause,* 63–142, argues that both nationalist and communist elites invented

enlightened and emancipated images of women to promote Ukrainian-Canadian community goals and help to integrate Ukrainian into Canadian society.

80 A. Hniazdovska, "Nehozhadani imigranty," *Ukrainskyi holos,* 20 June 1928, 11.

81 "Naivazhniima sprava," *Ukrainskyi holos,* 23 July 1924, 4; see also "Na uvahu farmeram i farmerskyii molodizhy," *Ukrainskyi holos,* 20 October 1920, 4; and "Postupaemo chy padaemo?," *Ukrainskyi holos,* 22 February 1922, 4.

82 Yasutarô Yamaga, "Dôhô no haiseki mondai," *Tairiku nippô,* 1 June 1926, 1.

83 See, for example, "Na uvahu farmeram i farmerskyii molodizhu," *Ukrainskyi holos,* 20 October 1924, 4.

84 "Naivazhniima sprava," *Ukrainskyi holos,* 23 July 1924, 4.

85 "Dobri ukraintsi i dobri kanadiitsi," *Ukrainskyi holos,* 6 November 1929, 4.

86 Yasutarô Yamaga, "Yamato minzoku hatten no kagi, 3," *Tairiku nippô,* 1 November 1934, 3.

87 Yamaga, "Yamato minzoku hatten no kagi, 3," *Tairiku nippô,* 1 November 1934, 3; See also his "Yamato minzoku hatten no kagi, 1," *Tairiku nippô,* 30 October 1934; and "Yamato minzoku hatten no kagi, 2," *Tairiku nippô,* 31 October 1934, 3.

88 "Zairyû dôhô ni taisuru kibô," *Tairiku nippô,* 27 August 1923, 1.

89 "Ukrainska kultura i chervoni ianychary," *Ukrainskyi holos,* 7 March 1923, 4.

90 F.T. Hawryliuk, "Nash kulturnyi rozvii v Kanadi," *Ukrainskyi holos,* 5 February 1936, 12.

91 Beaton Institute, University College of Cape Breton, MG 6-20, C 3, Joseph J. MacInnis Collection, 1924–39, Catherine MacKenzie, "Creating a New Scotland in Canada," n.d., 4.

92 "The Gael or Celt in Canada," *Gaelic Herald* 4, 9 (1932): 9. For Angus L. Macdonald's obsession with Gaelic, see McKay, "Tartanism Triumphant," 35–39.

93 Joseph D. Stetkewicz, "The Ukrainian Language," *Ukrainian Review,* 20 April 1937, 10.

94 Ibid.

95 "Nihongo gakkô mondai," *Tairiku nippô,* 8 October 1932, 3.

96 Ibid.

97 "Kanada zairyu dôhô no kakuriteki seikatsu," *Tairiku nippô,* 4 November 1932, 3.

98 "Dai nisei mondai to dôhôshakai no genjôtoppa," *Tairiku nippô,* 28 April 1932, 4.

99 Frances Swyripa has shown that "dual identity" of Ukrainians was fundamental to Canada's multicultural identity. See her *Wedded to the Cause.*

100 For Ukrainian nationalists' dual loyalty, see Swyripa, *Wedded to the Cause,* 157.

101 "Dobri ukraintsi i dobri kanadiitsi," *Ukrainskyi holos,* 6 November 1929, 4.

102 "Dainisei shidô seishin no kakuritsu ga hitsuyô da," *Tairiku nippô,* 2 April 1934, 2.

103 Loewen and Friesen, *Immigrants in Prairie Cities*, 5.
104 Swyripa, *Wedded to the Cause*, 9–10, and 259.
105 "Dobri ukraintsi i dobri kanadiitsi," *Ukrainskyi holos*, 6 November 1929, 4.
106 V. Sarchuk, "Harmonizatsiia dvokh kultur," *Ukrainskyi holos*, 21 September 1938, 11.
107 "Kanada no nihongo gakkô: Kyôikukai no sôkai," *Tairiku nippô*, 17 April 1933, 8.
108 Hisae Hirano, "Ideals of a Canadian-Born Japanese," *Tairiku nippô*, 12 November 1932, 7.
109 Eiko Henmi, "Ideals of a Canadian-Born Japanese," *Tairiku nippô*, 24 September 1932, 7.
110 LAC, John Buchan Fonds, MG 27, IIIA5 (M-8020), Lord Tweedsmuir, address to the Church of Scotland, "Scottish Church and the British Empire," Glasgow, May 1934.
111 LAC, John Buchan Fonds, MG 27, IIIA5 (M-8005), Lord Tweedsmuir, address to the Board of Trade Luncheon, Kitchener, May 1936.
112 Darcovich and Yuzyk, eds., *A Statistical Compendium*, Series 20.1–11.
113 The significance of the Prairies to Ukrainian identity and vice versa is best examined by Swyripa, *Storied Landscapes*.
114 "Za svoe pravo," *Ukrainskyi holos*, 13 June 1934, 5.
115 F.T. Havryliuk, "Nash kulturnyi rozvii v Kanadi," *Ukrainskyi holos*, 12 February 1936, 12.
116 Swyripa, *Storied Landscapes*, 29.
117 Darcovich and Yuzyk, *A Statistical Compendium*, Series 20.24–27.
118 Anderson, *Vancouver's Chinatown*.
119 "Nikkei dainisei no gyosha danketsu no yô o sakebu," *Tairiku nippô*, 9 May 1935, 2.
120 "Dainisei shidôseishin no kakuritsu ga hitsuyô da," *Tairiku nippô*, 31 March 1934, 3.
121 O.I. Bochkovsky, "Ukraintsi v Kanadi," *Ukrainskyi holos*, 21 August 1937, 4.
122 "Nisei no Tenshoku," *Tairiku nippô*, 21 January 1933, 4.
123 For the relationship between Canada and Japan in the 1930s, see John D. Meehan, "Pacific Beginnings: Canada and Japan Between Wars, 1929–41," in *Contradictory Impulses: Canada and Japan in the Twentieth Century*, ed. Greg Donaghy and Patricia E. Roy (Vancouver: University of British Columbia Press, 2008), 80–100.
124 Kenzô Ikago, "Zaika dainisei no kyôiku mondai ni tsuki," *Tairiku nippô*, 8 March 1935, 3.
124 LAC, John Buchan Fonds, MG 27, IIIA5 (M-8005), Lord Tweedsmuir, "The Meaning of Our Monarch," n.d. (1939?)
126 "Shinsaiin no nihonjin, shugasai ni dashi," *Tairiku nippô*, 11 May 1937, 5; and "Ukrainian Contribution to Welcome Week Parade," *Ukrainian Review*, May 1939, 1.
127 "Hail, Their Majesties!," *Ukrainian Review*, May 1939, 4.

128 "Bankuba o iyasu kehu no kangai," *Tairiku nippô,* 29 May 1939, 1.

129 Pittock, *Scottish Nationality,* 82. Hugh Trevor-Roper well explains how Highland cultures were invented. See his "The Invention of Tradition: The Highland Tradition of Scotland," in *The Invention of Tradition,* edited by Eric Hobsbawn and Terence Ranger (Cambridge, UK: Cambridge University Press, 1983), 15–41.

130 "Syn i batko narodu," *Ukrainskyi holos,* 10 March 1926, 4. See Swyripa, *Wedded to the Cause,* 104, 120–24, 215–16, 238, 255, for a discussion on the role of Cossack mythology in Ukrainian-Canadian women's organizations.

131 Wilson, *Ukrainian Nationalism in the 1990s,* 3.

132 Kiyoharu Kitô, "Kokumin kokka o sakanoboru," in *Kokumin Kokka o Tou,* edited by Rekishigaku Kenkyukai (Tokyo: Aoki Shoten, 1994), 228–29.

133 The theory that ethnicity was deeply rooted in a sense of being "chosen peoples" was best explored by Anthony D. Smith, *Chosen Peoples: Sacred Sources of National Identity* (Oxford: Oxford University Press, 2003). How Scots in Canada viewed themselves as a chosen people is discussed thoroughly by Ian McKay, "Tartanism Triumphant," 16–19.

134 Smith, *Myths and Memories of the Nation,* 149–50.

135 F.A. Morrison, "Toast to the Immortal Memory: Address before the Burns Club," Edmonton, on the anniversary of the birthday of Robert Burns, *Report,* 1925, 8.

136 For Ukrainian nationalists' politics and Shevchenko, see Swyripa, *Wedded to the Cause,* 48, 139–40.

137 "Sviato Shevchenka," *Ukrainskyi holos,* 10 March 1926, 5. See also "Pamiaty Shevchenka," *Ukrainskyi holos,* 9 March 1921, 4; "Shevchenka Sviata," *Ukrainskyi holos,* 23 March 1921, 4; "Ne pliuimo sobi v lytsie," *Ukrainskyi holos,* 19 March 1924, 4; "Mistsie Shevchenka," *Ukrainskyi holos,* 9 March 1932, 4; "9-ho bereznia—sviato Shevchenka," *Ukrainskyi holos,* 4 March 1936, 4; "Taras Shevchenko," *Ukrainskyi holos,* 3 March 1937, 4; and "Pamiati velykoho spivtsia Ukrainy," *Ukrainski visty,* 14 March 1934, 4.

138 Yoshikazu Matsui, ed., *Daijôsai no shisô to rekishi* (Tokyo: Nihonbunka kenkyûjo, 1990), 58.

139 Ibid., 58.

140 Hidematsu Wada, "Godaiten ni tsuite," *Tairiku nippô,* 9 October 1928, 1; 10 October 1928, 1; 11 October 1928, 1; 12 October 1928, 1; 13 October 1928, 1; 15 October 1928, 1; 16 October 1928, 1; 17 October 1928, 1; and 18 October 1928, 1.

141 *Daijôsai* was suspended during the era between Emperor Kashiwabara (1500–26) and Emperor Reigen (1663–87). After a short period of revival under Emperor Tôyama (1687–1709), it continued until the era of Emperor Kômei (1846–66). The modern version of *daijôsai* began when the Meiji emperor took the throne in 1868. See Matsui, *Daijôsai no shiô to rekishi,* 145–47.

142 Wada, "Godaiten ni tsuite," 18 October 1928, 1.

143 Takaya Nakamura, "Gotaiten to shinkoku nihon," *Tairiku nippô,* 29 October 1928, 3.

144 Masatake Tôgô, "Daiôsai no kazaritsuke," *Tairiku nippô,* 2 November 1928, 3; Masanao Sekine, "Gosokui no oshiki no shidai," *Tairiku nippô,* 5 November

1928, 3; "Daiôsai to okyô no gi," *Tairiku nippô,* 7 November 1928, 3; 8 November 1928, 3.

145 "Kansei shita 'nachi,'" *Tairiku nippô,* 19 October 1928, 7.

146 "Zairyûmin hôshukukai," *Tairiku nippô,* 28 December 1933, 5.

147 "Ishiiryôji no kôwa," *Tairiku nippô,* 24 April 1935, 3.

148 "Zaika nisei shokun no kyôiku mondai ni tsuki," *Tairiku nippô,* 23 February 1935, 3.

149 Hirokichi Nemichi, "Nihon no kokuryoku iyo kanpeki," *Tairiku nippô,* 7 July 1939, 3.

150 Eikichi Kagetsu, "Jiko no seishin o saikentô seyo," *Tairiku nippô,* 7 July 1939, 3. See also "Nihonjin no tachiba," *Tairiku nippô,* 27 February 1939, 4.

151 For the use of Ukrainian folk traditions as significant part of Canadian cultural mosaic see Swyripa, *Wedded to the Cause,* 159.

152 For Gibbon's role in creating national unity through folk arts, see Ian McKay, *The Quest of the Folk: Antimodernism and Cultural Selection in Twentieth-Century Nova Scotia* (Montreal: McGill-Queen's University Press, 1994), 57–58. See also Stuart Henderson, "'While There Is Still Time…': J. Murray Gibbon and the Spectacle of Difference in Three CPR Folk Festivals, 1928–1931," *Journal of Canadian Studies* 39, 1 (2005): 139–74.

153 Robert England, "Glimpse of Europe in Western Canada," *Canadian Geographical Journal* 5, 1 (1932): 15.

154 LAC, John Buchan Fonds, MG 27, IIIA5 (M-8005), Lord Tweedsmuir, address to the Dumfries Burns Club, 1930.

155 Gibbon, *Canadian Mosaic,* 299.

156 For Gibbon's comments on Ukrainians, see Swyripa, *Ukrainian Canadians,* 43–45.

157 John Murray Gibbon, "European Seeds in the Canadian Garden," *Transactions of the Royal Society of Canada* 17, 2 (1923): 123–24.

158 Ibid., 129.

159 Ibid., 303.

160 Watson Kirkconnell, *Canadian Overtones* (Winnipeg: Columbia Press, 1935), 76.

161 Swyripa, *Storied Landscapes,* 79.

162 The best exploration of the relationship between people and geographical territory in the rise of nationalism is by Smith, *Myths and Memories of the Nation,* 150.

163 McKay, "Tartanism Triumphant," 6. See also Steve Murdoch, "Cape Breton, Canada's 'Highland Island'?," *Northern Scotland* 18 (1998): 31–42.

164 Darcovich and Yuzyk, *A Statistical Compendium,* Series 20.49.

165 McKay, "Tartanism Triumphant," 9, 19. For myth making and the promotion of Scottishness, see also Norman Macdonald, "Putting on the Kilt: The Scottish Stereotype and Ethnic Community Survival in Cape Breton," *Canadian Ethnic Studies* 20, 3 (1988): 132–46.

166 Michael Vance, "Powerful Pathos: The Triumph of Scottishness in Nova Scotia," in *Transatlantic Scots,* edited by Celeste Ray (Tuscaloosa: University

of Alabama Press, 2005), 158. For Macdonald's fascination with the *Hector*, see McKay, "Tartanism Triumphant," 14. On romanticized histories of the *Hector* immigrants, see Lucille H. Campey, *After the* Hector: *The Scottish Pioneers of Nova Scotia and Cape Breton, 1773–1852* (Toronto: Natural Heritage, 2004); and Donald MacKay, *Scotland Farewell: The People of the* Hector (Toronto: Natural Heritage, 1996). Campey's book includes a list of passengers, their ages, their occupations, and other information.

167 Public Archives of Nova Scotia (hereafter PANS), MG 2, vol. 1507, file 436-1, Angus L. Macdonald, address to the St. Andrew's Society of New Glasgow, 1924, 5A.

168 Beaton Institute, MG 6-26, C 10, "New Scotland," n.d.

169 LAC, MG 27, IIIA5, John Buchan Collection, Lord Tweedsmuir, address at the Canadian Club, Halifax, 1937.

170 For Ukrainians' identification with the Prairies, see Swyripa, *Storied Landscapes.*

171 "Chy spravdi ukraintsi 'nebazhanyi' element v Kanadi?," *Zakhidni visty,* 16 January 1931, 4.

172 "Epopeia ukrainskykh pioniriv u Kanadi," *Ukrainskyi holos,* 20 July 1939, 3. See also "Novi kanadiitsi," *Ukrainskyi holos,* 26 July 1939, 10.

173 For example, see Baumgartner, "Central European Immigration," 183–92.

174 Ward, *White Canada Forever,* 117.

175 McKay, "Tartanism Triumphant," 19.

176 "The Gael or Celt in Canada," *Gaelic Herald* 4, 9 (1932): 9.

177 Ibid., 10.

178 See, for example, "V stolittia kanadiiskoi zalisnytsi," *Ukrainski visty,* 22 July 1936, 4.

179 "Nepryznani sasluhy," *Ukrainskyi holos,* 5 August 1925, 4. See also M. Luchkovich, "Ukrainian and Canadian Citizenship," *Ukrainskyi holos,* 6 July 1921, 2.

180 Swyripa, *Wedded to the Cause,* 221, argues that this sort of manipulation of "peasant pioneer myths" became common by the 1960s among Ukrainians.

181 "Epopeia ukrainskykh pioniriv u Kanadi," *Ukrainskyi holos,* 20 July 1939, 3.

182 "Gyodan to Stebusuton," *Tairiku nippô,* 14 December 1935, 5.

183 "Suson gyosha jizen dantai sôritsu sanjûgonen no shukugakai," *Tairiku nippô,* 17 December 1935, 4.

184 "Pauerugai ha hito no nami," *Tairiku nippô,* 13 August 1936, 5. See also "Sakuya no nihon odori," *Tairiku nippô,* 14 August 1936, 4; and "Nihonshu, omatsuri," *Tairiku nippô,* 27 August 1936, 3. It was argued that Powell Street could be one of the major tourist sites in Vancouver, and construction of a better "Japanese town" was emphasized. See Yoriki Iwasaki, "Nihonjingai hattensaku shian," *Tairiku nippô,* 13 August 1936, supplement.

185 "Kusawakejidai o kataru," *Tairiku nippô,* 1 January 1936, 1.

186 See "Shistdesiatylittia Kanady," *Ukrainskyi holos,* 29 July 1927, 9–10; and "Shistdesiat lit postupu vid konfederatsii," *Ukrainskyi holos,* 25 May 1927, 4. *Tairiku nippô* featured a series of articles, "Kenkoku rokujûnen no shukusai,"

10 June 1927, 2; 16 June 1927, 2; 20 June 1927, 2; 21 June 1927, 2; 22 June 1927, 2; 23 June 1927, 2; 25 June 1927, 2; and 28 June 1927, 2.

187 "Iuvylei Kanady," *Ukrainskyi holos,* 29 June 1927, 4.

188 "Obkhid iuvyleiu Kanady v Vinnipegu," *Ukrainskyi holos,* 6 July 1927, 1.

189 "Sviatkovannia iuvyleiu Kanady," *Ukrainskyi holos,* 29 June 1927, 1.

190 "Bankuba no daishukuga," *Tairiku nippô,* 28 June 1927, 5; "Daishukuga no nigiwai," *Tairiku nippô,* 2 July 1927, 5.

Chapter 3: Increasing Tensions and the Wartime Mosaic

1 On government internment policies in general, see John Stanton, "Government Internment Policy, 1939–1945," *Labour/Le travail* 31 (1993): 203–41.

2 See Martynowych, "Introduction," in *Prophets and Proletarians,* xxv–xxvi. The action that the government took against the ULFTA was attacked by mainstream MPs such as Dorise Nielsen of the CCF from Saskatchewan; see House of Commons, *Debates,* 15 July 1943, 4845–51.

3 Thomas M. Prymak, *Maple Leaf and Trident: The Ukrainian Canadians during the Second World War* (Toronto: Multicultural History Society of Ontario, 1988), 55–68.

4 For life in the camps, see, for example, Mary Taylor, *A Black Mark: The Japanese-Canadians in World War II* (Ottawa: Oberon Press, 2004); Keibo Oiwa, *Stone Voices: Wartime Writings of Japanese Canadian Isseis* (Montreal: Véhicule Press, 1991); Tom Sando, *Wild Daisies in the Sand: Life in a Canadian Internment Camp* (Edmonton: NeWest Press, 2002); and Shizue Takashima, *A Child in Prison Camp* (1971; reprint, Toronto: Tundra Books, 1998).

5 The establishment of the Ukrainian Canadian Committee (hereafter UCC) was not without conflicts among the various organizations. The roles that non-Ukrainian intervenors played in this process are examined, for example, in N. Fred Dreisziger, "Tracy Philipps and the Achievement of Ukrainian Canadian Unity," in *Canada's Ukrainians,* 326–41.

6 Watson Kirkconnell, *The Ukrainian Canadians and the War* (Toronto: Oxford University Press, 1940), 24.

7 G.W. Simpson, "The Ukrainian Problem," in *The Ukrainian Cause on Radio Waves* (Saskatoon: Ukrainian National Federation of Canada, 1939), 5.

8 W.L. Mackenzie King, in House of Commons, *Debates,* 17 February 1941, 815.

9 As a scholar, Henry F. Angus tried to present an objective image of Japanese Canadians, and his work in general was sympathetic. See his "The Effect of the War on Oriental Minorities in Canada," *Canadian Journal of Economics and Political Science* 7, 4 (1941): 506–16. For similar observations, see Forrest E. LaViolette, "Social Psychological Characteristics of Evacuated Japanese," *Canadian Journal of Economics and Political Science* 11, 3 (1945): 420–31.

10 Sunahara, *The Politics of Racism,* 7.

11 For a detailed description of Ian A. Mackenzie and his anti-Japanese stance, see ibid., 11–15.

12 Watson Kirkconnell, *Our Ukrainian Loyalists* (Winnipeg: UCC, 1943), 4. Kirkconnell had a great interest in Ukrainian history and the origins of the ideological conflict in Europe. His monograph describes the general background of Ukrainian nationalism and the communist revolution. See also his *Canada, Europe, and Hitler* (Toronto: Oxford University Press, 1939), 74–90.

13 Kirkconnell, *The Ukrainian Canadians and the War,* 7.

14 Kirkconnell, *Our Ukrainian Loyalists,* 20.

15 A.W. Neil, in House of Commons, *Debates,* 19 February 1942, 715.

16 Kordan, *Canada and the Ukrainian Question,* 37–40.

17 Prymak, *Maple Leaf and Trident,* 69–81.

18 Archbishop of York, "The Freedom for Which We Fight," *Presbyterian Record* 67, 2 (1942): 37.

19 "To the Task: The Call of 1912," *Presbyterian Record* 67, 1 (1942): 17.

20 R.J. Berlis, "An Address Delivered before the General Assembly of the Church of Scotland, Edinburgh, May 19th, 1942," *Presbyterian Record* 67, 10 (1942): 293.

21 Kordan, *Canada and the Ukrainian Question, 1939–1945.*

22 I. Havryliuk, "Vsi ukraintsi—razim!," *Ukrainskyi holos,* 8 May 1940, 4. For the necessity of Ukrainian unity, see also "Do porozuminnia," *Ukrainskyi holos,* 17 January 1940, 4; "V chim i na chim iednaemosia," *Ukrainskyi holos,* 29 May 1940, 4; and "Potreba iednosty," *Ukrainskyi holos,* 27 May 1942, 4.

23 Eikichi Kagetsu, "Nisei shokun ni teisu," *New Canadian,* 1 July 1940, 29. For an appeal to support Japan's cause, see also "Kaigai dôhôshoshi ni tsugu," *Tairiku nippô,* 9 January 1941, 1.

24 JCRC, box 17, file 6, Slocan Standing Meeting Committee, 17 June 1942.

25 "The Conflict of Loyalty and Affection," *New Canadian,* 25 December 1941, 4. See also "Nisei Reaffirm Loyalty to Canada," *Tairiku nippô,* 16 January 1941, 4; and "Zairyû no nihonjin ha kanadajin tare," *Tairiku nippô,* 1 April 1941, 4.

26 On the unity of Ukrainian nationalists, see, for example, "V chim i na chim iednaemosia," *Ukrainskyi holos,* 29 May 1940, 4; and "Potreba iednosty," *Ukrainskyi holos,* 27 May 1942, 4.

27 Adachi, *The Enemy that Never Was,* 237. See also Miki, *Redress: Inside the Japanese Canadian Call for Justice,* 44–46, 63.

28 The group resisted the order of mass evacuation that might mean the separation of family members. Their views conflicted with those of the *New Canadian.* On this point, see Patricia E. Roy et al., *Mutual Hostages: Canadians and Japanese during the Second World War* (Toronto: University of Toronto Press, 1990), 115; and Robert K. Okazaki, *The Nisei Mass Evacuation Group and P.O.W. Camp 101,* translated by Jean M. Okazaki and Curtis T. Okazaki (Scarborough: Markham Litho , 1996).

29 Adachi, *The Enemy that Never Was,* 269.

30 LAC, MG 28 V 7, Japanese Canadian Citizens Council, minutes, 12 May 1942, 1–3.

31 Prymak, *Maple Leaf and Trident,* 51. Mainstream Canadians also played a major part in this conflict. While Watson Kirkconnell, G.W. Simpson, and Tracy Philipps supported nationalists, communists such as R.A. Davies

criticized them for "favouring anti-allied, pro-fascist, and even outright fascist groups particularly the Ukrainian National Federation and the United Hetman Organizations." See R.A. Davies, *This Is Our Land: Ukrainian Canadians against Hitler* (Toronto: Progress Books, 1943), 85.

32 Prymak, *Maple Leaf and Trident*, 58–59.

33 UCC, "Preface," in *First All-Canadian Congress of Ukrainians in Canada* (Winnipeg: UCC, 1943), 4.

34 "Those Comfort Kits," *New Canadian*, 25 April 1941, 2.

35 Roy et al., *Mutual Hostages*, 130–31.

36 LAC, MG 28 V 7, Japanese Canadian Citizens Council, minutes, 17 May 1942, 1–3.

37 Takejirô Mitani, "Mohaya subete ha nisei no shakai," *New Canadian*, 2 May 1942, 3.

38 "Eigo o jiyûni hanasu nisei kyûsoku ni rikaisare shin'yôsaru," *New Canadian*, 6 June 1942, 3.

39 "For Canada and British Empire," *Ukrainskyi holos*, 6 September 1939, 1. See also "Na dvokh koniakh," *Ukrainskyi holos*, 5 June 1940, 4; "Treba peresterihaty," *Ukrainskyi holos*, 6 November 1940, 4; "Dobra pryznaka," *Ukrainskyi holos*, 20 May 1942, 4; and "100-protsentova loialnist," *Ukrainskyi holos*, 23 September 1942, 4.

40 "Nisei Canadianism," *New Canadian*, 22 November 1940, 2. See also "A Re-Dedication," *New Canadian*, 2 February 1940, 4.

41 "My ne imigranty," *Ukrainskyi holos*, 31 January 1940, 4.

42 "Hromadiany, chy hosti?," *Ukrainskyi holos*, 27 January 1943, 4.

43 "A Higher Education for Nisei—Hopeless?," *New Canadian*, 5 January 1940, 2.

44 "A Greater Task," *New Canadian*, 12 December 1941, 1.

45 W. Kossar, "Ukrainian Canadians in Canada's War Effort," in *First All-Canadian Congress of Ukrainians in Canada*, 42, 44.

46 G.E. Dragan, "Victory Loan," *Ukrainskyi holos*, 25 June 1941, 6.

47 See, for example, "Zhertviimo na Chervonyi Khrest," *Ukrainskyi holos*, 11 September 1940, 4.

48 "$1000 Donated to War Effort," *New Canadian*, 21 February 1941, 1.

49 "Victory Loan 1941," *New Canadian*, 5 June 1941, 1. See also "Japanese Canadians Give Freely to Red Cross and National Defense," *New Canadian*, 9 February 1940, 1; "First Japanese Canadian Red Cross Unit to Be Organized," *New Canadian*, 23 February 1940, 1; and "A Past Record of Loyalty the Japanese Canadians Will Uphold," *New Canadian*, 12 December 1941, 3.

50 "Community Plans Victory Loan Drive," *New Canadian*, 6 February 1942, 1. See also "Committee to Draft Final Plans for Victory Loan Drive," *New Canadian*, 11 February 1942, 1.

51 LAC, MG 28 V 7, vol. 1, file 3, B. Hisaoka to Major Austin C. Taylor, Chairman of the BC Security Commission, n.d.

52 PANS, MG 2, vol. 1506, file 419-20, George Farquhar to Angus L. Macdonald, 26 January 1940.

53 PANS, MG 2, vol. 1506, file 419-21, Angus L. Macdonald to George Farquhar, 23 January 1940.

54 See PANS, MG 2, vol. 1506, file 419-22, 23, 27, George Farquhar to Angus L. Macdonald, 5 March 1940; Angus L. Macdonald to Martin L. Fraser, 2 February 1940; and Angus L. Macdonald to George Farquhar, 6 March 1940.

55 PANS, MG 2, vol. 1506, file 419-22, Angus L. Macdonald to George Farquhar, 6 March 1940.

56 "Nedostatky demokratii," *Ukrainskyi holos,* 4 September 1940, 4. Democracy became one of the most popular concepts among Ukrainian nationalists. See, for example, "Teperishnia viina i oboviazok ukrainskoho zhinotstva v Kanadi," *Ukrainskyi holos,* 14 February 1940, 11; "Peresuvannia narodiv," *Ukrainskyi holos,* 8 October 1941, 4; "Demokratiiu treba boronyty," *Ukrainskyi holos,* 10 June 1942, 4; "Dlia sebe," *Ukrainskyi holos,* 3 March 1943, 4; and "Volia," *Ukrainskyi holos,* 23 February 1944, 4.

57 Kordan, *Canada and the Ukrainian Question,* 7–10.

58 Anthony Hlynka, in House of Commons, *Debates,* 2 February 1942, 231.

59 Acadia University Archives and Special Collections, Watson Kirkconnell Collection, vol. 45, file 9, memorandum of UCC to the Right Honourable W.L. Mackenzie King, Prime Minister and Minister for External Affairs Canada, 1943.

60 "Protection for Japanese Canadians," *New Canadian,* 14 February 1941, 2.

61 LAC, MG 28 V 7, vol. 1, file 1, JCCL, resolution to the sixth national JCCL council, n.d.

62 "It's Up to Us!," *New Canadian,* 5 June 1941, 2. The comparison between Japanese internment and Nazi racial persecution was also made by a few mainstream Canadians who wanted to protect Canada's image as a democratic nation. An editor of the *Marpole-Richmond Review,* for example, asked this question: "What is this, anyway—Hitler's country or a democracy?" *B.C. Teachers,* an organ of the provincial teachers' federation, also referred to Japanese in Canada as "Canadians." All these minority voices were publicized in the *New Canadian.* See "A Country Editor Views Evacuation," 17 March 1942, 2; "A National Problem," 6 April 1942, 2; W.R. McWilliams, "Problems of the Canadian-Born," 26 August 1942, 2; Audrey Alexandra Brown, "Need to Clear Away Our Prejudices," 22 May 1943, 3; "Christian Church Upholds Justice for Racial Groups," 17 June 1944, 1; "Let's Not Become as Nazis—*Ottawa Journal* Scorns Racism," 1 July 1944, 1; A. Drand, "No Reason for Persecution," 28 April 1945, 7; and Edith Fowke and F.G. Watson, "Democracy and the Japanese Canadian," 14 July 1945, 7. For other pro-Japanese articles, see the following in *Saturday Night:* Norman F. Black, "The Problem of Japanese Canadians and Solutions," 5 February 1943, 12; "Japanese Canadians," 24 June 1944, 3; L. Atkinson, "The Japanese Controversy Is Revising Liberalism," 15 July 1944, 6; and "The Japanese Canadians," 21 July 1945, 3.

63 "We Welcome a Statement," *New Canadian,* 13 May 1944, 1.

64 "Safeguarding Democratic Principles," *New Canadian,* 28 January 1942, 4.

65 J.R. Solomon, "Some Problems of Canadian Nationhood," in *First All-Canadian Congress of Ukrainians in Canada,* 91.

66 "The *Nisei*—Today and Tomorrow ...," *New Canadian,* 31 January 1941, 4. See also "National Unity," *New Canadian,* 29 March 1940, 2.

67 George T. Tamaki, "Notes on Nationality and Citizenship," *New Canadian,* 6 January 1945, 7.

68 "Re-Affirming a Purpose," *New Canadian,* 1 July 1944, 2.

69 For consolidation of the wartime mosaic, see Ivana Caccia, *Managing the Canadian Mosaic in Wartime: Shaping Citizenship Policy, 1939–1945* (Montreal: McGill-Queen's University Press, 2010). She focuses particularly on mainstream leaders' approach to ethnic diversity during World War II.

70 J. Murray Gibbon, "A Secular Bible for a New Canada," *Transactions of the Royal Society of Canada* 36, 2 (1942): 94.

71 Watson Kirkconnell, *Canadians All: A Primer of Canadian National Unity* (Ottawa: Director of Public Information, 1941), 7.

72 PANS, MG 2, vol. 1507, file 436-12, Donald Lewis MacDonald, address to the Highland Society of Antigonish, 30 November 1940, 5.

73 Watson Kirkconnell, *Twilight of Liberty* (Oxford: Oxford University Press, 1941).

74 Watson Kirkconnell, "The European-Canadians in Their Press," *Canadian Historical Association Report* (1940), 88. See also *"Our Communists and the New Canadians," an Address Delivered before a Meeting of the Canadian Club at Toronto, Canada, on Monday, February 1, 1943* (Toronto: Southam Press Toronto, 1943).

75 Kirkconnell, *Our Ukrainian Loyalists,* 20.

76 PANS, MG 2, vol. 1518, file 745-12, J.N. Wallis and J.J. MacInnis to Angus L. Macdonald, 16 December 1940.

77 PANS, MG 2, vol. 1506, file 419-16, A.W.R. Mackenzie to W.L. Mackenzie King, 2 May 1940.

78 Such use of ethnic cultural tradition was fully conceptualized by Frances Swyripa in her *Wedded to the Cause.*

79 C.H. Andrusyshen, "The Contributions of the Ukrainian Canadians to Canadian Culture," in *First All-Canadian Congress of Ukrainians in Canada,* 107.

80 "Folk Festival," *New Canadian,* 18 September 1940, 2. For folk festivals, see also other articles in *New Canadian* such as "*Nisei* of the Week," 14 February 1941, 2; "Community Contributes to Folk Festival Programs," 26 September 1941, 1; "Canadian Folk Society to Forge New Bonds of Common Interest and Unity," 28 November 1941, 1; "Kanada o ikuseisuru shominzoku," 30 September 1942, 3; and "Japanese Joined in Folk Festival," 13 November 1943, 8.

81 "Our Contacts with Canadian Society," *New Canadian,* 26 January 1942, 4.

82 "Our Festival of Peoples," *New Canadian,* 10 October 1941, 2.

83 Swyripa, *Wedded to the Cause,* 136.

84 Andrusyshen, "The Contributions of the Ukrainian Canadians to Canadian Culture," 108.

85 W.J. Sarchuk, "Ukrainian Contribution to Canadian Culture," in *First All-Canadian Congress of Ukrainians in Canada,* 109.

86 For Ukrainian nationalists' use of Lord Tweedsmuir's appreciation of Ukrainian folk culture, see Swyripa, *Wedded to the Cause.*

87 Anthony Hlynka, in House of Commons, *Debates,* 25 November 1940, 381.

88 Anthony Hlynka, in House of Commons, *Debates,* 18 February 1943, 521–22.

89 "Canadians All: *Nisei* Support Canada Says Gov't Book," *New Canadian,* 25 July 1941, 1. See also "Mosaic of Loyalty in Canada," *New Canadian,* 19 January 1940, 2; on the drama festival and the mosaic, "Nisei in Canadian Society," *New Canadian,* 9 February 1940, 4; and "Our Responsibility," *New Canadian,* 16 February 1940, 4.

90 "Peresuvannia narodiv," *Ukrainskyi holos,* 8 October 1941, 4.

91 Since the Cossacks and Bohdan Khmelnytsky were regarded as their symbols, nationalist Ukrainians opposed the use of them by communists. See "Shcho chorne, to ne bile," *Ukrainskyi holos,* 5 April 1944, 4.

92 The connection between democracy and the clan system made by Angus L. Macdonald during World War II is discussed by Ian McKay in "Tartanism Triumphant: The Construction of Scottishness in Nova Scotia," *Acadiensis* 21, 2 (1992): 41–42.

93 PANS, MG 2, vol. 1507, file 436-18, Angus L. Macdonald, address to the Ottawa Gaelic Society, 29 February 1944, 1.

94 Ibid., 3.

95 PANS, MG 2, vol. 1507, file 437-2, Angus L. Macdonald, "Gaelic Mod—Cape Breton," address, August 1942, 2.

96 PANS, MG 2, vol. 1518, file 746-47, T.C. Davis, address to the St. Andrew's Society of Melbourne, 30 November 1944, 13.

97 Basil Kushnir, "Post-War Reconstruction of the World," in *First All-Canadian Congress of Ukrainians in Canada,* 119.

98 J.L.W. McLean, "A Message for Sunday," *Presbyterian Record* 68, 7 (1943): 217.

99 PANS, MG 2, vol. 1507, file 436-12, Donald Lewis MacDonald, address to the Highland Society of Antigonish, 30 November 1940, 3.

100 PANS, MG 2, vol. 1507, file 436-18, Angus L. Macdonald, address to the Ottawa Gaelic Society, 29 February 1944, 1.

101 Anthony Hlynka, in House of Commons, *Debates,* 2 February 1942, 233.

102 "Demokratiia," *Ukrainskyi holos,* 3 June 1942, 4.

103 Anthony Hlynka, in House of Commons, *Debates,* 2 February 1942, 232.

104 PANS, MG 2, vol. 1507, file 436-18, Angus L. Macdonald, address to the Ottawa Gaelic Society, 29 February 1944, 2; O. Terletskyi, "Iak buduvav i iak ruinuvav ukrainskyi narod," *Kaliendar "Ukrainskyi holos"* (1941): 38; see also O. Ivakh, "Shevchenko—prorok ukrainy," *Kaliendar "Ukrainskyi holos"* (1942): 35–39.

Chapter 4: Democratic and Multicultural Citizenship

1 See Patricia E. Roy, *The Triumph of Citizenship: The Japanese and Chinese in Canada, 1941–67* (Vancouver: UBC Press, 2007); and Bangarth, *Voices Raised in Protest.*

2 See Iacovetta, *Gatekeepers*.

3 For mainstream Canadians' reaction to Ukrainian nationalists and communists, see Caccia, *Managing the Canadian Mosaic in Wartime*, 160–77.

4 On the Cold War, anticommunism, and new immigration that shaped postwar Canadian citizenship, see Iacovetta, *Gatekeepers*, 62.

5 Paul Martin, "Canada and the United Nations," *Dalhousie Review* 33, 4 (1954): 212.

6 This organization was established after a conference on education held on 20 November 1940 through the initiative of C.H. Blakeny, minister of education in New Brunswick, and D. McArthur, minister of education in Ontario. See LAC, MG 28 I 85, vol. 31, file: Annual Meeting—Report 1941, Canadian Council of Education for Citizenship, annual report, 31 December 1941. On the Canadian Citizenship Council and its ideals, see also Iacovetta, *Gatekeepers*, 62.

7 "United Nations Day," *Citizenship Items* 1, 2 (1948): 1.

8 Committee of the Canadian Teachers' Federation, *The Democratic Way: The Air We Breathe*, no. 1 (Ottawa: Canadian Citizenship Council; Toronto: Canadian Association for Adult Education, 1951), 1.

9 "Secretary's Desk," *New Canadian*, 23 December 1950, 15. For Japanese-Canadian internationalism, see also "Rule of War," *New Canadian*, 10 August 1949, 2; and "For a Better Canada, We Must Each Do Our Part," *New Canadian*, 28 October 1950, 1, 8.

10 "Unite as Ukrainians and as Canadians!," *Ukrainian Canadian*, 15 February 1956, 9.

11 "For Victory in AUUC Drive," *Ukrainian Canadian*, 1 April 1956, 5.

12 John Decore, in *Piatyi i shostyi kongres ukraintsiv Kanady*, edited by UCC (Winnipeg: Ukrainian National Publishers, 1956), 86.

13 How citizenship was imagined in a historical context is discussed in a collection of essays, Robert Adamoskyi, Dorothy D. Chunn, and Robert Menzie, eds., *Contesting Canadian Citizenship: Historical Readings* (Peterborough: Broadview Press, 2002).

14 "The Human Rights Charter," *Citizenship Items* 2, 1 (1949): 1.

15 Committee of the Canadian Teachers' Federation, *The Democratic Way: The Air We Breathe*, 6.

16 Committee of the Canadian Teachers' Federation, *The Democratic Way: I'm Free to Choose*, no. 2 (Ottawa: Canadian Citizenship Council; Toronto: Canadian Association for Adult Education, 1951), 5.

17 Committee of the Canadian Teachers' Federation, *The Democratic Way: Freedom of Conscience*, no. 4 (Ottawa: Canadian Citizenship Council; Toronto: Canadian Association for Adult Education, 1951), 5.

18 Louis St. Laurent, in *Chetvertyi vce-kanadiiskyi kongres ukraintsiv Kanady* (Winnipeg: Ukrainian National Publishers, 1953), 23.

19 Paul Martin, in House of Commons, *Debates*, 22 October 1945, 1337.

20 LAC, MG 28 I 85, vol. 31, file: Annual Meeting—Report 1941, Canadian Council of Education for Citizenship, annual report, 31 December 1941.

21 For the integration of postwar immigrants, see Iacovetta, *Gatekeepers*.

22 LAC, MG 28 I 85, vol. 45, file: Canadian Council of Education for Citizenship, Minute Book, 1944–1950, H.D.G. Crerar, Chairman, Executive Committee, Canadian Citizenship Council, memorandum on Training for Canadian Citizenship to Departments of Government and Organizations whose delegates attended the Conference on Citizenship Problems of Immigrants and Other Interested Bodies, 1948.

23 LAC, MG 28 I 85, vol. 31, file: Annual Meetings—Minutes and Financial Statements 1945–1955, Canadian Citizenship Council, minutes of annual meeting, 23 May 1950.

24 Ibid.

25 LAC, MG 28 I 85, vol. 31, file: Annual Meetings—Minutes and Financial Statements 1945–1955, Canadian Citizenship Council, annual report, 30 April 1954.

26 Roy, *The Triumph of Citizenship,* 188.

27 LAC, MG 32 C 67, vol. 15, file 30, Paul Yuzyk, "Citizenship Day in Winnipeg, Report to Ukrainian Section, IS-CBC," 20 May 1953.

28 LAC, MG 32 C 67, vol. 15, file 30, Paul Yuzyk, "Civic and Municipal Elections in Manitoba, News Report to the Ukrainian Section, IS-CBC," 1 November 1953.

29 "Vlasnymy sylamy," *Ukrainskyi holos,* 14 January 1948, 4. See also "Politychne a, b, v," *Ukrainskyi holos,* 6 February 1946, 4; and "V chim syla hromadianstva," *Ukrainskyi holos,* 25 December 1946, 4.

30 "We Are Canadian Citizens," *New Canadian,* 4 January 1947, 2. See also "New Years Day Marks Enforcement of New Canadian Citizenship Act," *New Canadian,* 4 January 1947, 1; Mas Sunada, "Citizenship Discussed at Alberta Youth Conference," *New Canadian,* 11 January 1947, 1; "Weakness in Citizenship Act Draws Many Criticisms," *New Canadian,* 18 January 1947, 1; "Mature Citizenship," *New Canadian,* 18 January 1947, 2; "Kanada shimin to natta hi no shinjô," *New Canadian,* 10 January 1948, 5; "Canada Recognizes Citizenship of Niseis, Naturalized Persons," *New Canadian,* 6 December 1947, 1; and "Canadian Citizenship," *New Canadian,* 21 May 1952, 2.

31 "1949—the Best Year for Japanese Canadians," *New Canadian,* 24 December 1949, 1. See also "A Day to Remember," *New Canadian,* 6 April 1949, 2; "Japanese Canadians Win Franchise: Measure Passed without Protest," *New Canadian,* 23 June 1948, 1; "A Pleasant Surprise," *New Canadian,* 26 January 1949, 2; "BC Japanese Canadians Win Franchise," *New Canadian,* 12 March 1949, 1; and "Credit Where Credit Is Due," *New Canadian,* 16 March 1949, 2.

32 "Zvidusiudy," *Ukrainskyi holos,* 16 January 1946, 2. For their attack on the communist definition of democratic practice in the Soviet Union, see, for example, "Shchyra mova," *Ukrainskyi holos,* 13 February 1946, 4; and "Ekonomichna demokratiia," *Ukrainskyi holos,* 20 November 1946, 4.

33 "Soiuz ukraintsiv samostiinykiv proty komunistychnoi roboty," *Ukrainskyi holos,* 9 January 1946, 1.

34 LAC, MG 30 D 403, vol. 24, file 31, William M. Teresio, President, Association of United Ukrainian Canadians, brief submitted to the Senate Committee on Immigration on behalf of the Association of United Ukrainian Canadians, the Ukrainian Labour-Farmer Temple Association (hereafter ULFTA), the

Workers' Benevolent Association, and the newspaper *Ukrainian Life*, Ottawa, 5 June 1947.

35 "Slavic Canadians! Let Our Voice Be Heard!," *Ukrainian Canadian*, 15 May 1955, 7. See also "USSR—Cornerstone of Slav Unity," *Ukrainian Canadian*, 15 January 1953, 7–8; and "The Address of John Boyd to the Congress," *Ukrainian Canadian*, 15 July 1955, 57.

36 Yasutarô Yamaga, "Hitotsu no hansei," *New Canadian*, 12 October 1946, 5.

37 Ibid. See also "Dai nisei no jidai to iukoto," *New Canadian*, 22 December 1956, 1.

38 Sunahara, *The Politics of Racism*, 109.

39 Adachi, *The Enemy that Never Was*, 333.

40 "Velyke pravo," *Ukrainskyi holos*, 26 January 1946, 4.

41 "Ukrainske pytannia v Ottavi," *Ukrainskyi holos*, 14 April 1954, 4. On the issue of nations that remained oppressed after World War II, see, for example, "Zabrekhanyi svit," *Ukrainskyi holos*, 16 January 1946, 4.

42 Basil Kushnir, "Ukrainska vyzvolna sprava na tri mizhnarodnoho polozhennia v sviti," in *Tretii vse-kanadiiskyi kongres ukraintsiv Kanady*, edited by UCC (Winnipeg: Ukrainian National Publishers, 1950), 58–59.

43 W.S. Kochan, "Politychi problemy," in *Piatyi i shostyi kongres ukraintsiv Kanady*, 144–45.

44 Many of the issues regarding the negotiations between the Canadian government and the Ukrainian-Canadian community and the role of Anthony Hlynka are discussed in Luciuk, *Searching for Place*.

45 Acadia University Special Collections, Watson Kirkconnell Collection, vol. 45, file 10, UCC, memorandum to W.L. Mackenzie King on Ukrainian Refugees, 23 May 1945. The UCC also presented a memorandum to the United Nations that can be found in *Ukrainskyi holos*, 13 November 1946, 4. On the refugee issue, see also, for example, "Obhovoriuetsia sprava imigratsii do Kanady," *Ukrainskyi holos*, 15 January 1947, 1; "Sprava imigratsii do Kanady," *Ukrainskyi holos*, 29 January 1947, 1; "Sprava imigratsii do Kanady," *Ukrainskyi holos*, 2 July 1947, 4; and "V spravi ukrainskoi imigratsii, Ukrainska delegatsiia v Ottavi," *Ukrainskyi holos*, 18 June 1947, 1.

46 Anthony Hlynka, in House of Commons, *Debates*, 24 September 1945, 386–87.

47 Anthony Hlynka, in House of Commons, *Debates*, 14 December 1945, 3528–29.

48 Ibid., 2529.

49 Oleh W. Gerus and Denis Hlynka, *The Honourable Member for Vegreville: The Memoirs and Diary of Anthony Hlynka, MP* (Calgary: University of Calgary Press, 2005), 139–42.

50 "Japanese Problem Can Be Solved," *New Canadian*, 30 March 1946, 2.

51 "We Must Continue the Fight," *New Canadian*, 23 February 1946, 2.

52 Norman Black, *From Citizens to Refugees—It's Happening Here!* (Toronto: Co-operative Committee on Japanese Canadians [hereafter CCJC], 1945), 1. On the Japanese lobby for the end of prewar and wartime restrictions, see, for example, "End Restrictions, JCCA Brief Urges," *New Canadian*, 13 March

1948, 1–3; and "Seek Vote for Japanese Canadians: Niseis Lobby for Elections Act Revision, Removal of Ban from Crown Timber Lands," *New Canadian*, 10 April 1948, 1.

53 See, for example, Edith Fowke, *They Made Democracy Work: The Story of the Co-operative Committee on Japanese Canadians* (Toronto: CCJC and Japanese Canadian Citizens Association [hereafter JCCA], 1951), 9.

54 "Orders-in-Council Challenged," *New Canadian*, 12 January 1946, 2.

55 Black, *From Citizens to Refugees—It's Happening Here!*, 1.

56 LAC, MG 31 E 26, vol. 1, Muriel Kitagawa, manuscript of speech to the National Council of Women, March 1948.

57 LAC, MG 28 V 1, vol. 1, file 1-2, Hugh MacMillan to Edith Fowke, CCJC, 19 May 1946. On deportation and racism, see also "The Bill vs. Deportation Orders," *New Canadian*, 11 May 1946, 2; "Expulsion?," *Nisei Affairs*, 20 July 1945, 2; "V-J Day," *Nisei Affairs*, 28 August 1945, 2; "Will Race Bigotry Triumph?," *Nisei Affairs*, 29 September 1945, 2; George T. Takami, "Deportation by Order-in-Council," *Nisei Affairs*, 31 October 1945, 1; and "Deportation Should Be Abandoned," *Nisei Affairs*, 19 January 1946, 1.

58 "Time to Protest," *New Canadian*, 19 July 1947, 2.

59 "How Can You Justify Racial Discrimination in Immigration, while Deploring It at Home?," *New Canadian*, 18 August 1956, 2.

60 *Tairiku jihô*, 3 December 1954, 4.

61 "Memorandum by Ukrainian Canadian Committee, Representing Canadian Citizens of Ukrainian Origin to Paris Peace Conference, September 1946," *Ukrainskyi holos*, 16 October 1946, 6.

62 S.W. Sawchuk, "Persha sesiia," in *Piatyi i shostyi kongres ukraintsiv Kanady*, 18–19.

63 Decore, in ibid., 87.

64 John Weir, "USSR—Cornerstone of Slav Unity," *Ukrainian Canadian*, 15 January 1953, 7.

65 John Kolasky, "Slavic Solidarity—a Ukrainian Tradition," *Ukrainian Canadian*, 15 January 1952, 5; Weir, "USSR—Cornerstone of Slav Unity," 7.

66 LAC, MG 28 V 1, vol. 1, file 3, CCJC, brief to W.L. Mackenzie King on Repatriation of Japanese Canadians, 25 July 1945.

67 Its official title was the Royal Commission to Investigate Complaints of Canadian Citizens of Japanese Origin Who Resided in British Columbia in 1941, that Their Real and Personal Property Had Been Disposed of by the Custodian of Enemy Property at Prices Less than the Fair Market Value.

68 "Wanted, a Report on Evacuation," *New Canadian*, 28 June 1946, 2.

69 Fowke, *They Made Democracy Work*, 32.

70 Harold Troper, "The Canadian Government and DPs, 1945–8," in *The Refugee Experience: Ukrainian Displaced Persons after World War II*, edited by Wsevolod W. Isajiw, Yury Boshyk, and Roman Senkus (Edmonton: Canadian Institute of Ukrainian Studies Press, 1992), 403.

71 Luciuk, *Searching for Place*, 79–81. The gap between the ideals of the Canadian government and the Ukrainian elite during World War II is best explored by Bohdan S. Kordan. He argues that the Canadian government,

while launching democratic principles and national sovereignty as policies, rarely supported Ukrainian nationalist causes, partly because of diplomatic relations with the Soviet Union. See his *Canada and the Ukrainian Question, 1939–1945* (Montreal: McGill-Queen's University Press, 2001), 4–5.

72 According to Luciuk, neither the British nor the American government showed sympathy for the independence of Ukraine. See his *Searching for Place,* 111–14.

73 Sunahara, *The Politics of Racism,* 117. Patricia E. Roy also argues that civil liberty and church groups took a pro-Japanese stance by this time in pursuit of democracy and human rights. See her "Lessons in Citizenship, 1945–1949: The Delayed Return of the Japanese to Canada's Pacific Coast," in *Nikkei in the Pacific Northwest: Japanese Americans and Japanese Canadians in the Twentieth Century,* edited by Louis Fiset and Gail M. Nomura (Seattle: University of Washington Press, 2000), 269.

74 For activities that advocated the rights of Japanese Canadians, see Bangarth, *Voices Raised in Protest.*

75 W.L. Mackenzie King, in House of Commons, *Debates,* 4 August 1944, 5915.

76 Sunahara, *The Politics of Racism,* 119–20.

77 Ibid., 128. Ross Lambertson provides a detailed account of the negotiation between the CCJC and the federal government over deportation of Japanese, recognizing the significance of the issue in the development of human rights in Canada. See his *Repression and Resistance: Canadian Human Rights Activists, 1930–1960* (Toronto: University of Toronto Press, 2005), 106–42.

78 On the attitudes of the Canadian government, see Myron Momryk, "Ukrainian DP Immigration and Government Policy in Canada, 1946–52," in Isajiw, Boshyk, and Senkus, *The Refugee Experience,* 413–33; and Troper, "The Canadian Government and DPs, 1945–8," 402–12.

79 Luciuk, *Searching for Place,* 82–83. Communist Ukrainians in Canada also expressed their resentment of Canada's acceptance of displaced persons; see, for example, "Deport Nazi DP Criminals!," *Ukrainian Canadian,* 15 January 1950, 1.

80 Anthony Hlynka, in House of Commons, *Debates,* 18 December 1945, 3718.

81 W.L. Mackenzie King, in House of Commons, *Debates,* 1 May 1947, 2645.

82 Troper, "The Canadian Government and DPs, 1945–8," 408; Momryk, "Ukrainian DP Immigration and Government Policy in Canada, 1946–52," 420.

83 Adachi, *The Enemy that Never Was,* 325–26. For the Japanese attack on the narrow definition of losses set by the royal commission, see "Terms of Reference Are Too Restricted," *New Canadian,* 18 August 1946, 2; "Indemnification for Losses," *New Canadian,* 1 February 1947, 2; "Basis for Compensation," *New Canadian,* 10 May 1947, 2; "A Satisfactory Proposal," *New Canadian,* 2 August 1947, 1; "A Request to the Commissioner," *New Canadian,* 8 November 1947, 2; and "The Claims Question," *New Canadian,* 21 June 1950, 8.

84 LAC, MG 28 V 1, vol. 1, file 1, CCJC, minutes, 24 February 1950.

85 LAC, MG 28 V 1, vol. 1, file 1, S. Takashima, Toronto Claimants' Committee, to Margaret K. Boos, Secretary, CCJC, n.d.

86 LAC, MG 28 I 85, vol. 31, file: Annual Meeting—Report 1941, Canadian Council of Education for Citizenship, first annual report, 31 December 1941.

87 LAC, MG 28 I 85, vol. 54, file: Canadian Citizenship Council Memorandum re: Its History and Activities, 1941–1955, Canadian Citizenship Council, memorandum, October 1955.

88 LAC, MG 28 I 85, vol. 45, file: Canadian Council of Education for Citizenship, Minute Book, 1944–1950, "Some Thoughts in Connection with Organization Pattern of the Canadian Citizenship Council," n.d.

89 The council was involved with the Jewish community in education and conferences. See, for example, LAC, MG 28 I 85, vol. 45, file: Canadian Council of Education for Citizenship, Minute Book, 1944–1950, Canadian Council of Education for Citizenship, minutes, 8 October 1949.

90 LAC, MG 28 I 85, vol. 45, file: Canadian Council of Education for Citizenship, Minute Book, 1944–1950, Canadian Citizenship Council, minutes of executive meeting, 5–6 November 1948.

91 "Ukrainska kultura," *Ukrainskyi holos,* 9 January 1946, 11. See also "Kulturna syla v nashomu zhyttiu," *Ukrainskyi holos,* 15 January 1947, 4; "Syla kultury v zhyttiu narodu," *Ukrainskyi holos,* 30 April 1947, 4; and "Chom ukraintsi v Kanadi svoimy spravamy interesuiutsia," *Ukrainskyi holos,* 18 June 1947, 4.

92 "Zahalnyi narodnyi zizd Soiuzu ukraintsiv samostiinykiv ta yoho soiuznik organizatsii v Vynypeg, Man.," *Ukrainskyi holos,* 30 January 1946, 7.

93 Ibid.

94 "Ukrainska mova v Alberti," *Ukrainskyi holos,* 3 September 1958, 4.

95 Michael Luchkovich, "V oboroni ukrainskoi movy," *Ukrainskyi holos,* 15 October 1958, 4. For bilingual education and school questions in the Prairies in the late nineteenth and early twentieth centuries, see Bill Maciejko, "Ukrainians and Prairie School Reform, 1896–1921: Ethnic and Domestic Ideologies in Modern State Formation," *Canadian Ethnic Studies* 22, 2 (1990): 19–40. For the historical development of Ukrainian education in Canada, see Manoly R. Lupul, "Ukrainian-Language Education in Canada's Public Schools," in *A Heritage in Transition,* 215–43.

96 "Korolivska komisiia i ukrainska mova v Manitobi," *Ukrainskyi holos,* 2 December 1959, 4.

97 On national communism, see Wilson, *Ukrainian Nationalism in the 1990s,* 93–116.

98 John Weir, "National Groups and the Canadian Character," *Ukrainian Canadian,* 1 May 1955, 9.

99 Ibid.

100 Hannah Polowy, "Ukrainians Have Role in Democratic Culture," *Ukrainian Canadian,* 1 May 1955, 11.

101 Peter Krawchuk, "October Revolution Gave Ukrainians Freedom," *Ukrainian Canadian,* 1 November 1955, 7.

102 For the call for a bill on fundamental human rights, see, for example, "Canada Needs a Bill of Rights," *New Canadian,* 15 March 1947, 2; "Canadians Ask for Rights Bill," *New Canadian,* 23 June 1948, 2; "Vancouver Minority and Labour Groups in Joint Action for Bill of Rights," *New Canadian,* 8 March 1950, 1;

"National JCCA to Urge Bill of Rights before Senate Committee at Ottawa," *New Canadian,* 29 April 1950, 1; "JCCA Brief Heard by Senate Committee, Urges Rights Bill," *New Canadian,* 13 May 1950, 1; and "To Confer with Prime Minister about Canadian Bill of Rights," *New Canadian,* 28 April 1951, 1.

103 S.W., "The Question of Assimilation," *New Canadian,* 24 August 1946, 2.

104 "Mature Citizenship," *New Canadian,* 18 January 1947, 18.

105 Martynowych, "Introduction," in *Prophets and Proletarians,* xxvi. See also "Some Problems Facing AUUC," *Ukrainian Canadian,* 1 January 1952, 6.

106 "JCCA Necessary to Safeguard Japanese Canadian Interests," *New Canadian,* 26 October 1949, 1. On the NJCCA survival, see also "George Tanaka Said: 'JCCA Important as Means of Fostering Democracy,'" *New Canadian,* 24 June 1953, 1; Ed Ide, "What 'JCCA' Means to Me," *New Canadian,* 22 December 1954, 4; "Whither JCCA?," *New Canadian,* 26 January 1955, 2; "National JCCA: A Backward Step?," *New Canadian,* 2 July 1955, 2; "Urge February Confab in Winnipeg to Decide Future of National JCCA," *New Canadian,* 10 November 1956, 1; "Nisei No Longer Dependent on Ethnic Community," *New Canadian,* 19 January 1957, 1; "What Do You Think about the National Confab?," *New Canadian,* 26 January 1957, 1; "JCCA: The Membership," *New Canadian,* 2 February 1957, 3; "Where Do We Go from Here?," *New Canadian,* 24 December 1958, 1; "Problems of JCCA in Vancouver," *Tairiku jihô,* 10 April 1959, 1 (English section); and "The JCCA—Reorganize or Disband?," *Tairiku jihô,* 28 April 1959, 1 (English section).

107 George Tanaka, "What Is JCCA?," *New Canadian,* 25 January 1958, 8.

Chapter 5: The Canadianization and Ethnicization of Myths, Collective Memories, and Symbols

1 See, for example, "Burns Glorified Scotland," *Globe and Mail,* 24 January 1947, 6; J.V. Mcakee, "Burns Not Bobby, but Rab or Rabby," *Globe and Mail,* 25 January 1947, 6; "A Tribute to Burns and His Poetry," *Globe and Mail,* 24 January 1948, 6; J.V. Mcakee, "Aberdeen Newspaper Two Centuries Old," *Globe and Mail,* 29 January 1948; and "Robert Burns," *Winnipeg Free Press,* 24 January 1953, 19.

2 McKay, "Tartanism Triumphant," 46–47.

3 For the relationship between ethnicity and past memories, see Anthony D. Smith, *Myths and Memories of the Nation* (Oxford: Oxford University Press, 1999), 174–208.

4 The term "the golden age" in this context was taken from Anthony D. Smith, *Chosen Peoples: Sacred Sources of National Identity* (Oxford: Oxford University Press, 2003), 191.

5 "I nesytyi ne vyore na dni moria polia," *Ukrainskyi holos,* 7 May 1947, 4.

6 "Bohdan Khmelnytskyi," *Ukrainskyi holos,* 4 June 1947, 9, and 11 June 1947, 9. For Cossacks as "freedom fighters" and the role of the grandmother of Volodymyr the Great in Ukrainian-Canadian women's mythology, see Swyripa, *Wedded to the Cause,* 103–42.

7 "Velych Shevchenka," *Ukrainskyi holos,* 7 March 1956, 4. See also "I necytyi ne vyore na dni moria polia," *Ukrainskyi holos,* 7 May 1947, 4; "Sviato Tarasa Shevchenka," *Ukrainskyi holos,* 26 February 1947, 4; "Obrikhuvachi

Shevchenka," *Ukrainskyi holos,* 20 June 1951, 4; "Nastilna knyha ukraintsia kobzar T. Shevchenka," *Ukrainskyi holos,* 26 September 1951, 4–5; and "Pamiatnyk Shevchenkovi," *Ukrainskyi holos,* 16 December 1959, 4.

8 "The chosen people" in this context is taken from Smith, *Chosen Peoples*, 51.

9 "Sviato Tarasa Shevchenka," *Ukrainskyi holos,* 26 February 1947, 4.

10 "I nesytyi ne vyore na dni moria polia," *Ukrainskyi holos,* 7 May 1947, 4.

11 The tendency of Scots in Nova Scotia to stress their superiority as a founding race and part of the British Empire is discussed by McKay, "Tartanism Triumphant," 19.

12 For Scots' mission to build peace in the postwar world, see also PANS, MG 2, vol. 1507, file 437-4, Angus L. Macdonald, address to the St. Andrew's Society of Philadelphia, 30 November 1948.

13 PANS, MG 2, vol. 1507, file 438-1, Angus L. Macdonald, "Response to the Toast to the Immortal Bard before the North British Society of Halifax, Nova Scotia, on the Occasion of Burns' Anniversary," 25 January 1951. On both Taras Shevchenko and Robert Burns, see also Frances Swyripa, "History, Ethnic Legitimacy, and Public Space: The Shevchenko Statues in Winnipeg and Washington," paper presented at the conference Cross-Stitching Cultural Borders: Comparing Ukrainian Experience in Canada and the United States, University of Toronto, 29–31 October 1998.

14 PANS, MG 2, vol. 1507, file 441-12, J. Keiller Mackay, "Response to the Toast to Scotland before the North British Society of Halifax Nova Scotia on the Occasion of Its One Hundred and Eighty-Third Annual Festival of St. Andrew," 30 November 1950, 5.

15 PANS, MG 2, vol. 1507, file 437-4, Angus L. Macdonald, address to the St. Andrew's Society of Philadelphia, 30 November 1948.

16 McKay, "Tartanism Triumphant," 27–29, also stresses the significance of the uprising of 1945 to Scots in Nova Scotia but does not relate it to the postwar context.

17 PANS, MG 2, vol. 1507, file 444-3, John A.Y. Macdonald, Deputy Attorney General, Nova Scotia, to All Members of the Clan Donald, 30 July 1952. See also Moray Mclaren, "Flora Macdonald and the Island of Her Heart," *Piper and Dancer Bulletin* (1952): 11–13.

18 The relationship between Scots and racism was explored by Michael Vance. According to him, an influential Scot, Reverend Duncan McDougall, promoted an anti-Asian movement in British Columbia in the 1920s. See his "A Brief History of Organized Scottishness in Canada," in *Transatlantic Scots,* edited by Celeste Ray (Tuscaloosa: University of Alabama Press, 2005), 106–07.

19 "Kokoro no hata o kakage hôgei junbi naru," *New Canadian,* 4 April 1953, 5.

20 "Nikka yûkô zôshin nozomu," *New Canadian,* 15 April 1953, 6.

21 "The Visit of Prince Akihito," *New Canadian,* 22 April 1953, 2.

22 "Nihon prinsu o mukaeta kimochi de nikkeijin no kanada kikan o yuruse," *Tairiku jihô,* 28 April 1953, 4. Racial discrimination in the entry of immigrants remained until the Immigration Regulations of 1967, designed to recruit skilled labourers. For changes in immigration policy, see Donald H.

Avery, *Reluctant Host: Canada's Response to Immigrant Workers* (Toronto: McClelland and Stewart, 1995), 186.

23 "Ippen no hanabira to ha o," *Tairiku jiho,* 28 April 1953, 2. For the enthusiasm of Japanese in Canada for this occasion, see also "Jûichinichikan no gonittei hajimeraru" and "Ensen de gokangei," *New Canadian,* 11 April 1953, 6; "Shûji egao de gorippa na taido," *New Canadian,* 15 April 1953, 6; "Mimei demo okirarete" and "Nikkei senamari ga sôgei," *New Canadian,* 18 April 1953, 5.

24 "Prince Akihito, Heir Apparent, Will Spend Eleven Days in Canada, Arrives on April 11," *New Canadian,* 28 March 1953, 1.

25 *Tairiku jihô,* 17 April 1953, 4.

26 Brass, "Elite Groups, Symbol Manipulation, and Ethnic Identity among the Muslims of South Asia," 41.

27 "Obrikhuvachi Shevchenka," *Ukrainskyi holos,* 20 June 1941, 4.

28 "The Legacy of Taras," *Ukrainian Canadian,* 1 February 1953, 4.

29 "Why Shevchenko Lives in Our Hearts," *Ukrainian Canadian,* 1 March 1951, 5.

30 "USSR—Cornerstone of Slav Unity," *Ukrainian Canadian,* 15 January 1953, 7.

31 "Ukraine's Birthday," *Ukrainian Canadian,* 15 December 1952, 4. Much of this argument reflected the fact that Khmelnytsky's Cossack state had no choice but to sign the Treaty of Pereiaslav in 1654 with Moscow, facing frequent attacks from Russians, Poles, and Tatars. For various interpretations of the treaty, see Andrew Wilson, *Ukrainian Nationalism in the 1990s,* 6–7.

32 For politicization of Shevchenko by both nationalist and communist Ukrainians and controversy over the monument, see Swyripa, "History, Ethnic Legitimacy, and Public Space."

33 "A Great Triumph," *Ukrainian Canadian,* 15 July 1951, 1. See also "Jubilee Festival and Shevchenko Monument, Museum, and Park," *Ukrainian Canadian,* 15 April 1951, 9; "Festival Concert Was Well Performed," *Ukrainian Canadian,* 1 August 1951, 2; "5000 at Eastern Canada Celebration," *Ukrainian Canadian,* 15 July 1952, 2; "True Canadian Spirit," *Ukrainian Canadian,* 15 July 1954, 4; "Bard of Ukraine: Taras Shevchenko," *Ukrainian Canadian,* 1 March 1955, 7–10; "Towards a Memorable Jubilee," *Ukrainian Canadian,* 1 September 1959, 3; Mitch Sago, "What Will the National Shevchenko Festival Be Like?," *Ukrainian Canadian,* 1 October 1959, 5; and "AUUC Issues Call for Stronger Peace Effort: Plan Shevchenko Festival in Palermo for July 1961," *Ukrainian Canadian,* 15 October 1959, 1.

34 "Nastilna knyha ukraintsia—kobzar T. Shevchenka," *Ukrainskyi holos,* 26 September 1951, 4.

35 Paul Yuzyk, "A New Monument on the Legislative Building Grounds," *Manitoba Pageant* 7, 1 (1961): 11. My ideas about the two Shevchenko statues draw on Swyripa, "History, Ethnic Legitimacy, and Public Space."

36 *Tairiku jihô,* 24 April 1953, 4.

37 Ethnic elites' strategy to combine their historic heroes with mainstream landmark events to position themselves in Canadian history was pointed out by Frances Swyripa in her "Ethnic Loyalists and Selkirk Settlers: The Ukrainians Rewrite Canadian History," paper presented at the Canadian Ethnic Studies Association Biennial Conference, Winnipeg, 23–26 October 1991.

38 "Iak vidbuvalosia sviato hromadianstva," *Ukrainskyi holos,* 22 January 1947, 5. For the symbolic significance of Eleniak to Ukrainian Canadians, see also "Wasyl Eleniak," *Ukrainskyi holos,* 18 January 1956, 4. For his message at the sixtieth anniversary of Ukrainian immigration to Canada, see "Pryvity z hahody sviatkuvan 60-littia ukrainskoho poselennia v Kanadi," *Ukrainskyi holos,* 19 September 1951, 5.

39 Vera Lysenko, *Men in Sheepskin Coats: A Study in Assimilation* (Toronto: Ryerson Press, 1947), 299. For communist enshrinement of another first Ukrainian to Canada, Ivan Pilipiw, see "The Pioneers' Long Trail to the Homestead," *Ukrainian Canadian,* 15 December 1950, 2; and "Ivan Pylypiv—First Settler," *Ukurainian Canadian,* 1 December 1950, 5. On the role of Eleniak in the Alberta golden jubilee in 1955, see Frances Swyripa, "1955: Celebrating Together, Celebrating Apart: Albertans and Their Golden Jubilee," in *Alberta Formed, Alberta Transformed,* edited by Michael Payne, Donald Wetherell, and Catherine Cavanaugh (Edmonton: University of Alberta Press; Calgary: University of Calgary Press, 2006), 604–05.

40 "Editor, Publisher, Exporter, Lumberman, Farmer, Chosen as Outstanding Japanese," *New Canadian,* 1 March 1950, 1.

41 "Dokusha ga eranda 'kôsekisha' sanjû roku mei kaku hômen o hukunda tokuhyôjun no kaobure," *New Canadian,* 1 March 1950, 5.

42 "Kôsekisha ni ageta riyû," *New Canadian,* 4 March 1950, 5.

43 "Z iuvileinykh sviatkuvan u Vynypegu," *Ukrainskyi holos,* 24 October 1951, 3. For the sixtieth anniversary of Ukrainian settlement in Canada, see also "Sviato ukraintsiv-pioniriv," *Ukrainskyi holos,* 16 May 1951, 4; "Skilky nas?," *Ukrainskyi holos,* 23 May 1951, 4; "Vanky z ukrainskymy prizvyshchamy," *Ukrainskyi holos,* 30 May 1951, 4; "Sviato ukrainskykh pioniriv u Prezent Hom, Man.," *Ukrainskyi holos,* 8 August 1951, 1; "Iuvileine sviatkuvannia 60-ykh rokovyn ukrainskykh pioniriv v Alberti," *Ukrainskyi holos,* 15 August 1951, 4–5; "60-littia ukrainskykh pioniriv," *Ukrainskyi holos,* 22 August 1951, 11; "1891—60-littia poselennia ukraintsiv v Kanadi—1951," *Ukrainskyi holos,* 5 September 1951, 1; "Iak ia pochav hospodariuvaty v Kanadi," *Ukrainskyi holos,* 5 September 1951, 6; and "Urochysto vshanovano ukrainskykh pioniriv," *Ukrainskyi holos,* 12 September 1951, 1.

44 "Thoughts on Canada Day," *Ukrainian Canadian,* 1 July 1956, 4. For the story of progress by communists, also see "Alberta—Land of Our Pioneers," *Ukrainian Canadian,* 1 July 1952, 2; and "Saskatchewan's Jubilee," *Ukrainian Canadian,* 15 June 1955, 3.

45 "Kaitaku seishin to shikyô," *New Canadian,* 21 October 1950, 5. For pioneer stories, see also "History of the First Arrivals to Canada from Japan," *New Canadian,* 22 March 1950, 1; Toyo Tanaka, "Saga of the Earliest Issei," *New Canadian,* 23 December 1950, 1, 16; "Ups and Downs of an Issei Pioneer," *New Canadian,* 12 May 1954, 2; "130–150 Issei Have Lived 50 Years in Canada," *New Canadian,* 24 December 1955, 9; and George Tanaka, "The Issei Generation," *New Canadian,* 24 December 1958, 5.

46 Alexandra Kruchka Glynn, "Vera Lysenko's *Men in Sheepskin Coats* (1947): The Untold Story," *Journal of Ukrainian Studies* 16, 1–2 (1991): 223.

47 Lysenko, *Men in Sheepskin Coats;* Alexandra Kruchka Glynn, "Reinforcing Vera Lysenko—Ukrainian Canadian Author," *Journal of Ukrainian Studies* 15, 1 (1990): 66.

48 Paul Yuzyk, *Ukrainians in Manitoba: A Social History* (Toronto: University of Toronto Press, 1953).See Swyripa, *Ukrainian Canadians*, 77.

49 "What Is the Japanese Canadian?," *New Canadian,* 2 October 1957, 8.

50 Frank Moritsugu, "The Years of Change," *New Canadian,* 9 August 1958, 1.

51 "National JCCA Commissions Adachi to Write JC History," *New Canadian,* 17 June 1959, 1, 8. On the Japanese-Canadian history project, see "Dôhô no rekishi o hozonseyo," *New Canadian,* 4 April 1951, 5; "Announce Winners of National JCCA History Contest," *New Canadian,* 6 December 1958, 1, 8; "National JCCA Launches History; Make Appeal for Funds, Adachi to Tour Canada," *New Canadian,* 19 September 1959, 1; "Urge Nation-Wide Support," *New Canadian,* 19 September 1959, 1; and "Nikkeijinshi no igi," *New Canadian,* 23 December 1959, 1. For people's response to the JCCA history project, see Jesse Nishihara, "Re: National JCCA Hopes for a History," *New Canadian,* 29 July 1959, 8; Sally Kamikawaji, "Re: National JCCA Hopes for a History," *New Canadian,* 1 August 1959, 8; and Hiroshi Takashima, "Nikkeijinshi ni tuite kibô," *New Canadian,* 16 September 1959, 5.

52 "Hope for History," *New Canadian,* 22 July 1959, 8.

53 Sunahara, *The Politics of Racism*, 1.

54 "Nature of the History," *New Canadian,* 19 September 1959, 1.

55 Ken Adachi, "History of Japanese Canadians in B.C., 1877–1958," *New Canadian,* 25 July 1959, 1.

56 This tendency did not begin during this period, however. In 1911, two scholars published what could be categorized as Scottish ethnic histories. See Gibbon, *Scots in Canada*; and Wilfred Campbell, *The Scotsman in Canada* (Toronto: Musson, 1911).

57 PANS, MG 2, vol. 1507, file 441-5, Angus L. Macdonald, address to Caledonian Clubs on St. Andrew's Night, 30 November 1949.

58 Charles W. Dunn, *Highland Settler: A Portrait of the Scottish Gael in Nova Scotia* (Toronto: University of Toronto Press, 1953), 11–23.

59 Ibid., 74. For the story of Highland Scots in Nova Scotia, see also Neil Macneil, *The Highland Heart of Nova Scotia: An American Peace* (New York: Charles Scribner's Sons, 1948).

60 He published a couple of books focussing on Pictou and Scots. See his *The Pictou Plantation* (Corner Brook: n.p., 1967) and *Country Roads: Rural Pictou Country Nova Scotia* (Halifax: Petheric Press, 1974).

61 For example, see LAC, MG 31 B4, Henry R. Beer Collection, Henry R. Beer to Director of Scottish Studies, Gaelic College, St. Ann's, Cape Breton, 15 September 1972; Henry R. Beer to J.L. Martin, Director of Cultural Services, Nova Scotia Museum, 15 January 1973; and Henry R. Beer to National Library of Scotland, 12 November 1972.

62 LAC, MG 31 B4, Henry R. Beer Collection, W.A. MacCulloch, Executive Manager, to Henry R. Beer, 21 December 1972.

63 LAC, MG 31 B4, Henry R. Beer Collection, Norman Mackenzie to Henry R. Beer, 23 November 1972.

64 Anthony D. Smith, *Myths and Memories of the Nation* (Oxford: Oxford University Press, 1999), 150.

65 See Frances Swyripa, "The Construction of Ethnic Identity in Canada: Comparing Asian and European Immigrant Peoples," paper presented at the University of Tsukuba, Tokyo, 20 February 2004. For the significance of the prairie region to various ethnic groups, see her *Storied Landscapes*.

66 For Ukrainians' regional myths, see Swyripa, *Storied Landscapes*.

67 McKay, *The Quest of the Folk*, 39.

68 P.I. Lazarovych, "Ekonomichni dociahnennia ukrainytsiv v Kanadi," in *Druhyi vse-kanadyiskyi kongres ukraintsiv Kanady*, edited by UCC (Winnipeg: Ukrainian National Publishers, 1946), 106. See also Lysenko, *Men in Sheepskin Coats*, 296.

69 For Ukrainian input into the provinces' golden jubilees, see Swyripa, *Storied Landscapes*, 92.

70 "Pivstolittia postupu," *Ukrainskyi holos*, 27 July 1955, 4. See also Swyripa, "1955," 604.

71 "Return to the Coast," *New Canadian*, 11 January 1947, 2. See also "Discrimination in Vancouver," *New Canadian*, 15 August 1951, 2.

72 "With Courage and Vision," *New Canadian*, 20 April 1946, 2.

73 "Gojûnensai kaneta rôdôsai," *New Canadian*, 13 September 1947, 5. See also "Sôidô no yoimen," *New Canadian*, 7 June 1952, 5; and "So. Alta. JC's Live in and with Community," *New Canadian*, 5 January 1955, 2.

74 "Gojûnensai kaneta rôdôsai," *New Canadian*, 13 September 1947, 5. Japanese were increasingly incorporated into the collective memory of Greenwood. Having one of the internment camps, the town of 200 became home to 1,177 Japanese after 1942, many of whom stayed after World War II. See Michael Kluckner, *Vanishing British Columbia* (Vancouver: UBC Press, 2005), 81.

75 "Gojûnensai kaneta rôdôsai," *New Canadian*, 13 September 1947, 5.

76 The tendency to look at the wartime internment positively, particularly among some *nisei*, as the basis of postwar success and the opportunity to get away from the *issei* community in British Columbia was criticized as "the blessing-in-disguise rationale" by Sunahara, *The Politics of Racism*, 148–50. According to her, economic development among Japanese during the postwar era had nothing to do with evacuation and internment. Although this argument is convincing, these *nisei* were rather using the positive myths to promote their status in new settlements. Kirsten Emiko McAllister's work explores the integration of Japanese Canadians in relocated places, see her *Terrain of Memory: A Japanese Canadian Memorial Project* (Vancouver: University of British Columbia Press, 2010), 168.

77 McKay, *The Quest of the Folk*, 25.

78 PANS, MG 2, vol. 1507, file 443-19, Collection of Gaelic Folklore and Foundation of a Gaelic Folklore Archive, dialogue between M. MacDonnell, St. Francis Xavier University, Antigonish, NS, and J.L. Campbell, Isle of Canna, Scotland, broadcast by Station CJFX, Antigonish, 7 June 1953.

79 Dunn, *Highland Settler*, 44–47.

80 Ibid., 37, 58, 138.

81 McKay, *The Quest of the Folk*, 25.

82 PANS, MG 2, vol. 1507, file 438-5, 11, Angus L. Macdonald, address to St. Andrew's Society, New Glasgow, 30 November 1951.

83 PANS, MG 2, vol. 1507, file 438-7, 6, Angus L. Macdonald, address to St. Andrew's Day Celebration in Winnipeg, 29 November 1952.

84 In different contexts, some scholars explored the idea of "lost homeland." See, for example, Masumi Izumi, "Reclaiming and Reinventing 'Powell Street': Reconstruction of the Japanese Canadian Community in Post-World War II Vancouver," in *Nikkei in the Pacific Northwest: Japanese Americans and Japanese Canadians in the Twentieth Century*, ed. Louis Fiset and Gial Nomura (Seattle and London: University of Washington Press, 2005), 308–33.

85 "The Changing Times," *New Canadian*, 24 December 1952, 2. See also "Familiar Van. Landmarks Changed or Vanished," *New Canadian*, 30 July 1952, 1, 8; and Tom Shoyama, "As I Remember a Bit of It—," *New Canadian*, 31 May 1958, 1, 2. *New Canadian* also published a poem by Mark Toyama, which had been written in 1940 and romanticized Powell Street; see "Powell St Knows," 31 May 1958, 1.

86 Ken Mori, "Only Ghost-Like Memories Remain," *New Canadian*, 18 July 1953, 1.

87 "So Let Me Sing My Tender Requiem," *New Canadian*, 29 July 1953, 8. See also "Powell Street of Ghosts," *New Canadian*, 8 March 1947, 7; Toyo Tanaka, "The Weekly Habit," *New Canadian*, 14 July 1951, 1; "Lil Tokyo Shifts from Powell," *New Canadian*, 19 August 1953, 2; and "Vancouver! Here We Come!," *Nisei Affairs*, 28 August 1945, 7.

88 A similar kind of provincial scheme could be seen in Manitoba when the premier announced Ukrainian Week on 15 January 1968, but his gesture did not match the scale with which Angus L. Macdonald promoted Scottishness in Nova Scotia. See LAC, MG 32 C 67, vol. 33, file 1, City of Winnipeg, proclamation of Ukrainian Week, 15 January 1968; and Province of Manitoba, proclamation of Ukrainian Week, 15 January 1968. On Japanese, see also "Toronto Proclaims Thursday, May 12th, as 'Japan Day,'" *New Canadian*, 11 May 1966, 1; and "Nihonê no gyôji," *New Canadian*, 11 May 1966, 5.

89 Ian McKay, "History and the Tourist Gaze: The Politics of Commemoration in Nova Scotia, 1935–1964," *Acadiensis* 22, 2 (1993): 106. See also his "Tartanism Triumphant," 26.

90 For the production of Scottish culture, see Jonathan Dembling, "You Play It as You Would Sing It: Cape Breton, Scottishness, and the Means of Cultural Production," in Ray, *Transatlantic Scots*, 180–97.

91 McKay, "Tartanism Triumphant," 27–28, calls the enshrinement of Flora Macdonald the premier's "filiopietistic view of Scottish history" and argues that it was irrelevant to the province's history. PANS, MG 2, vol. 1507, file 444-25, Angus L. Macdonald, address at the unveiling of the plaque for Flora Macdonald, Windsor, NS, 13 September 1951. Macdonald also stressed the connection between Flora Macdonald and Nova Scotia; see PANS, MG 2, vol.

1507, file 444-25, Angus L. Macdonald to Hugh M. Macdonald, 18 February 1953.

92 UCC, *Chetvertyi vse-kanadiiskyi kongres ukraintsiv Kanady,* 21.

Chapter 6: Ethnic Movements and the Road to Multiculturalism

1 Royal Commission on Bilingualism and Biculturalism, *The Cultural Contribution of the Other Ethnic Groups,* Book IV (1969; reprint, Ottawa: Minister of Supply and Services Canada, 1976).

2 Manoly R. Lupul, in *Multiculturalism and Ukrainian Canadians: Identity, Homeland Ties, and the Community's Future,* edited by Stella Hryniuk and Lubomyr Luciuk (Toronto: Multicultural History Society of Ontario, 1993), 8. Lupul was an active promoter of Ukrainian multiculturalism. He helped to lead the movement for bilingual programs in public schools in Alberta, served on the Alberta Cultural Heritage Council and the Canadian Consultative Council on Multiculturalism, and was the first director of the Canadian Institute of Ukrainian Studies at the University of Alberta. See his *The Politics of Multiculturalism: A Ukrainian-Canadian Memoir* (Edmonton: Canadian Institute of Ukrainian Studies Press, 2005).

3 Bohdan Bociurkiw, "The Federal Policy of Multiculturalism and the Ukrainian-Canadian Community," in *Ukrainian Canadians, Multiculturalism, and Separatism: An Assessment,* edited by Manoly R. Lupul (Edmonton: Canadian Institute of Ukrainian Studies Press, 1978), 101.

4 Many of the issues discussed in this chapter were first raised by Bociurkiw in "The Federal Policy of Multiculturalism and the Ukrainian-Canadian Community." Building on his framework of events, I analyze these issues in more depth and in comparison with Japanese.

5 On Ukrainian Canadians' long obsession with culture and language for both reasons, see, for example, Bociurkiw, "The Federal Policy of Multiculturalism and the Ukrainian-Canadian Community," 101; Manoly R. Lupul, "Multiculturalism and Canada's White Ethnics," *Canadian Ethnic Studies* 15, 1 (1983): 105; and Swyripa, *Wedded to the Cause,* 49–52.

6 By the 1960s, Ukrainians had three senators—William Wall (1955–62), John Hnatyshyn (1959–67), and Paul Yuzyk (1963–86)—as well as numerous MPs and MLAs; the first Japanese MP was elected only in 2004.

7 The B&B Commission was co-chaired by A. Davidson Dunton, president of Carleton University, and André Laurendeau, editor of *Le Devoir* (after 1968, replaced by Jean-Louis Gagnon, a Montreal journalist). Members included Clément Cormier (president of Saint Joseph's University in New Brunswick), Royce Frith (Toronto lawyer), Paul Lacoste (professor at l'Université de Montréal), Gertrude M. Laing (Sorbonne student from Calgary), André Raynauld (professor at l'Université de Montréal), F.R. Scott (professor at McGill University), and Paul Wyczynski (University of Ottawa professor, Polish).

8 On the value of ethnic votes, Bociurkiw, "The Federal Policy of Multiculturalism and the Ukrainian-Canadian Community," 101, argues that the opposition and minority government, in general, were particularly active in Ukrainian and other ethnic constituencies in the Prairies.

9 This question was explored by Bohdan Harasymiw, who convincingly suggests that ethnicity did not necessarily determine Ukrainians' voting patterns between 1904 and 1990. According to him, electors were much more influenced by circumstances, policies, and ideologies that varied over time. See his "Looking for the Ukrainian Vote," in *Canada's Ukrainians*, 362–76.

10 Yuzyk campaigned actively for Diefenbaker, calling him "a defender of the underdog, the forgotten and the neglected, a friend of the minority groups and fighter for justice and fair-play." See LAC, MG 32 C 67, vol. 17, file 4, Paul Yuzyk, "The Right Honourable John George Diefenbaker—Champion of Freedom and Justice," 24 January 1970.

11 LAC, MG 32 C 67, vol. 17, file 2, Paul Yuzyk to J.G. Diefenbaker, 20 March 1963.

12 LAC, MG 32 C 67, vol. 17, file 2, Paul Yuzyk to J.G. Diefenbaker, 12 January 1963.

13 Ibid.

14 LAC, MG 32 C 67, vol. 17, file 2, W. Kushnir to J.G. Diefenbaker, n.d.

15 Ibid.

16 LAC, MG 32 C 67, vol. 17, file 2, Paul Yuzyk to J.G. Diefenbaker, 20 September 1962.

17 Paul Yuzyk, "Canada: A Multicultural Nation, Delivered in the Senate of Canada, March 3, 1964," in *For a Better Canada: A Collection of Selected Speeches Delivered in the Senate of Canada and at Banquets and Conferences in Various Centres across Canada by Senator Paul Yuzyk* (Toronto: Ukrainian National Association, 1973), 30.

18 See, for example, "Bunka kenri o shuchô shite," *New Canadian*, 19 December 1968, 4; and "First Thinkers' Conference on Cultural Rights Slated Dec. 13, 14, 15," *New Canadian*, 13 November 1968, 1.

19 Bociurkiw, "The Federal Policy of Multiculturalism," 105.

20 "White Paper on the First Volume of the Final Report of the Royal Commission on Bilingualism and Biculturalism," *Ukrainskyi holos*, 7 February 1968, 2–3.

21 The number of briefs submitted to the B&B Commission were as follows: 118 from the French, thirty-nine from Ukrainians, three from Mennonites, and one each from Germans, Jews, Japanese, Icelanders, Belarusians, Poles, Italians, Hungarians, Estonians, Czechs, and Scandinavians. Bociurkiw also stresses Ukrainians' enthusiasm for submitting briefs; see his "The Federal Policy of Multiculturalism and the Ukrainian-Canadian Community,"105. See also "NJCCA to Submit Brief to Bicultural-Bilingual Meeting," *New Canadian*, 13 March 1965, 1.

22 Royal Commission on Bilingualism and Biculturalism, *The Cultural Contribution of the Other Ethnic Groups*, 3.

23 UCC, Headquarters, brief submitted to the B&B Commission, 1964 (Toronto: Micromedia, 1972).

24 UCC, Women's Council, brief submitted to the B&B Commission, n.d. (Toronto: Micromedia, 1972).

25 Kazumi Miyata, "Part One: A Capsule History of the Japanese Canadians by Kazumi Miyata," *New Canadian,* 13 August 1971, 1. See also T. Umezuki, "Long History of JC Suffering at Hands of Canadian Immigration Policy," *New Canadian,* 3 March 1965, 1; "Akumu no ato," *New Canadian,* 22 December 1965, 1; and "The Tojin and the Riot," *New Canadian,* 9 March 1966, 1, 8.

26 Paul Yuzyk, "The Ukrainian Fact in Canada, Article in Program of the Montreal Conference, June 9, 10, 11, 1972," in Yuzyk, *For a Better Canada,* 50–53. His comparison between French and Ukrainian contributions to Canada was pointed out by Swyripa in her "Ethnic Loyalists and Selkirk Settlers".

27 Yuzyk, "The Ukrainian Fact in Canada," 50–52.

28 Ukrainian Self-Reliance League (hereafter USRL), brief submitted to the B&B Commission, 1965 (Toronto: Micromedia, 1972).

29 "Tribute to Our Ukrainian Pioneers in Canada's First Century," *Ukrainian Canadian,* 1 April 1966, 10. See also "1966—a Special Year for 500,000 Canadians," *Ukrainian Canadian,* 1 January 1966, 1; and "Ukrainian Values in the Canadian Identity," *Ukrainian Canadian,* 1 May 1966, 9, 11–13. The AUUC also kept enshrining and honouring pioneers. See, for example, "A Message from Kin of Settlers from Neviliw," *Ukrainian Canadian,* 15 May 1966, 12–13; and "Honour Ukrainian Pioneers on Canada Day," *Ukrainian Canadian,* 15 July 1966, 3.

30 "National JCCA Brief," *New Canadian,* 3 August 1968, 8.

31 LAC, MG 32 C 67, vol. 45, file 16, Paul Yuzyk, "Are All Ethnic Groups Becoming English Canadians?," speech at the University of Toronto Conference The Changing Face of English Canada, 30 October 1964.

32 Ibid.

33 The Toronto JCCA, however, looked at the possibility and necessity of working with Chinese, organizing meetings with the Chinese Canadian Association to deal with racism. See "Toronto JCCA Discuss Closer Ties with Chinese Canadians," *New Canadian,* 13 January 1966, 1.

34 "Report of the Resolutions Committee," in *Concern: A Conference to Study Canada's Multicultural Patterns in the Sixties,* edited by Canadian Cultural Rights Committee (Ottawa: Canadian Cultural Rights Committee, 1968).

35 Approximately 6,000 Ukrainians were sent to internment camps during World War I. See Melnycky, "The Internment of Ukrainians in Canada," in *Loyalties in Conflict*, 1.

36 Swyripa, *Wedded to the Cause,* 182.

37 Heroism and sacrifice by Japanese-Canadian soldiers emerged much later, in the 1980s. See, for example, Roy Ito, *We Went to War: The Story of the Japanese Canadians Who Served during the First and Second World Wars* (Stittsville: Canada's Wings, 1984).

38 UCC, Winnipeg Branch, brief submitted to the B&B Commission, 1964.

39 Yuzyk, "Are All Ethnic Groups Becoming English Canadians?" On Ukrainian Canadians' commemoration of Konowal, see Luciuk, *Searching for Place,* 303–04.

40 Evidence suggests that Japanese also commemorated World War I veterans, but the memory of internment overwhelmed such heroism during this

period. See "Issei WWI Veteran Commemorates 50th Anniversary of Vimy Ridge Battle," *New Canadian,* 15 April 1967, 1.

41 A.B. Hotta, "The 'Nation' that Was Lost in British Columbia 28 Years Ago," *New Canadian,* Holiday Issue, 31 December 1970, Section III, 1.

42 *Tairiku jihô,* 8 December 1967, 4.

43 LAC, MG 32 C 67, vol. 22, file 11, official representatives of ethnic groups in Canada, brief on radio, television, and films in Canada submitted to the federal government, 1962. See also "Osnovy iednosty," *Ukrainskyi holos,* 20 May 1964, 4. The dilemma that the CBC faced in terms of ethnic programs and federal funding after 1971 was discussed by Bociurkiw in "The Federal Policy of Multiculturalism and the Ukrainian-Canadian Community," 112–15.

44 See "Sprava ukrainskoi movy v Manitobi," *Ukrainskyi holos,* 8 February 1961, 4; "Uriad Manitoby i ukrainska mova," *Ukrainskyi holos,* 12 April 1961, 4; "Ukrainsna mova v Manitobi," *Ukrainskyi holos,* 22 May 1963, 4; "Dopovid pro ukrainsku movu v shkolakh Manitoby," *Ukrainskyi holos,* 27 March 1963, 4; "V spravi ukrainskoi movy," *Ukrainskyi holos,* 8 April 1964, 4; and "Ukrainska mova," *Ukrainskyi holos,* 13 March 1968, 4.

45 UCC, Vancouver Branch, brief submitted to the B&B Commission, 1964 (Toronto: Micromedia, 1972).

46 Ukrainian Women's Association of Canada, brief submitted to the B&B Commission, 1964 (Toronto: Micromedia, 1972).

47 Ukrainian Self-Reliance Association, Alberta Branch, brief submitted to the B&B Commission, 1964 (Toronto: Micromedia, 1972).

48 LAC, MG 28 C 67, vol. 103, file 47, Bohdan Krawchenko, "Toward a Development of Multiculturalism," address at the Multicultural Conference, Toronto, 8 August 1970. For a Ukrainian-Canadian reaction to the B&B Commission report, see also Lupul, *The Politics of Multiculturalism,* 112–13.

49 "Jinshu tôgô no mondaiten," *New Canadian,* 22 April 1961, 5.

50 Thomas Hara, "Necessity of the JCCA," *New Canadian,* 29 September 1962, 2.

51 "NJCCA Reveals Royal Commission Bi & Bi Brief," *New Canadian,* 26 January 1966, 8.

52 Ibid.

53 "Future Role of the Centre … ," *New Canadian,* 6 June 1964, 8. See also Kunio Hidaka, "Future Role of the Centre," *Tairiku jihô,* 5 June 1964, 1.

54 "Japanese Canadian Centre, Its Philosophy and Purpose," *New Canadian,* 3 February 1960, 1.

55 Fred D. Kondo, "The Growth of an Idea," *Tairiku jihô,* 5 June 1964, 1.

56 "Pearson Says 'JC Evacuation Black Spot' in Canadian History," *New Canadian,* 10 June 1964, 1. See also "Icchi kyôryoku shite," *New Canadian,* 6 June 1964, 5.

57 *Tairiku jihô,* 12 June 1964, 4. For criticism, see "PM Says 'Black-Spot-Evac.' Speech Received Criticism," *New Canadian,* 30 October 1965, 1.

58 Lupul, "Multiculturalism and Canada's White Ethnics," 99–107. Ukrainians as white ethnics was also theorized by Vic Satzewich in comparison with the

Irish in his "Whiteness Limited: Racialization and the Social Construction of 'Peripheral Europeans,'" *Histoire sociale/Social History* 33, 66 (2000): 280–89.

59 In the 1980s, when discussion of visible minority rights became heated, Japanese challenged 1971 multiculturalism, designed to secure the cultural and linguistic rights of ethnic groups. According to them, visible minorities needed a combination of multiculturalism and human rights. See, for example, Laverne M. Lewycky, "Equality Now: The Issue of Japanese Canadian Redress and Multiculturalism," in *Asian Canadians: Contemporary Issues,* edited by K. Victor Ujimoto and Josephine Naidoo (n.p., 1986), 125. See also K. Victor Ujimoto and Gordon Hirabayashi, eds., *Visible Minorities and Multiculturalism: Asians in Canada* (Toronto: Butterworths, 1980).

60 On the impact of internment on Japanese identity, see Roy Miki, "Turning In, Turning Out: The Shifting Formations of 'Japanese Canadian' from Uprooting to Redress," in *Changing Japanese Identities in Multicultural Canada,* edited by Joseph F. Kess et al. (Victoria: University of Victoria Press, 2003), 25–45.

61 Bociurkiw calls it "multiple bilingualism," which means English and mother tongue; see his "The Federal Policy of Multiculturalism and the Ukrainian-Canadian Community," 105. Almost all briefs submitted to the B&B Commission supported this type of bilingualism outside Quebec.

62 UCC, Edmonton Branch, brief submitted to the B&B Commission, 1964 (Toronto: Micromedia, 1972). See also "Mnohomovna Kanada," *Ukrainskyi holos,* 29 May 1963, 4; "Ukrainske zvernennia v movno-kulturnii," *Ukrainskyi holos,* 15 January 1964, 2; "Dvomovnist u derzhavnii cluzhbi," *Ukrainskyi holos,* 5 February 1964, 5; "Zminy v Ottavi," *Ukrainskyi holos,* 29 January 1964, 4; and "Promova Premiera Pirsona," *Ukrainskyi holos,* 11 March 1964, 4.

63 LAC, MG 32 C 67, vol. 35, file 6, UCC, brief to the government of Canada on the Bill of Rights, 14 December 1968, 5.

64 Ibid., 6. See also "Pered oblychchiam novoho roku," *Ukrainskyi holos,* 10 January 1968, 4.

65 The Curatorium of Ukrainian Catholic Schools, Winnipeg, brief submitted to the B&B Commission, 1964 (Toronto: Micromedia, 1972). See also Bohdan Bociurkiw's view in "Bilingualism and Biculturalism as Seen by Western Canadians of Other Ethnic Origins," *Ukrainskyi holos,* 1 July 1964, 4.

66 LAC, MG 31 D 58, vol. 6, file 9, J.B. Rudnyckyj, "Vision globale du Canada: Un essai—'devoir de vacances,'" 1965.

67 Ibid.

68 LAC, MG 31 D 58, vol. 7, file 14, J.B. Rudnyckyj, "Regional Language: First Draft," 1967.

69 Ibid.

70 See, for example, LAC, MG 31 D 58, vol. 7, file 8, Ukrainian Canadian Council of Learned Societies, blueprint for the BNA Act, Section 133, a simplified version of B&B Rudnyckyj's formula, submitted to the government of Canada, 22 January 1968.

71 For example, see "'End Race Bias' Vote Gets Solid U.N. Backing," *New Canadian,* 27 November 1963, 1; "Nat. JCCA Issues Pamphlet to Obliterate Racial Epithet," *New Canadian,* 14 July 1965, 1; "Toronto JCCA Group Effort

Needed for Human Rights Fight," *New Canadian,* 20 July 1966, 1; "Fed. Manpower Offices Accept Discrimination Reveals Alan Borovoy," *New Canadian,* 19 April 1967, 1, 8; and "JCCA Supports Human Rights Inquiry Board," *New Canadian,* 4 July 1969, 1.

72 "No Real Answer to Racism?," *New Canadian,* 26 September 1969, 8.

73 Thomas Hara, "Necessity of the JCCA," *New Canadian,* 29 September 1962, 2. See also "JCCA—a Personal Point," *New Canadian,* 16 November 1960, 1, 8; "Why We Should Support the Toronto JCCA," *New Canadian,* 1 October 1960, 1; "Hope and Progress for 1961," *New Canadian,* 1 December 1960, 1; George K. Fujisawa, "Is the JCCA Necessary?," *New Canadian,* 28 June 1961, 7; and "Public Responsibility and Courage—JCCA," *New Canadian,* 15 February 1964, 1.

74 "The JCCA and What It Stands For," *New Canadian,* 20 April 1963, 1. See also "JCCA Membership Drive Vital for Human Rights Fight," *New Canadian,* 23 July 1966, 1.

75 JCRC, box 7, file 6, E. Ide, report on eighteenth biennial national JACL convention, Detroit, 4 July 1964. In the 1960s, the NJCCA sent delegates to the Japanese-American national convention. These representatives gave a report on the speeches and resolutions presented at the conference to the NJCCA's executive meeting. Since the civil rights movement was well under way, Japanese Americans focussed on the human rights of racial minorities. Masako Iino discusses American influence on Japanese-Canadian decision making in the context of the redress movement in *Nikkei kanadajin no rekishi* (Tokyo: University of Tokyo Press, 1997), 147–65.

76 The Ontario Human Rights Commission was established in 1961 to carry out Ontario's Human Rights Code, passed in 1962. It collected complaints and appeals from people who faced discrimination because of their backgrounds, which included race, sex, colour, and religion. Ontario was the first province to introduce this kind of code in Canada. See Carmela Patrias and Ruth A. Frager, "'This Is Our Country, These Are Our Rights': Minorities and the Origins of Ontario's Human Rights Campaign," *Canadian Historical Review* 82, 1 (2001): 1.

77 See, for example, "Nat. JCCA Issues Pamphlet to Obliterate Racial Epithet," *New Canadian,* 14 July 1965, 1; "JCCA Supports Human Rights Inquiry Board," *New Canadian,* 4 July 1969, 1; and "Human Rights Comm. Kills Epithet 'Jap' Advertising," *New Canadian,* 12 February 1971, 1.

78 A.B. Hotta, "A Question of Ethnicity?," *New Canadian,* 25 July 1969, 8.

79 Lucien C. Kurata, "Human Relations," *New Canadian,* 22 February 1964, 1, 8.

80 Bociurkiw points out that the AUUC conceptualized Quebec sovereignty in Stalin's framework of nations, recognizing its right of "self-determination" but opposing separatism. See his "The Federal Policy of Multiculturalism and the Ukrainian-Canadian Community," 106.

81 "On the Crisis of Confederation, Submission to the Royal Commission on Bilingualism and Biculturalism by Canadian Council of National Groups," *Ukrainian Canadian,* 1 February 1965, 5.

82 Ibid. See also "National Groups and the Crisis in French-English Relations," *Ukrainian Canadian,* 1 January 1967, 19; and "The 'Third' Element," *Ukrainian Canadian,* 1 May 1968, 9–10.

83 See, for example, "The Canadian Dilemma," *Ukrainian Canadian,* 15 August 1967, 4–6.

84 See, for example, "Launch Drive for Citizenship Rights of Foreign-Born," *Ukrainian Canadian,* 15 February 1962, 9–10; "Memorandum to the Minister of Citizenship and Immigration," *Ukrainian Canadian,* 1 March 1962, 5; "Citizenship Rights Vital to Freedom, Progress," *Ukrainian Canadian,* 1 August 1962, 2; "Memorandum to Minister Bell and MP's," *Ukrainian Canadian,* 15 November 1962, 11–13; and "Stress Human Rights on Canada Day," *Ukrainian Canadian,* 15 July 1965, 3.

85 "Only the Canadian Left Offers Goals and a Real Alternative," *Ukrainian Canadian,* 1 June 1968, 5.

86 For example, Krawchenko, "Toward a Development of Multiculturalism," stressed in 1970 that the report was not a finished work.

87 Harry Schachter, "B & B Commission Prof Wants Ukrainian, German as Regional Languages," *Manitoban,* 12 December 1967, 1. See also LAC, MG 31 D 58, vol. 8, file 18, Mark MacGuigan, "Constitutional Aspects of Ethnic Identity in Canada," Inter-University Committee on Canadian Slavs Symposium on Languages and Cultures in Multi-Ethnic Society, Ottawa, 22 May 1971.

88 LAC, MG 32 C 67, vol. 22, file 15, Arthur Stinson, Interim Executive Director, Multilogue Reaction Paper No. 1, Canadian Citizenship Council, 1967.

89 LAC, MG 32 C 67, vol. 22, file 15, Canadian Citizenship Council, "Declaration of Objective and National Purpose and Programme of Action," 1 October 1964.

90 "Samovyznachennia dlia vsikh, tilky ne dlia Ukrainy," *Ukrainskyi holos,* 8 July 1964, 4.

91 Although the Ukrainian Soviet Socialist Republic was one of the initial members of the United Nations, its delegate did not have a separate voice from that of the Soviet Union.

92 See, for example, LAC, MG 32 C 67, vol. 35, file 6, UCC, memoranda to the United Nations General Assembly, Fifteenth Session, September 1960; Sixteenth Session, November 1961; Seventeenth Session, December 1962; and Eighteenth Session, November 1963.

93 Paul Yuzyk, in Senate, *Senate Debates,* 26 October 1971, 1390.

94 Paul Yuzyk, in Senate, *Senate Debates,* 28 June 1971, 1224.

95 Yuzyk, Iin Senate, Senate Debates, 28 June 1971, 1224–25. See also Paul Yuzyk, "Trudeau's Apology to the Ukrainians?," in Yuzyk, *For a Better Canada,* 253.

96 Yuzyk, "Trudeau's Apology to the Ukrainians?," 253. See also "Senator Iuzyk demaskuie sovietskyi imperiialism," *Ukrainskyi holos,* 3 June 1964, 4.

97 LAC, MG 32 C 67, vol. 35, file 6, B. Kushnir, memorandum to Lester B. Pearson, 16 April 1968. For the violation of human rights and democracy in Ukraine by the Soviet Union, see also "Ha porozi novoho pivstorittia," *Ukrainskyi holos,* 18 May 1960, 4; and "Za odyn moralnyi pryntsyp," *Ukrainskyi holos,* 24 August 1960, 4.

98 LAC, MG 32 C 67, vol. 35, file 5, Paul Yuzyk, "Canadian Freedom and Ukrainian Freedom," 2 February 1974.

99 For discussion on the Centennial and Expo 67 as vehicles for spreading multiculturalism, see Bociurkiw, "The Federal Policy of Multiculturalism and the Ukrainian-Canadian Community," 103–04. For the incorporation of ethnic diversity, see also Gary Miedema, "For Canada's Sake: The Centennial Celebrations of 1967, State Legitimation, and the Restructuring of Canadian Public Life," *Journal of Canadian Studies* 34, 1 (1999): 139–61; his *For Canada's Sake: Public Religion, Centennial Celebrations, the Re-Making of Canada in the 1960s* (Montreal: McGill-Queen's University Press, 2005); and Peter H. Aykroyd, *The Anniversary Compulsion: Canada's Centennial Celebration: A Model of Mega-Anniversary* (Toronto: Dundurn Press, 1992).

100 "A Crisis of National Unity: The Quebec Viewpoint for Mr. Pearson," *Globe and Mail,* 21 December 1962, 7.

101 "Across the Land: Alberta," *Globe and Mail,* 14 October 1967, 7.

102 LAC, MG 32 C 67, vol. 30, file 10, W. Tarnopolsky, "Multi-Culturalism: A Logical Choice for Canada," 1971, 6. See also Yuzyk, "Are All Ethnic Groups Becoming English Canadians?," 11.

103 Yuzyk, "Are All Ethnic Groups Becoming English Canadians?," 15.

104 LAC, MG 28 I 85, vol. 7, file: Centennial Commission, R. Elliott, J. Fisher, etc., 1963–67, Canadian Citizenship Council, brief to the Centennial Commission, September 1965. See also "Promova P. Martina pry vidkryti pamiatkovoi tablytsi," *Ukrainskyi holos,* 30 August 1967, 2.

105 "1867–1967," *Ukrainskyi holos,* 11 January 1967, 4.

106 Tarnopolsky, "Multi-Culturalism," 6.

107 For Tweedsmuir, see LAC, MG 32 C 67, vol. 30, file 12, Paul Yuzyk, "Holovna tsil isnuvannia ukraintsiv Kanady," (1967?).

108 Yuzyk, "Are All Ethnic Groups Becoming English Canadians?," 15.

109 LAC, MG 32 C 67, vol. 113, file 3, Paul Yuzyk, "The Emerging New Force in the Emerging New Canada," paper presented at Thinkers' Conference on Cultural Rights, 13–15 December 1968, 7.

110 "1867–1967," *Ukrainskyi holos,* 11 January 1967, 4. See also "Na svitanku druhoho storichchia," *Ukrainskyi holos,* 5 July 1967, 4.

111 "Pislia zizdu," *Ukrainskyi holos,* 26 July 1974, 4.

112 Myron Shatulsky, "Our Contribution to Canadian Culture," *Ukrainian Canadian,* 15 May 1967, 11.

113 T. Umezuki, "Early Settlement and Full Citizenship for Immigrants," *New Canadian,* 25 January 1967, 1.

114 "Kenkoku dainiseiki no hajimeni," *New Canadian,* 14 June 1967, 16.

115 LAC, MG 28 I 85, vol. 7, file: Centennial Commission, R. Elliott, J. Fisher, etc., 1963–67, Canadian Citizenship Council, brief to the Centennial Commission, September 1965.

116 LAC, MG 32 C 67, vol. 25, file 3, Lester B. Pearson, address to the Conference to Establish a National Council for the Folk Arts, Ottawa, 8–9 November 1964.

117 LAC, MG 32 C 67, vol. 22, file 14, Judy LaMarsh, Secretary of State, speech prepared for delivery to the Sixth Annual Meeting of the Canadian Centenary Council, Ottawa, 26 May 1966.

118 For Canadian Folk Art Council, see Bociurkiw, "The Federal Policy of Multiculturalism," 103.

119 LAC, MG 32 C 67, vol. 24, file 7, Leon Kossar, "Canada's Newest and Oldest Cultural Movement," paper presented at the Second National Conference on Canadian Slavs, Ottawa, 1967.

120 "Ethnic Groups Invited to Participate at 1967 World Exhibition," *New Canadian*, 23 April 1966, 1.

121 "Ethnic Units Form Arts Council," *New Canadian*, 14 November 1964, 1. See also "Ethnic Groups Invited to Participate at 1967 World Exhibition," *New Canadian*, 23 April 1966, 1.

122 "Ukrainskyi dytiachyi festival v Saskatuni," *Ukrainskyi holos*, 5 July 1967, 7.

123 "Ukrainska propamiatna tablytsiia v Ottavi," *Ukrainskyi holos*, 16 August 1967, 1.

124 "Kanada hyakunen to nikkeijin," *New Canadian*, 14 June 1967, 16. See also "Kanada hyakunen iwau," *New Canadian*, 4 January 1967, 6; "$100,000 Budget Set by JC Centennial Committee," *New Canadian*, 18 January 1967, 1; and "Nikkei kanada shimin kyôkai no shimei, 1–5," *New Canadian*, 18 January 1967, 5; 21 January 1967, 5; 25 January 1967, 5; 28 January 1967, 5; 1 February 1967, 5.

125 "Nikkei kanada shimin kyôkai no shimei," *New Canadian*, 1 February 1967, 5. Albertan Japanese were often admired as "model" people for the Japanese elite, showing a "wonderful integration" with the local culture after the war. See "A-shû zaijû sanzenyomei no nikkeijin no migotona yûgô," *New Canadian*, 10 June 1959, 6.

126 "Ukrainians Will Light a Candle ... at Canada's Birthday Party," *Ukrainian Canadian*, 1 January 1967, 11.

127 "Centennial Summer," *Ukrainian Canadian*, 15 September 1967, 4.

128 "USSR at Expo," *Ukrainian Canadian*, 1 June 1967, 5.

129 "Greetings to Our Kinsmen on the National Day of Ukraine at Expo," *Ukrainian Canadian*, 15 August 1967, 8.

130 "$2 Million for Japan's Expo 67 Pavilion," *New Canadian*, 2 March 1966, 2.

131 Robert Hironaka, "Japanese Garden in Lethbridge," in *Nishiki: Nikkei Tapestry, a History of Southern Alberta Japanese Canadians*, edited by Lethbridge and District Japanese Canadian Association (Lethbridge: Lethbridge and District Japanese Canadian Association, 2001), 121–26.

132 "Celebrate Centennial in Shevchenko Park," *Ukrainian Canadian*, 15 July 1967, 3.

133 Peter Prokop, "Time to End This Discrimination!," *Ukrainian Canadian*, 1 March 1965, 5.

134 Ibid. See also "Delegates to Ottawa Arts Conference Unaware that Organizations Barred," *Ukrainian Canadian*, 15 November 1964, 1, 3; "We Ask Members of Parliament: Is the Centennial for All Canadians?," *Ukrainian Canadian*, 15 May 1965, 8; and "Discrimination," *Ukrainian Canadian*, 1 October 1965, 4–5.

135 "AUUC Protests to Lamontagne, Condemns Discrimination in '67 Policy," *Ukrainian Canadian*, 1 December 1964, 4–5.

136 LAC, MG 32 C 67, vol. 35, file 10, S.J. Kalba, Executive Director of the UCC, activity report 1966–68 of the UCC, 25 September 1968.

137 "Montreal Nisei Raps Japan Consulate Officials," *New Canadian,* 23 August 1967, 1. See also "Hyôban ha yokunai," *New Canadian,* 15 July 1967.

138 M. Asasuma, "Letter to the Editor," *Tairiku jihô,* 17 October 1967, 1.

SELECTED BIBLIOGRAPHY

Primary Sources

Books

Anderson, James T.M. *The Education of the New Canadian: A Treatise on Canada's Greatest Education Problem.* London: J.M. Dent and Sons, 1918.

Beer, Henry R. *Country Roads: Rural Pictou Country Nova Scotia.* Halifax: Petheric Press, 1974.

_____. *The Pictou Plantation.* Corner Brook: n.p., 1967.

Black, Norman. *From Citizens to Refugees—It's Happening Here!* Toronto: CCJC, 1945.

Calder, Jenni. *Scots in Canada.* Edinburgh: Luath Press, 2003.

Campbell, Wilfred. *The Scotsman in Canada.* London: S. Low Marston, 1911.

Committee of the Canadian Teachers' Federation. *The Democratic Way: The Air We Breathe.* No. 1. Ottawa: Canadian Citizenship Council; Toronto: Canadian Association for Adult Education, 1951.

_____. *The Democratic Way: Freedom of Conscience.* No. 4. Ottawa: Canadian Citizenship Council; Toronto: Canadian Association for Adult Education, 1951.

_____. *The Democratic Way: I'm Free to Choose.* No. 2. Ottawa: Canadian Citizenship Council; Toronto: Canadian Association for Adult Education, 1951.

Davies, R.A. *This Is Our Land: Ukrainian Canadians against Hitler.* Toronto: Progress Books, 1943.

Dawson, C.A. *Group Settlement: Ethnic Communities in Western Canada.* Toronto: Macmillan Company of Canada, 1936.

Dunn, Charles W. *Highland Settler: A Portrait of the Scottish Gael in Nova Scotia.* Toronto: University of Toronto Press, 1953.

England, Robert. *The Colonization of Western Canada: A Study of Contemporary Land Settlement.* London: P.S. King, 1936.

Foster, Kate A. *Our Canadian Mosaic.* Toronto: Dominion Council, YWCA, 1926.

Fowke, Edith. *They Made Democracy Work: The Story of the Co-operative Committee on Japanese Canadians.* Toronto: CCJC and JCCA, 1951.

Gerus, Oleh W., and Denis Hlynka, eds. *The Honourable Member for Vegreville: The Memoirs and Diary of Anthony Hlynka, MP.* Calgary: University of Calgary Press, 2005.

Gibbon, John M. *Canadian Mosaic: The Making of a Northern Nation.* Toronto: McClelland and Stewart, 1938.

______. *Scots in Canada: A History of the Settlement of the Dominion from the Earliest Days to the Present Time.* Toronto: Musson, 1911.

Glynn-Ward, Hilda. *The Writing on the Wall: Chinese and Japanese Immigration to BC, 1920.* 1921. Reprint, with an introduction by Patricia Roy, Toronto: University of Toronto Press, 1974.

Ito, Roy. *We Went to War: The Story of the Japanese Canadians Who Served during the First and Second World Wars.* Stittsville: Canada's Wings, 1984.

Kirkconnell, Watson. *Canada, Europe, and Hitler.* Toronto: University of Toronto Press, 1939.

______. *Canadians All.* Ottawa: Minister of National War Service, 1941.

______. *Canadian Overtones.* Winnipeg: Columbia Press, 1935.

______. *Our Communists and the New Canadians: An Address Delivered before a Meeting of the Canadian Club at Toronto, Canada, on Monday, February 1, 1943.* Toronto: Southam Press, 1943.

______. *Our Ukrainian Loyalists.* Winnipeg: UCC, 1943.

______. *Seven Pillars of Freedom: An Exposure of the Soviet World Conspiracy and Its Fifth Column in Canada.* 2nd ed. Toronto: Burns and MacEachern, 1952.

______. *Twilight of Liberty.* Oxford: Oxford University Press, 1941.

Lupul, Manoly R. *The Politics of Multiculturalism: A Ukrainian-Canadian Memoir.* Edmonton: Canadian Institute of Ukrainian Studies Press, 2005.

Lysenko, Vera. *Men in Sheepskin Coats: A Study in Assimilation.* Toronto: Ryerson Press, 1947.

MacNeil, Neil. *Highland Heart of Nova Scotia.* New York: Scribner, 1948.

Morrison, F.A. *Toast to the Immortal Memory, Address before the Burns Club, Edmonton, Alberta, on the Anniversary of the Birthday of Robert Burns.* Edmonton: Robert Burns Club, 1925.

Nakano, Takeo Ujo, and Leatrice Nakano. *Within the Barbed Wire Fence: A Japanese Man's Account of His Internment in Canada.* Halifax: Goodread Biographies, 1980.

Nakayama, Jinjiro. *Nikkeiimin Shiryôshû,* vol. 101922. Reprint, Tokyo: Nihon Tosho Senta, 1994.

Smith, W.G. *Building the Nation: A Study of Some Problems Concerning the Churches' Relation to the Immigrants.* Toronto: Canadian Council of the Missionary Education Movement, 1922.

_____. *A Study in Canadian Immigration.* Toronto: Ryerson Press, 1920.

Ukrainian Canadian Committee. *Chetvertyi vse-kanadiiskyi kongres ukraintsiv Kanady.* Winnipeg: Ukrainian National Publishers, 1953.

_____. *Druhyi vse-kanadyiskyi kongres ukraintsiv Kanady.* Winnipeg: Ukrainian National Publishers, 1946.

_____. *First All-Canadian Congress of Ukrainians in Canada.* Winnipeg: Ukrainian Canadian Committee, 1943.

_____. *Piatyi i shostyi kongresy ukraintsiv Kanady.* Winnipeg: Ukrainian National Publishers, 1956.

_____. *Tretii vce-kanadiiskyi kongres ukraintsiv Kanady.* Winnipeg: Ukrainian National Publishers, 1950.

Walker, James H. *A Scotsman in Canada.* London: J. Cape, 1935.

Watada, Terry. *Bukkyo Tozen: A History of Jodo Shinshu Buddhism in Canada.* Toronto: HPF Press and Toronto Buddhist Church, 1996.

Woodsworth, James S. *Strangers within Our Gates or Coming Canadians.* 1909. Reprint, with an introduction by Marilyn Barber, Toronto: University of Toronto Press, 1972.

Young, Charles H. *The Ukrainian Canadians: A Study in Assimilation.* Edited by Helen R.Y. Reid. Toronto: Thomas Nelson and Sons, 1931.

Young, Charles H., Helen R.Y. Reid, and W.A. Carrothers. *The Japanese Canadians.* Edited by H.A. Innis. Toronto: University of Toronto Press, 1938.

Yuzyk, Paul. *For a Better Canada: A Collection of Selected Speeches Delivered in the Senate of Canada and at Banquets and Conferences in Various Centres across Canada by Senator Paul Yuzyk.* Toronto: Ukrainian National Association, 1973.

_____. *The Ukrainian Canadians: Their Place and Role in Canadian Life.* Toronto: Ukrainian Business and Professional Federation, 1967.

_____. *Ukrainians in Manitoba: A Social History.* Toronto: University of Toronto Press, 1953.

Articles

Angus, Henry F. "The Effect of the War on Oriental Minorities in Canada." *Canadian Journal of Economics and Political Science* 7, 4 (1941): 506–16.

Anonymous. "Across the Land: Alberta." *Globe and Mail,* 14 October 1967, 7.

_____. "Burns Glorified Scotland." *Globe and Mail,* 24 January 1947, 6.

_____. "A Crisis of National Unity: The Quebec Viewpoint for Mr. Pearson." *Globe and Mail,* 21 December 1962, 7.

_____. "The Gael or Celt in Canada." *Gaelic Herald* 4, 9 (1932): 9–11.

_____. "The Human Rights Charter." *Citizenship Items* 2, 1 (1949): 1–3.

_____. "Robert Burns." *Winnipeg Free Press,* 24 January 1953, 19.

_____. "A Tribute to Burns and His Poetry." *Globe and Mail,* 24 January 1948, 6.

_____. "United Nations Day." *Citizenship Items* 1, 2 (1948): 1–3.

Baumgartner, F.W. "Central European Immigration." *Queen's Quarterly* 37, 4 (1930): 183–92.

England, Robert. "Glimpse of Europe in Western Canada." *Canadian Geographical Journal* 5, 1 (1932)

Frederick, Griffin. "Catching Up with Canada." *Star Weekly,* 1 December 1928, 3.

Gibbon, John M. "European Seeds in the Canadian Garden." *Transactions of the Royal Society of Canada* 17, 2 (1923): 119–29.

_____. "A Secular Bible for a New Canada." *Transactions of the Royal Society of Canada* 36, 2 (1942): 93–100.

Horton, A.L. "A Protest from Vegreville." *Maclean's,* 15 August 1930, 48.

Ivakh, O. "Shevchenko—prorok Ukrainy." *Kaliendar "Ukrainskyi holos"* (1942): 35–39.

Kirkconnell, Watson. "The European-Canadians in Their Press." *Canadian Historical Association Report* (1940): 85–92.

LaViolette, Forrest E. "Social Psychological Characteristics of Evacuated Japanese." *Canadian Journal of Economics and Political Science* 11, 3 (1945): 420–31.

Martin, Paul. "Canada and the United Nations." *Dalhousie Review* 33, 4 (1954): 211–26.

Mcakee, J.V. "Aberdeen Newspaper Two Centuries Old." *Globe and Mail,* 29 January 1948, 6.

_____. "Burns Not Bobby, but Rab or Rabby." *Globe and Mail,* 25 January 1947, 6.

Mclaren, Moray. "Flora Macdonald and the Island of Her Heart." *Piper and Danrer Bulletin* (1952): 11–13.

Ridout, Denzel G. "European Sources of Non-Anglo-Saxons in Canada." *Canadian Geographical Journal* 2 (1931): 201–23.

Schachter, Harry. "B & B Commission Prof Wants Ukrainian, German as Regional Languages." *Manitoban,* 12 December 1967, 1.

_____. "The Oriental Wants to Vote: Asiatic-Canadians, with a High Birth Rate, Are Creating a New Problem for British Columbia." *Maclean's,* 1 April 1937, 24, 44, 46.

Shaw, Charles Lugrin. "Japan's Finger in Canada." *Maclean's,* 15 October 1937, 11, 53.

Simpson, G.W. "The Ukrainian Problem." In *The Ukrainian Cause on Radio Waves.* Saskatoon: Ukrainian National Federation of Canada, 1939.

Terletskyi, O. "Iak buduvav i iak ruinuvav ukrainskyi narod." *Kaliendar "Ukrainskyi holos"* (1941): 33–43.

Thinkers' Conference on Cultural Rights. "Report of the Resolutions Committee." In *Concern: A Conference to Study Canada's Multicultural Patterns in the Sixties,* edited by Canadian Cultural Rights Committee. Ottawa: Canadian Cultural Rights Committee, 1968.

Whitton, Charlotte. "The Immigration Problem for Canada." *Queen's Quarterly* 31, 4 (1924): 388–420.

Yuzyk, Paul. "A New Monument on the Legislative Building Grounds." *Manitoba Pageant* 7, 1 (1961): 10–15.

Archives

Acadia University Archives and Special Collections, Wolfville, NS.
Watson Kirkconnell Collection.

Beaton Institute, University College of Cape Breton, Sydney, NS.
MG 6-26. Scottish Catholic Society Collection, 1920–46.
MG 6-20. Joseph J. MacInnis Collection.

University of British Columbia Archives, Vancouver, BC.
Japanese Canadian Research Collection.

Library and Archives Canada, Ottawa, ON.
MG 27, IIIA5. John Buchan Collection.
MG 28 I 85. Canadian Citizenship Council Collection.
MG 28 V 1. Co-operative Committee on Japanese Canadians Collection.
MG 28 V 2. St. Andrew's Society of Ottawa Collection.
MG 28 V 7. Japanese Canadian Citizens Association Collection.
MG 28 V 103. Ukrainian Canadian University Students' Union Collection.
MG 30 D 403. Peter Krawchuk Collection.
MG 31 B 4. Henry R. Beer Collection.
MG 31 D58. J.B. Rudnyckyj Collection.
MG 31 E 26. Muriel Kitagawa Collection.
MG 32 C 67. Paul Yuzyk Collection.

Presbyterian Church in Canada Archives, Toronto, Ontario.
Rev Alexander MacMillan and Family Collection. 2001–5002.

Public Archives of Nova Scotia, Halifax, NS.
MG 2. Angus L. Macdonald Collection.

Newspapers

New Canadian (1938–71)

Nisei Affairs (1945–47)

Presbyterian Records,(1942)

Saturday Night (1919–45)

Tairiku jihô ["Continental Times"] (1951–71)

Tairiku nippô ["Continental Daily"] (1919–41)

Ukrainskyi holos ["Ukrainian Voice"] (1919–71)

Ukrainian Canadian (1947–69)
Ukrainian Review (1937–39)
Zakhidni visty ["Western News"] (1928–39)

Government Publications

Canada. *Canada Year Book*. Ottawa: Dominion Bureau of Statistics, 1927–28.

______. Dominion Bureau of Statistics. *Census of Canada*. Ottawa: Dominion Bureau of Statistics, 1921–71.

______. House of Commons. *Debates*, 25 November 1940; 17 February 1941; 2 February 1942; 19 February 1942; 18 February 1943; 15 July 1943; 4 August 1944; 24 September 1945; 22 October 1945; 14 December 1945; 18 December 1945; 1 May 1947.

______. Senate. *Senate Debates*, 28 June 1971; 26 October 1971.

Royal Commission on Bilingualism and Biculturalism. *The Cultural Contribution of the Other Ethnic Groups*, Book IV. 1969. Reprint, Ottawa: Minister of Supply and Services Canada, 1976.

Briefs

National Japanese Canadian Citizens Association. Brief submitted to the Royal Commission on Bilingualism and Biculturalism, 1966. Toronto: Micromedia, 1972.

Ukrainian Canadian Committee. Edmonton Branch. Brief submitted to the Royal Commission on Bilingualism and Biculturalism, 1964. Toronto: Micromedia, 1972.

______. Headquarters. Brief submitted to the Royal Commission on Bilingualism and Biculturalism, 1964. Toronto: Micromedia, 1972.

______. Vancouver Branch. Brief submitted to the Royal Commission on Bilingualism and Biculturalism, 1964.Toronto: Micromedia, 1972.

______. Winnipeg Branch. Brief submitted to the Royal Commission on Bilingualism and Biculturalism, 1964. Toronto: Micromedia, 1972.

______. Women's Council. Brief submitted to the Royal Commission on Bilingualism and Biculturalism, n.d. Toronto: Micromedia, 1972.

Ukrainian Self-Reliance League. Alberta Branch. Brief submitted to the Royal Commission on Bilingualism and Biculturalism, 1964. Toronto: Micromedia, 1972.

______. Headquarters. Brief submitted to the Royal Commission on Bilingualism and Biculturalism, 1965. Toronto: Micromedia, 1972.

Ukrainian Women's Association of Canada. Brief submitted to the Royal Commission on Bilingualism and Biculturalism, 1964. Toronto: Micromedia, 1972.

Secondary Sources

Books

Adachi, Ken. *The Enemy that Never Was: An Account of the Deplorable Treatment Inflicted on Japanese Canadians during World War Two.* Toronto: McClelland and Stewart, 1976.

Adamoskyi, Robert, Dorothy D. Chunn, and Robert Menzie, eds. *Contesting Canadian Citizenship: Historical Readings.* Peterborough: Broadview Press, 2002.

Anderson, Benedict. *Imagined Communities: Reflections on the Origin and Spread of Nationalism.* London: Verso, 1983.

Anderson, Kay. *Vancouver's Chinatown: Racial Discourse in Canada, 1875–1980.* Montreal and Kingston: McGill-Queen's University Press, 1991.

Andrews, Allen. *The Scottish Canadians.* Toronto: Van Nostrand Reinhold, 1981.

Aykroyd, Peter H. *The Anniversary Compulsion: Canada's Centennial Celebration: A Model of Mega-Anniversary.* Toronto: Dundurn Press, 1992.

Bangarth, Stephanie. *Voices Raised in Protest: Defending North American Citizens of Japanese Ancestry, 1942–49.* Vancouver: UBC Press, 2008.

Berger, Carl. *Sense of Power: Studies in the Idea of Canadian Imperialism, 1867–1914.* Toronto: University of Toronto Press, 1970.

Broadfoot, Barry. *Years of Sorrow, Years of Shame: The Stories of Japanese Canadians in World War II.* Don Mills: Paperjacks, 1977.

Bumsted, J.M. *The Scots in Canada.* Ottawa: Canadian Historical Association, 1982.

Butcher, Dennis L., ed. *Prairie Spirit: Perspectives on the Heritage of the United Church of Canada in the West.* Winnipeg: University of Manitoba Press, 1985.

Caccia, Ivana. *Managing the Canadian Mosaic in Wartime: Shaping Citizenship Policy, 1939–1945.* Montreal: McGill-Queen's University Press, 2010.

Campbell, D., and R.A. MacLean. *Beyond the Atlantic Roar: A Study of the Nova Scotian Scots.* Toronto: McClelland and Stewart, 1974.

Campey, Lucille H. *After the* Hector: *The Scottish Pioneers of Nova Scotia and Cape Breton, 1773–1852.* Toronto: Natural Heritage, 2004.

Champion, C.P. *The Strange Demise of British Canada: The Liberals and Canadian Nationalism, 1964–1968.* Montreal: McGill-Queen's University Press, 2010.

Cowan, Paul. *How the Scots Created Canada.* Edmonton: Dragon Hill, 2006.

Darcovich, William, and Paul Yuzyk, eds. *A Statistical Compendium on the Ukrainians in Canada, 1891–1976.* Ottawa: University of Ottawa Press, 1980.

Driedger, Leo. *Race and Ethnicity: Finding Identities and Equalities.* Oxford: Oxford University Press, 2003.

Ferguson, Barry, ed. *The Anglican Church and the World of Western Canada, 1820–1970.* Regina: Canadian Plains Research Center, University of Regina, 1991.

Geertz, Clifford. *The Interpretation of Cultures: Selected Essays by Clifford Geertz.* New York: Basic Books, 1973.

Goa, David J., ed. *The Ukrainian Religious Experience: Tradition and the Canadian Cultural Context.* Edmonton: Canadian Institute of Ukrainian Studies Press, 1989.

Harding, John S., Hori, Victor S., and Soucy, Alexander, eds. *Wild Geese: Buddism in Canada.* Montreal and Kingston: McGill-Queen's University Press, 2010.

Harvie, Christopher. *Scotland and Nationalism: Scottish Society and Politics, 1707 to the Present.* 3rd ed. London: Routledge, 1998.

Herman, Arthur. *How the Scots Invented the Modern World.* New York: Three Rivers Press, 2001.

Hobsbawm, Eric J. *Nations and Nationalism since 1780: Programme, Myth, Reality.* Cambridge, UK: Cambridge University Press, 1990.

Hryniuk, Stella, and Lubomyr Luciuk, eds. *Multiculturalism and Ukrainian Canadians: Identity, Homeland Ties, and the Community's Future.* Toronto: Multicultural History Society of Ontario, 1993.

Iacovetta, Franca. *Gatekeepers: Reshaping Immigrant Lives in Cold War Canada.* Toronto: Between the Lines, 2006.

Igartua, José. *The Other Quiet Revolution: National Identities in English Canada, 1945–1971.* Vancouver: UBC Press, 2006.

Iino, Masako. *Nikkei Kanadajin No Rekishi.* Tokyo: University of Tokyo Press, 1997.

Kluckner, Michael. *Vanishing British Columbia.* Vancouver: UBC Press, 2005.

Kordan, Bohdan S. *Canada and the Ukrainian Question, 1939–1945.* Montreal: McGill-Queen's University Press, 1991.

Kymlicka, Will. *Multicultural Citizenship: A Liberal Theory of Minority Rights.* Oxford: Clarendon Press, 1995.

Lambertson, Ross. *Repression and Resistance: Canadian Human Rights Activists, 1930–1960.* Toronto: University of Toronto Press, 2005.

Lee, Jo-Anne, and John Lutz, eds. *Situating Race and Racisms in Time, Space, and Theory: Critical Essays for Activists and Scholars.* Montreal: McGill-Queen's University Press, 2005.

Loewen, Royden, and Gerald Friesen. *Immigrants in Prairie Cities: Ethnic Diversity in Twentieth-Century Canada.* Toronto: University of Toronto Press, 2009.

Luciuk, Lubomyr. *Searching for Place: Ukrainian Displaced Persons, Canada, and the Migration of Memory.* Toronto: University of Toronto Press, 2001.

Luciuk, Lubomyr, and Stella Hryniuk, eds. *Canada's Ukrainians: Negotiating an Identity*. Toronto: University of Toronto Press, 1991.

MacKay, Donald. *Scotland Farewell: The People of the* Hector. Toronto: Natural Heritage, 1996.

Magocsi, Paul R., ed. *Encyclopedia of Canada's Peoples*. Toronto: University of Toronto Press, 1999.

Martynowych, Orest T. *Ukrainians in Canada: The Formative Years, 1891–1924*. Edmonton: Canadian Institute of Ukrainian Studies Press, 1991.

Marunchak, M.H. *The Ukrainian Canadians: A History*. Winnipeg: Ukrainian Academy of Arts and Sciences in Canada, 1982.

Matsui, Yoshikazu, ed. *Daijôsai no Shisô to Rekishi*. Tokyo: Nihonbunka Kenkyûjo, 1990.

McAllister, Kirsten Emiko. *Terrain of Memory: A Japanese Canadian Memorial Project*. Vancouver: University of British Columbia Press, 2010.

McKay, Ian. *The Quest of the Folk: Antimodernism and Cultural Selection in Twentieth-Century Nova Scotia*. Montreal: McGill-Queen's University Press, 1994.

Miedema, Gary. *For Canada's Sake: Public Religion, Centennial Celebrations, the Re-Making of Canada in the 1960s*. Montreal: McGill-Queen's University Press, 2005.

Miki, Roy. *Redress: Inside the Japanese Canadian Call for Justice*. Vancouver: Raincoast Books, 2004.

Oiwa, Keibo, ed. *Stone Voices: Wartime Writings of Japanese Canadian Isseis*. Montreal: Véhicule Press, 1991.

Okazaki, Robert K. *The Nisei Mass Evacuation Group and P.O.W. Camp 101*. Translated by Jean M. Okazaki and Curtis T. Okazaki. Scarborough: Markham Litho, 1996.

Omatsu, Maryka. *Bittersweet Passage: Redress and the Japanese Canadian Experience*. Toronto: Between the Lines, 1992.

Pringsheim, Klaus H. *Neighbours across the Pacific: Canadian-Japanese Relations, 1870–1982*. Oakville: Mosaic Press, 1983.

Prymak, Thomas M. *Maple Leaf and Trident: The Ukrainian Canadians during the Second World War*. Toronto: Multicultural History Society of Ontario, 1988.

Ray, Celeste, ed. *Transatlantic Scots*. Tuscaloosa: University of Alabama Press, 2005.

Reid, W. Stanford, ed. *The Scottish Tradition in Canada*. Toronto: McClelland and Stewart, 1976.

Rider, Peter E., and Heather McNabb, eds. *A Kingdom of the Mind: How the Scots Helped Make Canada*. Montreal: McGill-Queen's University Press, 2006.

Roy, Patricia E. *The Oriental Question: Consolidating a White Man's Province, 1914–1941*. Vancouver: UBC Press, 2003.

_____. *The Triumph of Citizenship: The Japanese and Chinese in Canada, 1941–67.* Vancouver: UBC Press, 2007.

Roy, Patricia E., J.L. Granatstein, Masako Ino, and Hiroko Takamura. *Mutual Hostages: Canadians and Japanese during the Second World War.* Toronto: University of Toronto Press, 1990.

Sando, Tom. *Wild Daisies in the Sand: Life in a Canadian Internment Camp.* Edmonton: NeWest Press, 2002.

Shaw, Matthew. *Great Scots! How the Scots Created Canada.* Winnipeg: Heartland Associates, 2003.

Shinpo, Mitsuru, Tamura, Novio, and Shiramizu, Shigehiko. *Kanada No Nihango Shinbun: Minzokuidô No Shakaishi.* Tokyo: PMC Shuppan, 1991.

Smith, Anthony D. *Chosen Peoples: Sacred Sources of National Identity.* Oxford: Oxford University Press, 2003.

_____. *The Ethnic Origins of Nations.* Oxford: Blackwell, 1986.

_____. *Myths and Memories of the Nation.* Oxford: Oxford University Press, 1999.

Sunahara, Ann. *The Politics of Racism: The Uprooting of the Japanese Canadians during the Second World War.* Toronto: J. Lorimer, 1981.

Swyripa, Frances. *Storied Landscapes: Ethno-Religious Identity and the Canadian Prairies.* Winnipeg: University of Manitoba Press, 2010.

_____. *Ukrainian Canadians: A Survey of Their Portrayal in English Language Works.* Edmonton: University of Alberta Press, 1978.

_____. *Wedded to the Cause: Ukrainian-Canadian Women and Ethnic Identity, 1891–1991.* Toronto: University of Toronto Press, 1993.

Takashima, Shizue. *A Child in Prison Camp.* 1971. Reprint, Toronto: Tundra Books, 1998.

Taylor, Mary. *A Black Mark: The Japanese-Canadians in World War II.* Ottawa: Oberon Press, 2004.

Ujimoto, K. Victor, and Gordon Hirabayashi. *Visible Minorities and Multiculturalism: Asians in Canada.* Toronto: Butterworths, 1980.

Ward, W. Peter. *White Canada Forever: Popular Attitudes and Public Policy toward Orientals in British Columbia.* Montreal: McGill-Queen's University Press, 1978.

Watada, Terry. *Bukkyo Tozen: A History of Jodo Shinshu Buddhism in Canada.* Toronto: HPF Press and Toronto Buddhist Church, 1996.

Waterston, Elizabeth. *Rapt in Plaid: Canadian Literature and Scottish Tradition.* Toronto: University of Toronto Press, 2001.

Wilson, Andrew. *Ukrainian Nationalism in the 1990s: A Minority Faith.* Cambridge, UK: Cambridge University Press, 1997.

Articles

Barth, Fredrik. "Introduction." In *Ethnic Groups and Boundaries: The Social Organization of Culture Difference,* edited by Fredrik Barth, 9–38. Boston: Little, Brown and Company, 1969.

Bociurkiw, Bohdan. "The Federal Policy of Multiculturalism and the Ukrainian-Canadian Community." In *Ukrainian Canadians, Multiculturalism, and Separatism: An Assessment,* edited by Manoly R. Lupul, 98–128. Edmonton: Canadian Institute of Ukrainian Studies Press, 1978.

Brass, Paul R. "Elite Groups, Symbol Manipulation, and Ethnic Identity among the Muslims of South Asia." In *Political Identity in South Asia,* edited by David Taylor and Malcolm Yapp, 35–77. London: Curzon Press, 1979.

Epp, Marlene. "Pioneers, Refugees, Exiles, and Transnationals: Gendering Diaspora in an Ethno-Religious Context." *Journal of the Canadian Historical Association* 12 (2001): 137–53.

Gans, Herbert J. "Symbolic Ethnicity and Symbolic Religiosity: Towards a Comparison of Ethnic and Religious Acculturation." *Ethnic and Racial Studies* 17, 4 (1994): 577–92.

_____. "Symbolic Ethnicity: The Future of Ethnic Groups and Cultures in America." In *On the Making of Americans: Essays in Honor of David Riesman,* edited by Herbert J. Gans, 193–220. Philadelphia: University of Pennsylvania Press, 1979.

Gulka-Tiechko, Myron. "Ukrainian Immigration to Canada under the Railways Agreement, 1925–30." *Journal of Ukrainian Studies* 16, 1–2 (1991): 29–60.

Hall, David J. "Clifford Sifton: Immigration and Settlement Policy, 1896–1905." In *The Settlement of the West,* edited by Howard Palmer, 60–85. Calgary: University of Calgary Press, 1977.

Hechter, Michael. "A Rational Choice Approach to Race and Ethnic Relations." In *Theories of Race and Ethnic Relations,* edited by D. Mason and J. Rex, 268–77. Cambridge, UK: Cambridge University Press, 1986.

Iacovetta, Franca. "Manly Militants, Cohesive Communities, and Defiant Domestics: Writing about Immigrants in Canadian Historical Scholarship." *Labour/Le travail* 36 (1995): 217–52.

Ichikawa, Akira. "A Test of Religious Tolerance: Canadian Government and Jodo Shinshu Buddhism during the Pacific War, 1941–1945." *Canadian Ethnic Studies* 26, 2 (1994): 46–69.

Iino, Masako: "Bukkyôkai and Japanese Canadians Community in Canada." In *Issei Buddhism in the Americas*, edited by Duncan Williams and Tomoe Moriya, 27–44. University of Illinois Press, 2010.

Isajiw, Wsevolod W. "Multiculturalism and the Integration of the Canadian Community." *Canadian Ethnic Studies* 15, 2 (1983): 107–17.

Izumi, Yasuo. "Buddhists in British Columbia." In *Circle of Voices: A History of the Religious Communities of British Columbia,* edited by Charles P. Anderson, Tirthankar Bose, and Joseph I. Richardson, 27–33. Lantzville: Oolichan Books, 1983.

Kitô, Kiyoharu. "Kokumin kokka o sakanoboru." In *Kokumin Kokka o Tô*, edited by Rekishigaku Kenkyukai, 219–41.Tokyo: Aoki Shoten, 1994.

Kordan, Bohdan S. "The Intelligentsia and the Development of Ukrainian Ethnic Consciousness in Canada: A Prolegomenon to Research." *Canadian Ethnic Studies* 17, 1 (1985): 22–33.

Kruchka-Glynn, Alexandra. "Reinforcing Vera Lysenko—Ukrainian Canadian Author." *Journal of Ukrainian Studies* 15, 1 (1990): 53–70.

_____. "Vera Lysenko's *Men in Sheepskin Coats* (1947): The Untold Story." *Journal of Ukrainian Studies* 16, 1–2 (1991): 219–29.

Macdonald, Norman. "Putting on the Kilt: The Scottish Stereotype and Ethnic Community Survival in Cape Breton." *Canadian Ethnic Studies* 20, 3 (1988): 132–46.

Makuch, Andrij. "Narodni Domy in East Central Alberta." In *Continuity and Change: The Cultural Life of Alberta's First Ukrainians,* edited by Manoly R. Lupul, 202–10. Edmonton: Canadian Institute of Ukrainian Studies Press, 1988.

Martynowych, Orest T. "Introduction." In *Prophets and Proletariats: History of the Rise and Decline of Ukrainian Communism in Canada,* edited by John Kolasky, xv–xix. Edmonton: Canadian Institute of Ukrainian Studies Press, 1990.

McKay, Ian. "History and the Tourist Gaze: The Politics of Commemoration in Nova Scotia, 1935–1964," *Acadiensis* 22, 2 (1993): 102–38.

_____. "Tartanism Triumphant: The Construction of Scottishness in Nova Scotia, 1933–1954." *Acadiensis* 11, 2 (1992): 5–47.

Melnycky, Peter. "The Internment of Ukrainians in Canada." In *Loyalties in Conflict: Ukrainians in Canada during the Great War,* edited by Frances Swyripa and John Herd Thompson, 1–24. Edmonton: Canadian Institute of Ukrainian Studies Press, 1983.

Miedema, Gary. "For Canada's Sake: The Centennial Celebrations of 1967, State Legitimation, and the Restructuring of Canadian Public Life." *Journal of Canadian Studies* 34, 1 (1999): 139–61.

Miki, Roy. "Turning In, Turning Out: The Shifting Formations of 'Japanese Canadian' from Uprooting to Redress." In *Changing Japanese Identities in Multicultural Canada,* edited by Joseph F. Kess, Hiroko Noro, Midge M. Ayukawa, and Helen Lansdowne, 25–45. Victoria: University of Victoria Press, 2003.

Momryk, Myron. "Ukrainian DP Immigration and Government Policy in Canada, 1946–52." In *The Refugee Experience: Ukrainian Displaced Persons after World War II,* edited by Wsevolod W. Isajiw, Yury Boshyk, and Roman Senkus, 413–33. Edmonton: Canadian Institute of Ukrainian Studies Press, 1992.

Murdoch, Steve. "Cape Breton, Canada's 'Highland Island'?" *Northern Scotland* 18 (1998): 31–42.

Patrias, Carmela, and Ruth A. Frager. "'This Is Our Country, These Are Our Rights': Minorities and the Origins of Ontario's Human Rights Campaign." *Canadian Historical Review* 82, 1 (2001): 1–35.

Patterson, Orlando. "Context and Choice in Ethnic Allegiance: A Theoretical Framework and Caribbean Case Study." In *Ethnicity: Theory and Experience,* edited by Nathan Glazer and Daniel P. Moynihan, 305–49. Cambridge, MA: Harvard University Press, 1975.

Perin, Roberto. "Writing about Ethnicity." In *Writing about Canada: A Handbook for Modern Canadian History,* edited by John Schultz, 201–03. Scarborough: Prentice-Hall Canada, 1990.

Placzek, James, and Devries, Larry. "Buddhism in British Columbia." In *Buddhism in Canada,* edited by Bruce Matthews, 1–29. New York: Routledge, 2006.

Roy, Patricia E. "Lessons in Citizenship, 1945–1949: The Delayed Return of the Japanese to Canada's Pacific Coast." In *Nikkei in the Pacific Northwest: Japanese Americans and Japanese Canadians in the Twentieth Century,* edited by Louis Fiset and Gail M. Nomura, 254–77. Seattle: University of Washington Press, 2000.

Satzewich, Vic. "Whiteness Limited: Racialization and the Social Construction of 'Peripheral Europeans.'" *Histoire sociale/Social History* 33, 66 (2000): 280–89.

Stanton, John. "Government Internment Policy, 1939–1945." *Labour/Le travail* 31, 1 (1993): 230–41.

Swyripa, Frances. "1955: Celebrating Together, Celebrating Apart: Albertans and Their Golden Jubilee." In *Alberta Formed, Alberta Transformed,* edited by Michael Payne, Donald Wetherell, and Catherine Cavanaugh, 589–610. Edmonton: University of Alberta Press; Calgary: University of Calgary Press, 2006.

Takamura, Hiroko. "The Tangled Identity of Issei Japanese in Their Fight for Franchise, 1900–1931." In *Changing Japanese Identities in Multicultural Canada,* edited by Joseph F. Kess, Hiroko Noro, Midge M. Ayukawa, and Helen Lansdowne, 233–40. Victoria: University of Victoria Press, 2003.

Trevor-Roper, Hugh. "The Invention of Tradition: The Highland Tradition of Scotland." In *The Invention of Tradition,* edited by Eric Hobsbawm and Terence Ranger, 15–41. Cambridge, UK: Cambridge University Press, 1983.

Troper, Harold. "The Canadian Government and DPs, 1945–8." In *The Refugee Experience: Ukrainian Displaced Persons after World War II,* edited by Wsevolod W. Isajiw, Yury Boshyk, and Roman Senkus, 402–12. Edmonton: Canadian Institute of Ukrainian Studies Press, 1992.

Vance, Michael. "A Brief History of Organized Scottishness in Canada." In *Transatlantic Scots,* edited by Celeste Ray, 96–119. Tuscaloosa: University of Alabama Press, 2005.

_____. "Powerful Pathos: The Triumph of Scottishness in Nova Scotia." In *Transatlantic Scots,* edited by Celeste Ray, 156–79. Tuscaloosa: University of Alabama Press, 2005.

Walker, James W. "Human Rights in a Multicultural Framework: Defining Canadian Citizenship, 1945–1970." *Canadian Issues* 24, 1 (2002): 32–34.

Walker, James W. "Race and Recruitment in World War I: Enlistment of Visible Minorities in Canadian Expeditionary Forces" *Canadian Historical Review* 70, 1 (1989): 1–26.

Weber, Max. "Ethnic Groups." In *Theories of Ethnicity: A Classical Reader,* edited by Werner Sollors, 52–66. New York: New York University Press, 1996.

Yuzyk, Paul. "Religious Life." In *A Heritage in Transition: Essays in the History of Ukrainians in Canada,* edited by Manoly R. Lupul, 143–72. Toronto: McClelland and Stewart, 1982.

Conference Presentations

Swyripa, Frances. "The Construction of Ethnic Identity in Canada: Comparing Asian and European Immigrant Peoples." Paper presented at the University of Tsukuba, Tokyo, 20 February 2004.

_____. "Ethnic Loyalists and Selkirk Settlers: The Ukrainians Rewrite Canadian History." Paper presented at the Canadian Ethnic Studies Association Biennial Conference, Winnipeg, 23–26 October 1991.

_____. "History, Ethnic Legitimacy, and Public Space: The Shevchenko Statues in Winnipeg and Washington." Paper presented at the conference Cross-Stitching Cultural Borders: Comparing Ukrainian Experience in Canada and the United States, University of Toronto, 29–31 October 1998.

Theses

Bellay, Susan. "Pluralism and Race/Ethnic Relations in Canadian Social Science, 1880–1939." PhD diss., University of Manitoba, 2001.

Nakahara, Yoko Urata. "Ethnic Identity among Japanese Canadians in Edmonton: The Case of Pre-World War II Immigrants and Their Descendants." PhD diss., University of Alberta, 1991.

INDEX